Third World
STUDIES

GARY Y. OKIHIRO

Third World STUDIES

THEORIZING LIBERATION

DUKE UNIVERSITY PRESS

DURHAM AND LONDON   2016

© 2016 Duke University Press
All rights reserved
Printed in the United States of America on acid-free paper ∞
Designed by Heather Hensley
Typeset in Garamond Premiere Pro by Copperline

Library of Congress Cataloging-in-Publication Data
Names: Okihiro, Gary Y., [date] author.
Title: Third World studies : theorizing liberation / Gary Y. Okihiro.
Description: Durham : Duke University Press, 2016. |
Includes bibliographical references and index.
Identifiers: LCCN 2016011264
ISBN 9780822362098 (hardcover : alk. paper)
ISBN 9780822362319 (pbk. : alk. paper)
ISBN 9780822373834 (ebook)
Subjects: LCSH: Developing countries—Study and teaching—
United States. | Minorities—Study and teaching—United States. |
Decolonization—Study and teaching—United States.
Classification: LCC D16.4.D44 O35 2016 | DDC 909/.09724—dc23
LC record available at http://lccn.loc.gov/2016011264

FOR MY STUDENTS

CONTENTS

Acknowledgments ix

Introduction 1

CHAPTER 1
Subjects 15

CHAPTER 2
Nationalism 37

CHAPTER 3
Imperialism 57

CHAPTER 4
World-System 77

CHAPTER 5
Education 93

CHAPTER 6
Subjectification 107

CHAPTER 7
Racial Formation 121

CHAPTER 8
Social Formation 139

CHAPTER 9
Syntheses 155

NOTES 173   BIBLIOGRAPHY 187   INDEX 201

ACKNOWLEDGMENTS

This book would have been impossible without my students. They are the reason I teach and write. They inspire and impart meaning to my life. *Third World Studies: Theorizing Liberation* draws from my dialogues with them.

Elfriede Michi Barall was indispensable as a remarkable research assistant and an able manuscript reader for this project. I owe her an immense debt of gratitude. Thankfully, during the summer of 2015 Katie Julia Zheng assisted me with research for this book, and for her excellence and generosity I am grateful.

The anonymous reviewers of this manuscript were terrific; they knew the subject matter, offered sage advice, and thereby made this book much better than originally submitted. I thank them as valuable colleagues and as, I am certain, allies of the masses in struggle fighting the power(s).

I have known Ken Wissoker for decades. Years ago we spoke about a Duke University Press series on social formation, which I theorize herein. The series came to naught because of my neglect. Now I thank Ken for accepting what I consider a summation of my intellectual labors.

INTRODUCTION

Third World Studies: Theorizing Liberation introduces an academic field of inquiry that never existed because it was extinguished at birth. Its brief life was no accident. Third World studies began in 1968 at San Francisco State College as a revolutionary student movement led by the Third World Liberation Front (TWLF). For democracy's sake, the TWLF declared, US higher education must address the masses as well as the ruling elites who predominate in the textbooks and courses peddled by the academy. As a corrective, the TWLF proposed a "Third World curriculum." Instead college administrators and faculty granted the students "ethnic studies," which is a deception but is the term widely recognized today. This textbook revisits the scene of that crime, tracks where the genealogies of Third World and ethnic studies converge and depart, and posits theories and methods that might constitute the field of Third World studies, which is yet to emerge. This, then, is a work of imagination.

To clear the deck, Third World studies is not identity politics, multiculturalism, or intellectual affirmative action. Third World studies is not a gift of white liberals to benighted colored folk to right past wrongs; Third World studies is not a minor note in a grand symphony of US history. Within the United States diversity and pluralist versions of the nation trivialize the intellectual and political claims of Third World studies, reducing power relations and their interventions to cultural celebrations, difference, and competence. Moreover Third World studies is not about teaching students "to resent or hate other races or classes of people," as Arizona's SB 2281 (2010) alleges in legislation that rendered ethnic and Chicana/o studies illegal in the public schools. Accompanying that curbing of intellectual freedom was the banning of books offensive to the ruling class from school libraries.

Rather than a retreat into provincialism Third World studies is about society and the human condition broadly; Third World studies is about the United States in its entirety and its place in the world. The social formation or the forms and movements of society, its structures, relations, and changes over time are the deep and capacious subject matter of Third World studies. Power or agency and its articulations exhibited in the formations of race, gender, sexuality, class, and nation as discrepant and intersecting constructions and practices conceive and cultivate the social formation. Attending to the multiplicity of those forces ceaselessly at work in the locations and exercises of power, the social formation demands a complexity in our thinking and action to engage and resist the forces that oppress us all.

Since its institutionalization in US higher education, (post-1968) ethnic studies as an academic subject matter remains largely undefined.[1] There are no agreed upon methodologies and theories particular to and definitive of the field. That absence is astonishing and revealing, considering the hundreds of ethnic studies programs in the United States, thousands of classes taught each year, and tens of thousands of students who enroll in those classes. By contrast, the allied academic fields of feminist and queer studies have a host of books on theories and methods that define and animate them.

Ethnic studies as we now know it has resisted a unified approach mainly because, in the name of self-determination, the field began as discrete, separate, and, some claimed, exceptional formations of African American studies, American Indian studies, Asian American studies, and Chicana/o or Latina/o studies. Self-determination, the key demand of the TWLF, came to mean for (post-1968) ethnic studies each group speaking for and about itself mainly within the US nation-state. Rare, as a consequence, are institutionalized arrangements of comparative ethnic studies; most segregate the faculty, curricula, and students of each racialized group. That pattern mirrors and, I believe, succumbs to the organization of knowledge by distinctive disciplines and fields with their own tribal members, hierarchies, histories, literatures, cultures, and professional journals and organizations.

In that sense abandoning Third World studies for (post-1968) ethnic studies can be correctly called identity politics and intellectual segregation. I count myself among that generation of scholars. I once wrote that Asian American studies was by, about, and for Asian Americans; as far as I was concerned those outside that community mattered little to the field I helped create. I have long since abandoned that position, which is commonly called cultural nationalism. Despite its contrary claims, cultural nationalism subscribes to European national or racialized categories, often to the marginalization of gender, sexuality, and class, and its principal pivots are the relations between (a binary construction) whites, the dominant group, and nonwhites, the subordinate group. Black (or brown, red, and yellow) power is a potent antidote to the poison of white supremacy, but it follows and is in reaction to white power and is accordingly limited by its model and prior condition.

I appreciate the centrality of African Americans to US history and culture, but I also apprehend as oppressive the white-and-black racialized binary. While I agree with the distinction of indigeneity for Native Americans, including American Indians and Pacific Islanders, I deny the claims of priority and possession even as I reject the legitimacy of imperial expansion. I know conquest, the imposition of national borders, and migrant labor particularizes the Latinx[2] experience, and only Asians were classified as "aliens ineligible to citizenship" from 1790 to 1952. Yet I hold that there is more that connects than divides our struggles for self-determination and freedom. Third World studies constitutes a unified, coherent field of study. I intend to show those propositions in the pages that follow.

A brief explanation of how this text came into being. I had the rare opportunity to teach "comparative ethnic studies" at Columbia University. Although in Harlem and New York City, Columbia's entry into (post-1968) ethnic studies was inexcusably late: in 1993, when Manning Marable began the Institute for Research in African-American Studies, and in 1999, when I became the founding director of the Center for the Study of Ethnicity and Race. However, freed from the turf wars that were common on many campuses with long-standing (post-1968) ethnic studies programs, I was at liberty to install a curriculum attentive to the particularities of people of color—African, Asian, Native American, and Latinx—and one that compared those racial formations across their divides while integrating them with related theories of gender, sexuality, class, and nation. But without faculty trained in comparative ethnic studies I had the responsibility of devising and teaching that introductory course on the subject.

At first I took a "great books" approach to the class, assigning authors I had read during the beginnings of (post-1968) ethnic studies, including Frantz Fanon, Karl Marx, Mao Zedong, and Paulo Freire. The approach failed to hang together because the readings had no theoretical organization. Thus began my search for theory. After all, I knew, all disciplines had theories, methods, and subject matter particular to them, defining them as autonomous fields of study. This introductory book is the outcome of that extended, exhilarating pursuit. There were, of necessity, numerous iterations resulting from self-criticism and dialogue with my patient, discerning students. This text is the written form of my oral lectures; always delivered without notes, my lectures are oral versions of my notes, handwritten from my readings. Readings, notes, lectures, textbook—oral and written traditions—these I consider the sum total of my nearly forty-year labor in and commitment to the subject and striving I herein call Third World studies.

The Book

I was born and grew up on a sugar plantation in Hawai'i. My parents, like their parents, were sugar plantation workers. The plantation, with its social hierarchies of race, ethnicity, gender, sexuality, class, and nation, was the start of my education. My world beyond the cane fields was, in Mark Twain's memorable words, the "loveliest fleet of islands." In plain view from my home was Pu'uloa, called Pearl Harbor and chosen by US militarists for their navy; the anchorage facilitated US imperial ambitions in the Pacific. Gone was the independent kingdom of Hawai'i; greatly diminished primarily by introduced diseases were its native peoples; and surging numbers of Asian migrant laborers tended the vast tropical estates of sugar and pineapple. I came of age in that social formation.

After graduating from a Christian mission high school, unlike most of my peers I was fortunate to continue my education. California was not yet a Third World state, and the US war in Southeast Asia was raging. As an undergraduate I majored in history, and as a graduate student at UCLA I studied African history. To escape the draft I joined the Peace Corps, which sent me for training among African Americans in Frogmore, South Carolina, and stationed me in Botswana, southern Africa. A former British colony, the independent black-ruled nation of Botswana was at the time hemmed in by white supremacist states to its south, north, east, and west. Apartheid South Africa dominated the region. Living and working for three years in Botswana was transformative, and I returned to UCLA and back to Botswana to complete my studies in African history.

Meanwhile students had gained (post-1968) ethnic studies, and I was among the first cohort of graduate students at UCLA in Asian American studies. My PhD, though, was in African history, which was the dominion of whites mainly and a few blacks. I might have been the first Asian recipient of that degree in the United States and failed to land a job in African history. Instead, in affirmation of identity politics, I secured a position in Asian American studies and have been so appointed throughout my academic career. The formations I count as central to my education and consciousness remain colonial Hawai'i and postcolonial Botswana. Spatially Hawai'i and Botswana are earth's antipodes, but intellectually they connect and cohere within my subject-self.

Authors write from their subject positions. In that sense their writings are autobiographical. There are still those who reject that proposition; they believe scholars can conceive of truths and that artists create works transcendent of their time and place. They refuse to see the writer and social contexts embedded within the text. Instead I call your attention to my presence in this work, especially because the Third World curriculum proposed in 1968 was neither explained nor implemented. My version of Third World studies is accordingly idiosyncratic, though not completely. There are guideposts.

Clearly the Third World Liberation Front's course of study was directed at liberation, called self-determination. The Third World curriculum was designed to create "a new humanity, a new humanism, a New World Consciousness," in the TWLF's words, lifted from the Third World writer and revolutionary Frantz Fanon. Certainly the subjects were peoples of the Third World—Africa, Asia (and Oceania), and Latin America (and the Caribbean)—but also of the First and Second Worlds, the so-called West (capitalist world) and East (socialist world). In those worlds were the oppressed, the masses, the earth's "wretched," so named by Fanon, and they are the subject of chapter 1.

Notable are the students' subjectivities as members of the *Third World* and not *national* liberation fronts, as was the case in Algeria and Vietnam, two revolutions that inspired their movement for educational transformation. The Third World referred not to nation-states but to regions, areas of the world once conquered, colonized, and impoverished by Europeans. In 1900 the African American scholar and activist W. E. B. Du Bois delineated that global color line as the problem of the twentieth century, which was colonialism (material relations) and racism (discourse), the ideology that upheld white supremacy and nonwhite subservience. Third World studies descends from that lineage of anticolonial, antiracist struggles identified and described by Du Bois, among others. That global contest was waged over power, of course, the power to know and the power to rule. The oppressed and their relations to power, then, are the subjects of Third World studies.

Racist discourse endorsed and advanced European imperialism that ruled the world for about four hundred years, beginning in about the sixteenth century. About the time of Du Bois's color line declaration, racists warned against a peril produced by colonialism: the uplift and stirring of nonwhite peoples and their migration to the imperial centers of Europe and the United States. Fields of study to contain and mitigate the problem were race relations and ethnic studies. In the United States sociologists at the University of Chicago were the foremost proponents of both race relations and ethnic studies. The former sought to understand and control the challenges posed by nonwhites to white rule, while the latter conceived of ethnicities or cultures as the way to preserve white supremacy by assimilating problem minorities into the dominant group. This brand of ethnic studies I refer to as (Chicago) ethnic studies.

The sociologist Robert E. Park, a leading figure in race relations and (Chicago) ethnic studies, learned race relations while serving as Booker T. Washington's research assistant at the Tuskegee Institute in Alabama. Washington was the primary architect of the Atlanta Compromise (1895), which promised African American docility and submission in exchange for white funding for black education. He was also a dutiful student of Samuel Chapman Armstrong, a son of missionaries to Hawai'i and the founder of the Hampton Institute, which educated African Americans and American Indians to work with their hands and not minds. Race relations and (Chicago) ethnic studies, as instruments of colonialism, thus were antithetical to the emancipatory aims of Third World studies.

But at its inception Third World studies gained institutionalization as (Chicago) ethnic studies and, like the independence movements in the Third World, the field turned to (cultural) nationalism and the nation-state. Chapter 2 considers that retreat and surrender, which betrayed the broadminded understandings of the Pan-African Conference of 1900 and the African and Asian meeting at Bandung in 1955. The latter, convened in the midst of the Cold War, expressed a remarkable vision of a world free from racism and colonial rule and with the achievement of lasting world peace. Contrarily Third World independence installed the sovereign nation-state, patterned on the European model with an elite ruling over the oppressed, exploited masses. Similarly in the United States, cultural nationalism was upheld as the highest expression of self-determination and as an end in itself, not as a strategic, albeit necessary, step toward liberation. At the same time, many leading cultural nationalists were staunch internationalists; they knew that imperialism abroad consorted with social relations at home.

The sovereign nation-state is both spatial and social. It is marked by borders within which rulers rule over people. In the narrative of nation the people were related biologically and were thus referred to as races. They shared a common descent and were of one blood. In addition, under patriarchy men occupied the public sphere or the state because of their alleged virtues, while women were confined to the domestic sphere because of their presumed deficiencies. Families constituted the nation, and sexuality and marriage were thus state prerogatives. Under capitalism inviolate was the bedrock of possession or property, including land, goods, and dependents—women, children, slaves. The nation-state accordingly was designed to install and interpellate hierarchies of race, gender, sexuality, class, and (national) citizenship. Those relations of power privilege the few and oppress the many.

As the old imperial order crumbled and colonies gained independence, a new empire, a world-system of nation-states, emerged. The internecine First and Second World Wars, waged by Europeans over national sovereignty and imperial holdings, proved to be the old empire's undoing. Under the new dispensation global peace was pursued through instruments like the League of Nations and its successor, the United Nations, both composed of nation-states bound by juridical agreements. At the same time, the League of Nations opposed antiracism and decolonization, and only in 1960 did the UN declare that colonization violates fundamental human rights. Capitalism financed and profited from that hegemony of nation-states, which the United States called multilateralism. The world economy was restructured through institutions like the World Bank and the International Monetary Fund and international trade agreements and organizations, producing economic, political, and cultural dependency as well as, across the color line, generating immense wealth for the few and abject poverty for the many.

The Third World Liberation Front's choice of a spatial and ideological affiliation with the Third World and its peoples, not the nation-state, suggests a curriculum built around the discourses and manifestations of imperialism and colonialism globally, the subjects of chapters 3 and 4. Imperialism, or extraterritorial expansion, was impelled by capitalism and underwritten by discourses to impose order and subjection. From ancient Greece emerged ideas of geographical and biological determinism; the former conceived of life forms, including humans, as shaped by geography and climate; the latter, as decreed by biology or blood. The (European) Enlightenment demarcated the earth by continents—Europe, Asia, Africa, and America—and those divides delineated the four major races with their particular natures. Whether determined by geography or inheritance and blood, the superior race possessed virtues and hence rights over the inferior races. That project of segregating, naming, and attributing, the discourse of taxonomy, was an imperial exertion of power over the planet and all of its inhabitants.

That language and ideology (discourses) of rule materialized the world-system, which tracks the career of capitalism. Mercantile or trade-based capitalism produced profits, and, beginning in the eleventh century with the Italian city-states, trade with Asia was the principal means for acquiring wealth and influence. The Atlantic world eclipsed the Mediterranean around the fifteenth century. With foundations in the Mediterranean, the Atlantic perfected the arts of conquest and colonization. Enslaved Africans supplied the labor for sugar plantations on islands off the West African coast and later in the Caribbean. African slaves and sugar sold in Europe provided capital to finance the long and arduous journey around Africa to the Indian Ocean and Asia. Across the Atlantic, American Indians, after their conquest, mined the gold and silver that enriched Spain, and the bullion was traded in the Pacific world for Asian goods. Settler colonies secured the imperial, oceanic highways, and capital, labor (migrant labor), and culture moved across the world-system.

In that designed and imposed global web the core accumulated wealth at the expense of its peripheries, resulting in Europe's development and the Third World's underdevelopment. Those connections were related and structured; they were not commerce in the usual sense of exchange, but exploitation. A Spanish colonizer called the highly profitable traffic "an inheritance," gesturing to the privileges of blood and race. Colonies existed to generate wealth for their owners. Conquest was both material and discursive, and it involved military might but also sexual violence. Rape of the land and people, mainly women, was a method of subjugation and the means for producing and reproducing dependencies. Language was a crucial weapon in the colonizer's arsenal. Native languages and therewith ideologies were removed, replaced with the conqueror's tongue, producing colonized minds. Without a consciousness of the subject-self, self-determination was more easily denied.

Like language, education, considered in chapter 5, is an apparatus of the state to colonize and mold useful, docile subjects and citizens, but it also can enable resistance to oppression and exploitation. It was therefore a battleground for what some called the culture or canon wars of the 1980s and 1990s, sparked in part by the Third World Liberation Front's 1968 strike. However, long before that historic student uprising, American education was established to manufacture preachers and teachers to school the untutored masses, rendering them safe for democracy. White men from the elite assumed that (white man's) burden, while white women were at first excluded and later nurtured in schools for mothers of the republic to reproduce the next generation of pliant citizens. Missionaries similarly tended to the maternal instruction of childlike American Indians, and their Foreign Mission School, established in

1816, civilized into subservience native peoples, including American Indians, Pacific Islanders, and Asians.

Samuel Armstrong found his calling in that ministry to the republic's "darkies"—Hawaiians, African Americans, and American Indians—to defer their dreams of equality and teach them to remain contentedly within their assigned places. Another educator, Richard Henry Pratt, was like Armstrong a commander of African American troops during the Civil War. He admired Armstrong's pedagogy, sent some of his American Indian war captives to Hampton, and established the Carlisle Indian Industrial School. Pratt's educational mission was, in his words, to "kill the Indian in him, and save the man." Armstrong agreed and gave that brand of miseducation a practical rationale: it is cheaper to civilize Indians than to exterminate them. As the African American educator Carter G. Woodson discovered, when you control a person's thinking, you will not need to fear any opposition or uprising. Miseducation inculcates obedience.

But education can also inspire rebellion. That was a motivation for masters to forbid literacy and learning among their enslaved laborers. The master's tools can enslave as well as free. Students of the Third World Liberation Front had freedom in mind when they engaged in the fight for a "national culture," which, Fanon explained, was nothing less than the creation of a people who had been denied a history and culture. Consciousness, the Brazilian educator Paulo Freire added, can be obtained through a "pedagogy of the oppressed," which humanizes teachers and students alike and disrupts the relation of teacher as colonizer and student as colonized. Contrary to miseducation, that dialogic pedagogy generates consciousness and intervention, critical thinking and action, creating subjects (not objects) who are agents of history, rendering them "truly human."

Discussion of the formation of that subject-self or subjectification follows in chapter 6. While Freirian consciousness grounds the subject-self within society, humanism of the (European) Enlightenment extols the primacy of the self over self's others. "I think, therefore I am" is the optimistic, positivist formulation of the self—the center—and with that consciousness, humanism. Humans, the discourse maintained, have the ability to shape their own destinies and possessed the power to rule over and even subdue nature. Not all humans, however, were equal; in fact nonwhites and women might approach but could never achieve the status and rights of white men. That humanism consorted with racism, patriarchy, and imperialism to justify and advance nationalism, conquest, colonization, and the capitalist world-system. Although the Third World Liberation Front and Fanon advocated a "new humanism," whether old or new, humanism arises from within that discourse of white men and the colonizers. Accordingly even a new humanism might not result in liberation and self-determination, the objects of a Third World curriculum.

Post-Enlightenment intellectuals offer us trenchant criticisms of humanism's sovereign subjects. Humans are not completely autonomous. Marx argued that the relations of production shape consciousness, and Freud revealed the unconscious dimensions of the self that are inaccessible to thought. Saussure contended that nothing exists outside of language; thus language structures consciousness and the subject-self. Lacan found that the subject is created through language in a process called subjectification, and Gramsci, Althusser, and Foucault point to the state and its apparatuses in the production of the subject-self. Subjects are made through discourse, which is language and ideology, Foucault explained. Those insights of structuralism and poststructuralism, not humanism, supply Third World studies with its analytical category: the subject-self of self-determination.

As noted, race was the distinguishing mark of race relations, culture, of (Chicago) ethnic studies, and both discourses functioned to maintain the relations of power. By the time the Third World Liberation Front was established, (Chicago) ethnic studies was the prevailing ideology in US society. That is, races were reduced to cultures, and the celebration of ethnicity and diversity was the ticket to the big tent of inclusion, citizenship, and rights—the perceived goals of the civil rights movement. For the ruling class ethnicity ensured domestic tranquility. As the US sociologists Michael Omi and Howard Winant explain, the theory of racial formation, examined in chapter 7, arose in opposition to that dominance of the ethnic model in sociology, and it swept the newly instituted field misnamed "ethnic studies" (post-1968). Racial formation theory contends that race is persistent, central, and irreducible within US history and society because race is a creation of and, in turn, exerts influences over economic, political, and social forces—the sum total of society and the nation-state. At the same time race is a social construction and is mobile, always in formation.

In a complementary work the social and political philosopher Charles W. Mills argues that philosophy, like US sociology, glosses over race despite its long-standing and pervasive presence in the writings of major figures of the (European) Enlightenment, including Hobbes, Locke, Rousseau, and Kant. That failure, which is an "episteme of ignorance," circulates within the "racial contract" that is at the heart of not merely modern social contract theory but the regimes of slavery and colonialism. By "racial contract" Mills refers to the assumption of superior whites and inferior nonwhites that enshrines privileges for whites and bestows subservience on nonwhites. Whiteness accordingly is not simply a race or color but a set of power relations—the discursive and material powers of whites over nonwhites.

Whiteness in fact is the starting point of racial formation theory; whites named themselves and their inferior others. Critical race theory builds upon that insight. The *critical* in critical race theory arises from a critique of structuralism, materialism, and positivism in the disillusionment that followed the twentieth century's world wars. The nineteenth century's faith in science, capitalism, and human progress was undermined by those European conflicts, and the sovereign nation-state and its instruments were revealed as oppressive to the masses. Marxism and socialism, critical theory believed, offered antidotes to the poisons of capitalism and materialism, and deconstruction in literary criticism considered texts, like self and society, as constructed and mediated. Critical legal studies adopted critical theory's positions on power, ideology, discourse, and the material conditions, but its failure to consider race and racism as central to the constitution of legal theory and practice led to the rise of critical race theory. As a pivotal apparatus of the nation-state, the law, while complex and contingent, creates race and racial meanings and confers privileges and poverties, according to critical race theory. Whiteness, then, is the protected category, although assumed and thereby rendered invisible in the racial contract. Critical white studies aims to expose that racial contract and deconstruct white power by making it visible.

While a central axis, race is not the entirety of the social formation or society and the locations and articulations of power. Third World women (organic) intellectuals led the search for a new language to express and theory to explain their everyday experiences as women of color, queers, the poor, and migrants. The problems they faced were more nuanced and complicated than the answers provided by racial formation theory alone. In 1968 the African American feminist Frances Beale outlined the impact of racism, sexism, and capitalism on the lives of African American women; she formed the Black Women's Liberation Caucus that evolved into the Third World Women's Alliance because "the complexities of intersecting oppressions [are] more resilient than the distinctions of the particular groups." That is, women of color and Third World women faced similar forces of oppression and exploitation that cut across racialized divides. Moreover, Beale held, a Third World consciousness would enable a more robust political movement for social change than one based on cultural nationalism. That revolutionary idea is the subject of chapter 8.

Beale's "intersecting oppressions," later theorized as intersectionalism, are the essential feature of my social formation theory. It is important to note that a Third World consciousness sustains the theory and that intersectionalism draws from the lived experiences of the subjects of Third World studies— the oppressed, the masses. Social formation theory purports to explain the structures of society in their totality and their changes over space/time. The theory understands power or agency as the means by which societies are organized and changed, and social structures involve primarily race, gender, sexuality, class, and nation. Those discourses materialize social categories and hierarchies such as white and nonwhite, man and woman, straight and queer, owner and worker, and citizen and alien. While power is suspect, diffuse, and constantly in motion, it has abilities and effects. Social formation theory thus insists on locating power to name the oppressors and the oppressed and to create alternative, liberating discourses and practices.

Self-determination, the goal of Third World studies, requires a strategic mastery of the language and ideologies of the ruling class to engage and up-end oppression. But liberation also demands discourses and practices not of the master's creation. The idea of intersectionalism and its progeny, social formation theory, are attempts to articulate new languages, ideologies, and practices, which is the future of Third World studies. Chapter 9 concludes this version of Third World studies with two syntheses that reveal the particularities and ties that bind across the imposed divides of race, gender, sexuality, class, and nation.

Synthesis 1 identifies some theories of relevance to Third World studies drawn from feminist, queer, and (post-1968) ethnic studies. Feminist and (post-1968) ethnic studies form parallels in their movements for social change. Both began as the pursuit of integration and civil rights within the nation-state, and strands in both abandoned that focus for self-determination and the locations and articulations of power in society and the world. Performance, invisibility of the normal, and the making of subjects, as explained by feminist and queer scholars, enhance our understanding of subjectivity. In comparative (post-1968) ethnic studies, land and labor constitute the common ground, while Native American studies underscores the importance of indigeneity and sovereignty; African American studies, transnational community (Pan-Africanism); Asian American studies, migrant labor; and Chicana/o studies, borderlands. Those discourses and practices unite as well as point to the particularities of each field, and they clarify and explain the subjects of Third World studies.

Third World studies, as Synthesis 2 shows, engages discourses of the ruling class in the colonizer's tongue, of necessity, but also in creolized languages.

In that the Third World appropriated First World discourses of sovereignty, equality, and self-determination, which freed even as they imprisoned; (European) humanism was never intended to embrace Third World peoples. In fact by tracing the intellectual histories of discourses such as nation and race, imperialism and colonialism, modernity and postmodernity, we see clearly their workings in the material relations and conditions of exploitation and oppression, the elite and the masses. Rising from the old must emerge novel, truly liberating discourses and material conditions. To rephrase the Third World Liberation Front's 1968 objective for its Third World studies curriculum, Third World studies is designed to create and nurture "a new language, a new ideology, a new world consciousness." That revolutionary conclusion is the ambition of this introduction to Third World studies reborn.

Summary

In 1998 and 1999, when a colleague proposed Latina/o studies and I, Asian American studies at Columbia University, both undergraduate majors were quickly approved. They were almost certainly seen as ethnic or cultural studies of groups that added to the colors of multicultural Columbia and America. Later, by contrast, when I proposed a major in comparative ethnic studies and explained the field as a study of power in society, the college dean and chair of the undergraduate committee on instruction queried me about that claim. "What is power?" he chided me. While the dean might have been incapable of apprehending power in the abstract, he clearly knew how to wield it, keeping the proposal in limbo for three years by requiring evidence of the field's academic legitimacy and demanding several revisions of the proposal. The dean likely saw the study of power from the perspective of comparative ethnic studies as potentially disruptive of the extant relations of power.

I recount that fairly recent past to underscore the disparate receptions of (Chicago) ethnic studies and what I herein call Third World studies. That contemporary response, it is significant to recall, mirrored the actions of faculty and administrators in 1968, when the Third World Liberation Front proposed a Third World curriculum. They welcomed race relations and (Chicago) ethnic studies while turning their backs to Third World studies. They had accomplices in (post-1968) ethnic studies faculty who fled the Third World for the United States, seeking asylum in civil rights and the nation-state. Cultural nationalism and segregation into cells of races named and interpellated by those with power dominated the field called ethnic studies (post-1968). Race was the defining subject matter. In that acquiescence and insofar as they have become ends, like the independent Third World nation-state, and not a strategic choice and a temporary position in the war against oppression, we have willingly complied with our hegemony and subordination.

I must stress nonetheless that there is a difference between the ethnic studies of Robert Park and Chicago sociology and the misnamed ethnic studies of 1968. In the 1960s black (and brown, red, and yellow) power threatened white supremacy, even as independent Third World nation-states opposed European colonialism and racism. Cultural nationalism and the nation-state were effective vehicles toward liberation, but only as instruments in transit. Antonio Gramsci, the Italian Marxist, conceived of that strategy as a mobile war of positions.

Indeed not all post-1968 ethnic studies scholars saw race and the nation-state as the sole or even primary subjects of their field, and in recent years, to distinguish themselves from the (post-1968) ethnic studies that has become the prevailing norm, some refer to their scholarship and practice as "critical ethnic studies." Moreover new generations of scholars have published innovative and courageous works cutting across disciplines and the social formation that, while they might not have been written under the sign of (post-1968) ethnic studies, have advanced the field of (critical) ethnic studies. Liberation remains the object of those varieties of post-1968 and critical ethnic studies, which can be seen as an appropriation of the Chicago name and variety. Yet it is useful to remind ourselves of the origins and purposes of (Chicago) ethnic studies and the imperative to abandon the master's language and ideology for more liberating taxonomies and discourses of our choosing and design.

Third World Studies: Theorizing Liberation is a conjuring, a haunting from a past that refuses to die. The spirit of the global Third World anticolonial struggles for self-determination and antiracism lives on. In this articulation of the field, Third World studies retains the original drive for universal liberation (self-determination) against all forms of oppression, material and discursive. This introduction merely starts a conversation. As such *Third World Studies* invites dialogue and engagement, agreement and dissent. Only then, in the formation and practice of ideology and language, will Third World studies compose a field of inquiry and action worthy of its student founders and their magnificent, enduring cause and movement, making history.

ONE

SUBJECTS

Third World studies is the systematic examination of power and its locations and articulations involving race, gender, sexuality, class, and nation—what I herein call the social formation. Power in the physical world is expressed as energy; power in the social realm is realized as agency. As Foucault points out in his critique of the sovereign model of power that reduces complex relations to a single dialectic, power is dispersed throughout the social order. That fragmentation, however, does not preclude the possibility, indeed the necessity of locating power, apprehending its workings, and contesting its consequences. Third World studies subscribes to that species of positivism for the imperative of pointing to privilege and poverty, exploitation and oppression, revolution and liberation.

The Oppressed

Third World studies began in 1968 at San Francisco State College, where students of the Third World Liberation Front (TWLF) identified and affiliated with the disempowered, the oppressed, the exploited Third World peoples. The field thus emerged from a commitment to "the people," not "we, the people" of the US Constitution. "The people, united, will never be defeated!" and, as the Black Panthers declared, "All power to the people!" were more than empty slogans for the TWLF. "Serve the people" was their guide, and "for my people" they labored.

In their statement of purpose the TWLF declared, "As Third World students, as Third World people, as so-called minorities, we are being exploited to the fullest extent in this racist white America and we are therefore preparing ourselves and our people for a prolonged struggle for freedom from this yoke of oppression." The people, the oppressed, the TWLF understood, extended beyond the borders of the nation. "We adhere to the struggles in Asia, Africa, and Latin America, ideologically, spiritually, and culturally.... We have decided to fuse ourselves with the masses of Third World people, which are a majority of the world's peoples, to create, through struggles, a new humanity, a new humanism, a New World Consciousness, and within the text [*sic*] collectively control our own destinies."[1]

Following Marxist ideology, the people were also "the masses." Activist Pat Sumi recalled reading Marx and Lenin and studying revolutionary movements. As Third World peoples, as oppressed peoples, she explained, the goal was to organize "on a mass level" for revolutionary change.[2] The principal architect of black studies at San Francisco State (SFS), Nathan Hare, described black studies at its best as "a mass movement and a mass struggle" conceived "to rid the world of racism and achieve black self-determination." That project, he believed, was a revolutionary movement.[3] It is important to remember that Marxism's masses were the proletariat or working class, and the struggle between capital and labor was an international contest.

Closely related to the idea of "the people" was the notion of "the community." At times the community came to campus, opening elite institutions of higher learning to the masses and rendering them more democratic. Just south of SFS, the College of San Mateo instituted a College Readiness Program to recruit and retain students of color. In the summer of 1966 only thirty-nine African American students participated in the program. The following year the program expanded to recruit "brothers and sisters on the block," a designation for inner-city, working-class students who were unlikely to attend college, and to include Asian Americans and Latinxs. From East Palo Alto and San Francisco Chinatown and the Fillmore and Mission districts they came from predominantly African, Asian, and Latinx communities.[4] The community came to campus, and by the fall of 1968 the program had grown to nearly five hundred students.

The campus also went to the community. At the College of San Mateo, Robert Hoover, codirector of the College Readiness Program, explained, "We try to change the students' whole value system towards themselves and their communities, so they can help themselves and bring the help back to their people."[5] Hare wrote that integral to black studies was an ideology of black liberation and practice that linked the campus with "the community." Black studies must work "to transform the black community," which is "a laboratory" wherein students can serve apprenticeships, Hare proposed,[6] much like the University of Chicago's Sociology Department, where he earned his doctorate.

The South African patriot Nelson Mandela, a major figure for many in the Third World liberation movement, expressed succinctly the subjects of Third World studies. At his Rivonia trial on April 20, 1964, he described his purpose in fighting to dismantle the apartheid regime: "To serve my people and make my humble contribution to their freedom struggle." He resolved, "It [a free society] is an ideal which I hope to live for and to achieve. But if needs be, it is an ideal for which I am prepared to die."[7] Mandela, we remember, lived to see the improbable happen in 1994 with apartheid's fall and his election as free South Africa's first black president.

Third World Curriculum

In his revolutionary anthem, *The Wretched of the Earth* (1961), Frantz Fanon, a Martinican and French-trained psychiatrist, described the cosmos or order imposed by European colonizers, which segregated the colonizer and colonized into worlds separate and unequal. That divide and hierarchy of race and class placed white, capitalist expansionists from the First World over colored, native workers of the Third World. The former were humans and individuals; the latter, nonhumans and faceless masses. Because of those conditions bred by colonialism, Fanon wrote, Third World liberation is necessarily a revolutionary process, replacing a certain "species" with another "species" of men and altering the consciousness of both the colonizer and the colonized.

That renewal of the colonial universe is not merely destructive, Fanon wrote; it is also a work of creation. The revolution gives birth to "new men" with a "new language and a new humanity." We, the colonized, Fanon urged, must "change our ways" from a "nauseating mimicry" that copies the European example and pattern. "Leave this Europe," he exhorted, move "in a new direction," fashion "the whole man," and thereby, as Third World peoples, begin "a new history of Man."[8] Fanon's emphatic call for rebirth, regeneration, and re-creation of the European cosmos was truly revolutionary.

As described by Fanon, the "Third World," conceived about midcentury and comprising Africa, Asia (and Oceania), and Latin America (and the Caribbean), was a project by the periphery to solve the core's problems of imperialism, wars, and systems of bondage.[9] Indonesian president Ahmed Sukarno told the 1955 Bandung Conference of newly independent African and Asian nations that the Third World's historic turn was directed at "the liberation of man from his bonds of fear, his bonds of poverty, the liberation of man from the physical, spiritual and intellectual bonds which have for long stunted the development of humanity's majority."[10]

Indeed the Third World's rise and with it the end of formal European empires marked a turning point in some four hundred years of world history. That achievement along the global color line was, indeed, momentous.[11]

| | |

The students of the TWLF were aware of that history when they demanded a "Third World curriculum" and declared their intention to create, through struggle, "a new humanity, a new humanism, a New World Consciousness."[12] That "New World Consciousness" drew from anticolonial writers like Fanon and Albert Memmi, a Tunisian Jewish intellectual who denounced the erasure of the colonized from history and their resulting "cultural estrangement" from self and society. Colonization "disfigures," wrote Memmi, and requires a restoration of "a whole and free man"; Fanon urged the creation of "a new humanity . . . a new humanism."[13]

Like Fanon in his call for a Third World revolution, TWLF students explained, "We offer a positive program. We are not anti-white; we are anti-white-racist-oppression and it is this powerful and just determinant that is the genesis of our movement, but the growth of the movement is affirmative; an affirmation of our humanity, our strength, our beauty, our dignity and our pride. Our programs are working programs. Our direction is revolutionary. Our method is organization. Our goal is Third World Power. Our essence is a New World Consciousness of oppressed peoples."[14]

Third World students understood the revolutionary nature of their demand for Third World studies when situated within world history. Barbara Williams, an African American student at SFS, wrote insightfully of the Third World movement on campus and its purposes, "We are conscious of our blackness, brownness, redness, yellowness and are moving with that knowledge back into our communities. We intend to reveal to the world our own place in this world's history and to mark our place in space and time." George Murray, a graduate student and part-time English Department instructor at SFS and the Black Panther Party's minister of education, added, "When we talk about becoming free, we have to talk about power, getting all the goods, services, and land, and returning them equally to the oppressed and enslaved Mexicans, Blacks, Indians, Puerto Ricans, and poor whites in the US and to the rest of the oppressed and hungry people in the world."[15]

Across San Francisco Bay, at the University of California, Berkeley, students organized that campus's Third World Liberation Front to demand Third World studies. That Third World consciousness can be seen in a 1971 foundational text, *Asian Women*, edited by a collective drawn from a course at UC Berkeley. A prominent section was devoted to Third World women. In selecting chapters for that section, the editors highlighted the solidarity among Third World women in America and Asia sutured by the red thread of resistance to oppression and exploitation.

Central was the Indochinese Women's Conference held in Vancouver in April 1971 that brought together Third World and women's liberation concerns and engaged over 150 Canadian and US activists and a six-woman delegation from Vietnam.[16] "As Third World people," a conference report asserted, "we share similar struggles in fighting racist conditions and attitudes in our communities and our everyday lives. Our people—Blacks, Chicanos, Asians, Native Americans, and Native Hawaiians—have had our land ripped off by the whites, our women raped, our homes plundered, and our men drafted to further this country's imperialist ventures into Third World countries. . . . [Accordingly] we see a need for learning about each other's history as Third World people and of informing each other about our movements for self-determination."[17]

Turning the Third World curriculum into ethnic studies, which transpired in the fall of 1968 and spring of 1969 at SFS and Berkeley, trivialized that declaration of global solidarity with the liberation and antiracist struggles of Third World peoples. That move not only domesticated an international alliance and struggle; it reduced its revolutionary potential and power by grafting it onto the trunk of race relations and ethnic studies as explicated by sociologists at the University of Chicago (called the Chicago school of sociology).

Color Line

At the century's start, in 1900, the African American and Harvard-trained historian W. E. B. Du Bois famously declared, "The problem of the twentieth century is the problem of the color line."[18] He delivered that prophetic announcement, appropriately, in London, the seat of the British Empire, on which the sun never set. Imperialism closed the nineteenth century, and its counter, the decolonization struggles of Africa and Asia, ushered in the twentieth century. Self-determination and antiracism, the dismantling of the ideology that justified and supported colonialism, were the central elements of those liberation movements, which promised a new dispensation for humanity and, after two global wars and the Cold War's onset, world peace.

Early in the century, in the midst of World War I, Du Bois explained that colonialism, the exploitation of the lands and peoples of the "darker races"—"Chinese, East Indian, Negroes, and South American Indians"—produced European empires containing material conditions of oppression and exploitation affirmed and advanced by the discourses of religion and science. The Berlin Conference of 1884–85, he recalled, parceled out Africa, synonymous with "bestiality and barbarism," for European possession and colonization, exemplifying how racism resolved rhetorical incongruities such as declarations of universal human equality and paid real dividends for Europe. At stake in the present war, Du Bois wrote, were those colonies and the discourse of white supremacy that warranted them. Lasting peace, he concluded, will only descend with the abolition of racism and the inauguration of a "new democracy of all races: a great humanity of equal men."[19]

The First World War, ostensibly waged for democracy, was never intended to include people of color, wrote a skeptical Hubert H. Harrison, the West Indian intellectual. "The white world has been playing with catch-words of democracy while ruthlessly ruling an overwhelming majority of black, brown and yellow peoples to whom these catch-words were never intended to apply." At its core the war was a fratricidal conflict, "a war of the white race" over empire to possess the lands and determine the destinies of the "colored majority in Asia, Africa and the islands of the sea."[20]

For racists and antiracists alike, the problem of the twentieth century was the problem of the color line, which sustained, in Du Bois's words, the "greed for wealth and power." The problem for racists like the journalist Lothrop Stoddard was "the rising tide of color" that threatened to swamp "white world-supremacy."[21] For antiracists like Du Bois, the problem was European colonial rule and the need for Third World self-determination and the eradication of racism.[22]

In 1905, a mere decade after Kaiser Wilhelm II of Germany exhorted Europe to rise above its parochial disputes to defend "your holiest possession"—Christianity and European civilization—against the impending threat of the "Yellow Peril,"[23] Japan defeated Russia. The event prompted a young Oxford University lecturer, Alfred Zimmern, to put aside his lesson on Greek history to announce to his class "the most historical event which has happened, or is likely to happen, in our lifetime; the victory of a non-white people over a white people."[24]

Du Bois agreed with Zimmern's assessment. "The Russo-Japanese war has marked an epoch," he exulted. "The magic of the word 'white' is already broken. . . . The awakening of the yellow races is certain. That the awakening of the brown and black races will follow in time, no unprejudiced student of history can doubt."[25] Japan's victory, a historian concurs, broke the myth of white invincibility and influenced a regeneration of Asia broadly.[26] It signaled the prospect of colored resistance to white supremacy globally, as Du Bois and others hoped for, and awakened anxieties and fears over the West's decline among those invested in imperial order and white supremacy.

For Sun Yat-sen, the father of Chinese nationalism, Japan's defeat of Russia supplied a lesson for the decolonization movement. Twenty years after the event, in a speech delivered in Japan, Sun recalled sailing through the Suez Canal soon after news of Japan's victory had spread. When the ship docked, Arabs flocked around Sun, congratulating him on his nation's achievement. Even after Sun corrected their misidentification, the group continued to celebrate their solidarity with him against European imperialism. The lesson, Sun observed in his speech, was the need for oppressed Asians to unite on the bases of race and culture against white supremacy and imperial rule.[27]

Race Relations

The impending global conflict along the color line produced a discourse and a field of study, *race relations*, to manage the problem of the twentieth century and forestall the prospect of a "race war."[28] Its purpose was to study "racial tensions" and "racial conflicts" as social problems with an eye toward ameliorating those conditions. The cure, race relations scholars prescribed, was racial "adjustments" on the part of the colonized to conform to the will of the colonizers. Assimilation or conformity was evolutionary and designed to preserve the status quo by moving in a single direction, toward and in compliance with the ruling class.[29]

In the United States, the Institute of Race Relations was charged with studying native peoples to install "effective government" and continue their economic dependency, and the prime objective of the Institute of Pacific Relations, established in 1925, was "to prevent a possible Oriental-Occidental war arising . . . out of an increasing bitterness over racial, religious, economic and political differences."[30] That "bitterness," however, did not emerge from "differences" but from the relations of power, involving conquest, colonization, and exploitation.

Later framed as "problems," colored subjects and their abilities were at first solutions to white masters when useful to them, as in supplying efficient, pliant labor, but they caused apprehension, even dread when they aspired to full equality and a measure of self-determination. "One speaks of race relations when there is a race problem," declared the University of Chicago sociologist Robert E. Park, one of the founding figures of the field. To illustrate he wrote of the "race problem" in South Africa, where "the African does, to be sure, constitute a problem."[31] Of course from the African perspective, that is, from the San, Khoikhoi, Nguni, and Sotho point of view, the invading European was the problem.

The field of race relations thrived in the United States, especially during the interwar period, and it took turns particular to the United States and Britain.[32] During the 1920s, revealing of the field's origins and objectives, an influential US sociology textbook from the Chicago school likened race conflict to nationalism and the drive of subject peoples for freedom and self-determination.[33] In that context of global race relations, Park isolated and dissected the "Negro problem" and the "Oriental problem" in the United States. On the eve of World War II a conference on the state of the field of race relations cautiously diagnosed an obvious condition: "The world seems to be reorganizing to some extent along racial lines"[34]—the problem of the twentieth century.

Ethnic Studies

Chicago sociology's *ethnic studies* hearkened back to the field of worldwide race relations and its problems approach to maintaining colonial rule. The Chicago school's ambition for race relations and ethnic studies was to distinguish US from European sociology by highlighting social processes it claimed were unique to the US environment. Additionally Chicago sociology advanced the field through the new concept of "ethnicity" in place of "race," which had dominated US sociology.[35]

Sociology in the United States surfaced in a swirling sea of domestic, social currents during the late nineteenth century. Urbanization and immigration from southern and eastern Europe, unprecedented in numbers and colors, languages, and religions, and their attendant problems, including housing, sanitation, poverty, ethnic and labor strife, social disorganization, and crime and juvenile delinquency, prompted the rise of the social gospel and various reform and nativist movements such as the campaign for "Americanization." During the 1880s and 1890s the first courses offered in US sociology departments addressed social "pathologies" as exercises in problem solving.[36] Sociology was thus a science of society for the management of its afflictions.

Robert Park, a central figure in establishing a US brand of sociology at the University of Chicago, was especially concerned with the "Negro" and

"Oriental" problems as samples to test his general propositions about US modernity. He observed, "The study of the Negro in America, representing, as he does, every type of man from the primitive barbarian to the latest and most finished product of civilization, offers an opportunity to study . . . the historic social process by which modern society has developed. The Negro in his American environment is a social laboratory."[37] Park had learned race relations under Booker T. Washington while serving as Washington's research assistant and director of public relations at the Tuskegee Institute. As we will see, Washington was a devoted student of Samuel Chapman Armstrong, the son of missionaries to Hawai'i and founder of the Hampton Institute.

The consequences of Chicago sociology were both paradigmatic and far-reaching. Its students and faculty, notably Park, Louis Wirth, and William I. Thomas, who had recruited Park to Chicago, focused on urban sociology and devised a "natural history" of ethnic and race relations in that teeming habitat. US cities were considered social laboratories and spatial fields to test the tenets of modernization broadly, and African and Asian Americans, like European ethnic groups, were experimental subjects in the advance of progress.[38] Additionally and importantly, at Columbia University the anthropologist Franz Boas had distinguished race from culture,[39] and ethnicity or culture thus bore the prospect of problem solving, especially in racial conflicts, through the cultural assimilation of the inferior group.

Within that flattened world of the modernizing, homogenizing city, Chicago sociology abandoned race for ethnicity, and European ethnic immigrant groups constituted the model for the progressive ethnic cycle of immigration, contact and interaction, competition and conflict, and accommodation and assimilation. African Americans in the urban North, migrants from the rural South, and Asian migrants in the agrarian West were like Polish peasants in northern cities, according to the Chicago school. Modernity's capacity to civilize denizens of the urban jungle dissolved the affiliations of race, enabling a single frame of reference and direction for disparate peoples.[40] That optimism was ultimately diminished by the durability of racism, called "racial prejudice," evident in the experiences of African and Asian Americans.

Perhaps pivotal in that regard was the Chicago race riot of July 1919 that lasted over a week and resulted in the deaths of fifteen whites and twenty-three blacks and injuries to 537 and left over a thousand people homeless. The Chicago riot was the worst of several instances of racial violence during that summer, in which 120 people died. In its wake the governor of Illinois appointed a commission to study its causes and make recommendations for remediation.[41] Charles S. Johnson, an African American sociology graduate student at the University of Chicago, led the commission's research staff and was the principal author of the final report, *The Negro in Chicago*.[42] Although the Chicago school's ethnic cycle of immigration, contact, competition, conflict, and assimilation formed the organizing framework of the study, *The Negro in Chicago* documented the persistence and deleterious effects of racism on African Americans, revealed in inferior housing, schools, and recreational facilities, poverty, and unstable family life. It was clear to the commission that the African American experience in Chicago failed to fit the European ethnic model.

The 1924–26 Pacific Coast Survey of Race Relations, headed by Park, similarly tested the applicability of the ethnic cycle to a non-European race. The study assumed that the problems of Europeans in northern cities and Asians in the West were similar enough to sustain comparison. Instigated by the Institute of Social and Religious Research in New York City, the Race Relations Survey was to ascertain the causes of anti-Japanese hatred on the Pacific Coast. Instead, however, Park conceived of the project as a study in assimilation or the ethnic cycle, especially of second-generation Japanese Americans.

As was shown in later studies, notably by Emory Bogardus, a former Chicago sociology student, social distance and discriminatory laws retarded assimilation's advance, resulting in some amalgamation but also segregation. Even members of the so-called assimilated Chinese, Japanese, Filipino, and Mexican second generation, Bogardus found, were partially alienated from both American culture and the culture of their immigrant parents, resulting in the "marginal man."[43]

As Park himself came to acknowledge, "Japanese, Chinese, and Negroes cannot move among us with the same freedom as the members of other races because they bear marks which identify them as members of their race." That fact of race isolates them. Segregation and isolation lead to prejudice, and prejudice to isolation and segregation.[44] Because of their "racial badges," Park went on to explain, "Negroes" and "Orientals" were unable to assimilate; "the chief obstacle[s] to assimilation of the Negro and Oriental are not mental but physical traits," he wrote. That racial distinctiveness constituted, in the language of race relations, the "Negro problem" and the "Oriental problem."[45]

Exceptional, then, were African and Asian Americans to the primacy and general rule of ethnicity, the ethnic cycle, and eventual triumph of assimilation.[46] They belonged to the field of race relations. European immigrants, by contrast, affirmed the ideas of (Chicago) ethnic studies. They sustained the foundational, mythical narrative of the United States as a nation of immigrants. African and Asian Americans could not assimilate with whites because of their color and white racial prejudice, which, Thomas and Park held, was "a spontaneous, more or less instinctive defense-reaction." In the US wilderness white racism was a natural survival mechanism. Segregation and even slavery, accordingly, were solutions to the race problem as required by natural law because under slavery and Jim Crow, both groups, masters and servants, knew their places. That view agreed with US sociology's founding fathers. When people of color, the oppressed, observed the rules and relations of subordination, social order prevailed, but when they claimed democracy's promise, demanding equality with whites, they became social problems.[47]

Sustaining those ideas of "natural" and "instinctual" responses to social conflict was the Chicago school's analogy of social relations with evolution, natural selection, and biological competition, thereby procuring the endorsement of science. Thus, in the language of ecological succession, the "invading race," as posed by Park, whether black, brown, or yellow, was the problem, not white supremacy or the ideology and material environments and conditions that sustained white rule.[48] Biological determinism and fixity, unlike cultural change, were key features of race relations, and human nature, not human institutions, held the answer to the race problem.

Race thinking globally, it appears, fell out of favor when Third World elites claimed the allegedly universal values of European humanism and emulated their white supremacist rulers by crafting identifications and solidarity along race lines. The calls of "Africa for Africans" and "Asia for Asians" made by the decolonization movements in Africa and Asia employed racialized categories made in Europe, and their galvanizing powers threatened to disrupt race relations in the imperial order. White supremacy and its eugenicist "final solution," taken to its logical, obscene end by the Nazis during World War II, ultimately spelled the demise of race relations and influenced the turn to ethnicity and (Chicago) ethnic studies.

Culture or ethnicity did not have the sharp edges of race and racism, and assimilation offered a gentler means of absorption, or subjugation by another name. French colonizers were particularly adept at that paternal siring and policing of dependent subjects through the education of a native elite, creating an "ex-native," as described by Sartre. In his preface to Fanon's *Wretched of the Earth*, Sartre penned an acid critique of that violation:

> Not so very long ago, the earth numbered two thousand million inhabitants: five hundred million men, and one thousand five hundred million natives. The former had the Word; the others had the use of it. . . . The European elite undertook to manufacture a native elite. They picked out

promising adolescents; they branded them, as with a red-hot iron, with the principles of Western culture; they stuffed their mouths full with high-sounding phrases, grand glutinous words that stuck to the teeth. After a short stay in the mother country they were sent home, whitewashed. These walking lies had nothing left to say to their brothers; they only echoed. From Paris, from London, from Amsterdam we would utter the words, "Parthenon! Brotherhood!" and somewhere in Africa or Asia lips would open " . . . thenon! . . . therhood!" It was the golden age.[49]

Assimilation produced a "colonized mentality," in Memmi's words, and "miseducation," described by the African American educator Carter G. Woodson, was the apparatus by which to ensure dependency. Schooling, Woodson found in his *Mis-education of the Negro* (1933), inspires the oppressor and crushes the spirit of the oppressed by teaching that whites possessed great civilizations and blacks produced nothing of significance. "Lead the Negro to believe this and thus control his thinking," he wrote. "If you can thereby determine what he will think, you will not need to worry about what he will do. You will not have to tell him to go to the back door. He will go without being told; and if there is no back door, he will have one cut for his special benefit."[50]

A member of the Latin American Students Organization and TWLF at SFS in 1968 applied Woodson's concept of miseducation. Schools, that astute student observed, purposefully excluded certain peoples and their cultures and histories from the curriculum. "It's a process of mis-education," he explained. "It has a purpose. . . . One is to teach us not how to change our community, or even live in it, but how to escape it by denying that we are a part of it. . . . The condition of black people, brown people, yellow people, and red people is essentially that we are all oppressed systematically as individuals and as a people by society."[51]

Chicago sociology's ethnic studies gained traction especially in research on Asian Americans. As noted, Park's Survey of Race Relations, despite its claim to race relations, was a survey of ethnicity, not race, and the processes of assimilation. The marginal status of the second generation as neither Asian nor American was a central feature of that project and those that followed. Asian Americans studied at Chicago and became prominent sociologists, and other former Chicago sociology students trained cadres of students at the University of Washington, the University of Southern California, and the University of Hawai'i who went on to produce works on Asian American marginality and assimilation.[52] In academic discourse after World War II and in the popular imagination of the "model minority" of the 1960s, Asian Americans were positioned and well on their way toward moving from race relations to (Chicago) ethnic studies.[53]

Ethnic Studies Redux

As we will see, while the students of the TWLF demanded a unified Third World curriculum, administrators and faculty made a distinction between African American studies, which they treated as race relations, and Asian, Mexican, and Native American studies, which they considered ethnic studies. Those faculty and administrators might not have been fully cognizant of the intellectual genealogy of or even the discourses surrounding race relations and (Chicago) ethnic studies, but many, I suspect, understood Third World to exude notions of revolution and possibly the specter of Marxism.

Students were susceptible to the claimed prerogatives of administrative and faculty governance and to the authority of academic language and bureaucracy. Roger Alvarado, a member of the TWLF, observed of that process of mystification, "You go to someone's office, they tell you to go elsewhere. You go there, this cat explains how this function is really a little different from what that cat said, so he can only do this much for you, you got to go somewhere else. . . . It's the way the institution is laid out, man." Alvarado concluded insightfully, "Anyone can do whatever he wants to as long as he doesn't make any changes in the institution."[54]

Black studies supplied the opening for (Chicago) ethnic studies. As early as 1965 sympathetic SFS faculty sponsored black studies as experimental courses, and the Black Students Union (BSU) organized courses through the Experimental College and high school tutorial programs such that by March 1968 they had enrolled nearly three thousand students. On February 9, 1968, SFS president John Summerskill appointed Nathan Hare "to help design a curriculum of Black Studies." In April of that year Hare proposed a department of black studies, while the TWLF demanded an increase in minority student admission and "the establishment of a Third World curriculum, along the lines of the Black Studies Program." Meanwhile the SFS academic senate considered a recommendation from its instructional policies committee to establish a program of ethnic studies.[55]

In April and May 1968 student library workers struck for union recognition, Third World students demanded influence over admissions and the hiring of more faculty of color, and the Students for a Democratic Society demanded the eviction of the Air Force ROTC from campus. Summerskill called the San Francisco tactical squad, police trained to stamp out urban riots, to

A beaten, bleeding student, Don McAllister, in police custody, San Francisco State, 1968. Photo by Terry Schmitt. Courtesy of San Francisco State University.

remove student protesters from the administration building, and in the skirmish the police arrested twenty-six students and injured at least eleven. More sit-ins, demonstrations, and arrests rocked SFS for days, and on May 24, 1968, the students reached an agreement with the administration.[56] On that day Summerskill resigned, and on June 1 Robert Smith assumed the presidency. In August the trustees considered a proposal for a black studies major, and the following month Smith announced the formation of a department of black studies and appointed Hare as its chair.

On November 6, 1968, after the dismissal of George Murray, the part-time English Department instructor, the BSU launched the strike that eventuated in a School of Ethnic Studies.[57] As the Black Panther Party's minister of education, Murray had expressed the party's vow to fight until "colonized Africans, Asians and Latin Americans in the United States and throughout the world have become free. . . . That is the historic duty of black people in the United States to bring about the complete, absolute and unconditional end of racism and neocolonialism by smashing, shattering and destroying the imperialist domains of North America."[58] The immediate demands of the strike, however, were far less ambitious: petitioning for a larger black studies program and

Murray's reinstatement. Other student organizations of the TWLF joined the BSU a few days later.

Meanwhile, in the November 4 issue of the official SFS newsletter *On the Record*, President Smith issued "Statement on Black and Ethnic Studies," in which he refers to "black and ethnic" students, including "young adults of minority racial and ethnic backgrounds" and "Spanish-speaking cultural backgrounds." Thereby Smith makes a distinction between race in reference to blacks, and ethnicity to nonblacks. A December academic senate report reinforced that differentiation when it endorsed the implementation of a black studies program and the creation of a task force to study the feasibility of "non-black Ethnic programs" and "to explore policies and procedures for ethnic studies."[59]

Student activists mirrored the distinction between black studies and ethnic studies, which some called "ethnic area studies," reflecting, ironically, the wider academic convention since the cold war of African, Asian, and Latin American area studies. "Ethnic area studies," the students explained in a position paper, was the term used at least since June 1968, when the TWLF sought to implement "ethnic area studies" and institute "a school of ethnic area studies" to respond to Third World needs.[60] That choice of "area studies," a weapon of the Cold War, misnames the students' intention for their Third World curriculum. Area studies in the United States was originally funded and designed to contain the spread of communism, especially in the Third World. Moreover, as was the convention in area studies, the United States was the home and center and not an area of the world marked for strategic study. To their credit the TWLF ultimately dropped that designation. The term ethnic studies nonetheless endured.

Two sets of demands followed the initial petitions to expand black studies and rehire Murray. The first came from the BSU's "10 Demands," which addressed the expansion of black studies but did not include a provision for Third World or ethnic (area) studies. The second, "Third World Liberation Front Demands," proposed that a "School of Ethnic Studies for the ethnic groups involved in the Third World be set up with students in each particular ethnic organization having the authority and control of the hiring and retention of any faculty member." Among the TWLF's five demands was a provision for fifty faculty positions for a school of ethnic studies, with twenty of those set aside for a program in black studies.[61]

When the BSU and TWLF signed the joint agreement on March 18, 1969, that ended the longest student strike in the history of US higher education, they settled for the language: "that a school of ethnic studies for the ethnic groups involved in the third world be set up with the students in each."[62] The name ethnic studies remains at San Francisco State in the College of Ethnic Studies that opened in the fall of 1969, along with the separation of each group in its own program, although some students and faculty continued to employ the term Third World through at least 1970.[63]

The move from Third World to (post-1968) ethnic studies involved several steps. San Francisco State's administrators racialized African Americans and labeled American Indians, Asians, and Mexicans ethnic or cultural groups. College faculty referenced black studies and "non-black Ethnic programs" when students demanded Third World studies. Students deployed "ethnic area studies" to link the condition of Africans, Asians, and Mexicans in the United States with the peoples of Africa, Asia, and Latin America—the Third World.[64] In the end ethnic studies became shorthand for members of the TWLF, embracing African Americans, American Indians, Asian Americans, and Mexican Americans and Latinx.

Before that final agreement Hare submitted his proposal for a black studies curriculum on April 29, 1968. In his introduction Hare acknowledged that the impetus for black studies at SFS came from African American students and the BSU. The idea, Hare warned, "not only reflects their cries—echoed by others across the country—for relevant education; it also represents the greatest and last hope for rectifying an old wrong and halting the decay now gnawing away at American society."[65]

A key component of the black studies program, Hare proposed, was its focus on "community involvement . . . to inspire and sustain a sense of collective destiny as a people and a consciousness of the value of education in a technological society." The academic program would constitute "a cultural base" for the black community to celebrate "black holidays, festivities and celebrations." Black information centers would increase awareness within black communities and distribute "propaganda" aimed at black children to motivate them to complete their education.[66]

Hare's tentative black studies major included four core courses on black history, black psychology, black arts and humanities, and a method and theory course in the sciences. He proposed a black arts concentration, comprising music, writing, literature, painting, and sculpture, and a behavioral and social sciences concentration, involving black politics, sociology, geography, counseling, leadership, and community. The only course not centered in the United States that might have gestured toward the Third World was a course titled "Black Consciousness and the International Community."[67]

Black studies graduates, Hare believed, would share a commitment "to the struggle to build the black community," and graduates employed outside the black community would possess "a keener sense of security as individuals and would be better equipped to present the black perspective. This would benefit the black community indirectly and perhaps assist those members of the white community who, like the black studies program, seek, in a roundabout way, a better society for all of its members."[68]

Black studies, so conceived, was limited to the US nation-state and directed at African American uplift through community development and a collective sense of peoplehood. Black or national culture, black ethnicity, was central to that project, which featured the nation-state and its black and white "communities." In seeking "a better society for all of its members," black studies mirrored the problem solving and culture of ethnic studies of Chicago sociology and the civil rights movement's drive for national inclusion and belonging, not the self-determination and antiracism of the Third World liberation movement or the internationalism of Third World women and TWLF.[69] In May 1967, a year before Hare submitted his proposal, college deans considered black studies as a place "wherein the Negro student could get something to help him find his place in American society."[70] It was that version of black studies that Hare endorsed, SFS president Smith approved, and the academic senate considered, blending Chicago sociology's race relations with ethnic studies.

Absent in that discourse of (post-1968) ethnic studies is the revolutionary movement, ideology, and language that changed over four hundred years of world history wrought by the struggles of Third World peoples along the color line. In that post-1968 version of ethnic studies, patriarchal nationalism eclipsed Third World consciousness and solidarity even as in the Third World the nation-state was seen as the final expression of self-determination. Meanwhile internal colonialism in the United States and neocolonialism in the Third World descended as soon as self-determination and independence dawned, and imperialism and capitalism found new life in a national and transnational new world order.

Terry Collins, a member of the central committee of San Francisco State's BSU, reflected on that drift to nationalism and patriarchy. In the spring of 1968, Collins recalled, a handful of "dominant personalities . . . tyrannically reigned over the other students" in the movement. "Factionalism was rampant, potential revolutionary brothers were disillusioned, sisters were used and abused in the name of 'blackness.' It was the era of bourgeois cultural nationalism." The cults of personality and authenticity, nationalism and culture, Collins noted, divided and diverted the focus of black students from "the real enemy."[71]

Black Colony

Dissident stirrings appear in the writings of African American sociologists trained at Chicago. While Chicago sociologists held that their ethnic cycle followed the natural history of evolution from instability to equilibrium, like the German sociologist Georg Simmel (1858–1918), they argued that caste and slave systems of rule and subordination were natural states for peoples William Thomas called "culturally undeveloped material." E. Franklin Frazier, Charles S. Johnson, William O. Brown, and Bertram Doyle, African American Chicago sociologists, found those theories difficult to reconcile with the realities of black life. Frazier, for instance, stressed racial segregation rather than assimilation, and saw conflict, not accommodation, as the central feature of black-white relations. Black "traditional intellectuals," to use the distinction made by Gramsci, chafed under white hegemony.

The masses too were discontent. Black "organic intellectuals," another of Gramsci's terms, learned in the act of mobilizing campus and community, and they read and debated ideas drawn from Third World thinkers and revolutionaries. Du Bois, Hubert Harrison, Paul Robeson, the singer, actor, and social activist, and others had long described African Americans as a colonized people and their struggles for liberation as a part of the Third World anti-imperialist, decolonization movement. Three months before passage of the Civil Rights Act (1964), Malcolm X resuscitated that understanding when he spoke in Cleveland on "the ballot or the bullet." Black freedom, he urged, should not be pursued as domestic civil rights but as international human rights in unity with "our African brothers and our Asian brothers and our Latin-American brothers."[72]

Max Stanford, founder of the Revolutionary Action Movement (RAM), a black nationalist group in Philadelphia, wrote in 1965, "We are revolutionary black nationalist[s], not based on ideas of national superiority, but striving for justice and liberation of all the oppressed peoples of the world. . . . There can be no liberty as long as black people are oppressed and the peoples of Africa, Asia and Latin America are oppressed by Yankee imperialism and neo-colonialism. After four hundred years of oppression, we realize that slavery, racism and imperialism are all interrelated and that liberty and justice for all cannot exist peacefully with imperialism."[73] The words and deeds of Fanon, Mao, and Che Guevara informed the ideology and politics of RAM and Stanford, who considered African Americans colonial subjects, not US citizens. On July 4, 1965, RAM declared solidarity with the Vietnamese people in their struggle against US imperialism and opposed African American military service in the US war in Southeast Asia.

Robert F. Williams, president of the Monroe, North Carolina, chapter of the National Association for the Advancement of Colored People, advocated armed self-defense for black people in the face of white violence. The Ku Klux Klan, with the collaboration of white leaders and police, terrorized African American communities in the South. When equal justice under the law fails, Williams held, citizens must resort to self-defense to preserve rights and the rule of law.[74] In 1961, after the state leveled criminal charges against him, Williams fled the country for Cuba, and in 1963 he traveled to China to live and work there and secure from Mao a statement in support of the African American freedom struggle.

In his August 8, 1963, "Statement" Mao called on "the workers, peasants, revolutionary intellectuals, enlightened elements of the bourgeoisie and other enlightened persons of all colours in the world, whether white, black, yellow or brown, to unite to oppose racial discrimination practised by US imperialism and to support the American Negroes in their struggle against racial discrimination." He cited US imperialism as the cause of oppression in the world and predicted, "The evil system of colonialism and imperialism arose and throve with the enslavement of Negroes and the trade in Negroes, and it will surely come to its end with the complete emancipation of the black people."[75]

Three years later, during a rally in Beijing, Williams, who published his newsletter, *The Crusader*, while in exile in China, thanked Mao and the Chinese people for their support. "The thunder of BLACK POWER echoes throughout the land," he reported of the United States. "A mighty firestorm sweeps through the black ghettoes rife with rebellion.... What is the meaning of this cry BLACK POWER in a land dominated by the unmerciful power of white intruders who murdered and all but exterminated the rightful owners, the American Indians? Black Power means that black men want to have some control over their own lives, to have a respected voice in public affairs that affect them. They resent being a colonial people, treated as third class citizens in their own native land." Together with the Vietnamese people suffering under US imperialism, Williams declared, "We are oppressed people."[76]

In 1961, before his exile, Williams visited the University of California, Berkeley. About two months later Malcolm X followed. Invited by Berkeley's Afro-American Association (AAA), an activist and study group, Williams and Malcolm X were influential in opening those young minds to the international significance of the African American freedom struggle. One of those youth was Huey P. Newton, the future leader of the Black Panther Party who was greatly impressed by Williams's life and courage. While in Cuba Williams met with Stanford of RAM and Ernest Allen, founder of the Soul Students Advisory Council at Oakland's Merritt College, which became a prototype for student activism. Newton was a student at Merritt College and a member of AAA, which had expanded from Berkeley to Oakland and San Francisco.

The AAA fostered black solidarity, Pan-Africanism, and the politics of Third World liberation. At the height of its powers in 1963 the AAA had its largest following at Merritt College, which enrolled students mainly from the black working class who had migrated to Oakland from the US South. Anne Williams, an AAA member at Oakland City College, remembered AAA study groups reading and debating armed self-defense, Marxism, women's liberation, existentialism, and black consciousness. Williams went to Cuba in the spring of 1962, and there she met Robert Williams and his wife, Mabel. The trip, she said, changed her life in that it exposed her to the wider world.[77]

Under student pressure in 1964, Merritt College offered black studies classes in its experimental program. Working-class blacks, military veterans, and older people enrolled in those classes, including cofounders and future Panther leaders Bobby Seale and Huey Newton, Ernest Allen, Richard Thorne, and Marvin Jackman. Between 1964 and 1966 Allen's Soul Students Advisory Council pressed the college to hire more black faculty and expand the black studies curriculum. In 1966 the council changed its name to the Black Student Union, and in June 1968 the BSU submitted a resolution to California's State Board of Education to initiate a new credential major in Afro-American studies. In October of that year Afro-American studies became a temporary program at Merritt College, and by the end of 1968 the college instituted a black studies department. Of that remarkable success Newton explained, "Everyone—from Warden [Donald Warden, an AAA leader] and the Afro-American Association to Malcolm X and the Muslims to all the other groups active in the Bay Area at the time—believed strongly that the failure to include Black history in the college curriculum was a scandal. We all set out to do something about it."[78]

Begun in 1966, the Black Panther Party became a major force in the assertion of black power. In May 1967 the party announced its Ten Point Program, "What We Want Now! What We Believe." It began with the electrifying "We want freedom. We want power to determine the destiny of our Black Community," which is the essence of black power: agency. Other desires were full employment, decent housing, an end to police brutality, exemption from military service, freedom for all black prisoners, trial by black juries, and "land, bread, housing, education, clothing, justice and peace." Regarding education the program stated, "We want education that teaches us our true history and our role in the present day society." The program referenced "the black colony" and "black colonial subject."[79]

That summer Newton published a series of articles in the *Black Panther*, the party's official organ. He drew from Fanon, Mao, and Malcolm X and expanded on the RAM idea of African America as a colony within the US Empire. Citing Fanon, he noted the effects of colonization on the black psyche, accounting for a colonial mentality, and he likened the police to a foreign occupying army. Linking those conditions with US imperialism in Asia, Newton wrote, "There is a great similarity between the occupying army in Southeast Asia and the occupation of our communities by the racist police."[80] The anticolonial struggles in Asia and throughout the world, Newton advanced, forged connections with the African American liberation movement.

As early as 1966 San Francisco State's BSU leader James Garrett called the black struggle "no different from that of the Vietnamese.... We are struggling for self-determination ... for our black communities; and self-determination for black education." In August 1968, just before the BSU and TWLF strike for Third World studies at San Francisco State, George Murray of the BSU, Nation of Islam, and Black Panther Party attended the Organization of Solidarity with the People of Asia, Africa and Latin America conference held in Cuba. Speaking for the Black Panther Party, Murray promised the delegates, "We have vowed not to put down our guns or stop making Molotov cocktails until colonized Africans, Asians and Latin Americans in the United States and throughout the world are free." Black liberation required a global revolution against imperialism, he declared, and promised, "If it means our lives, that is but a small price to pay for the freedom of humanity."[81] Interviewed in Havana, Murray testified, "Our thinking is inspired by Che Guevara, Malcolm X, Lumumba, Ho Chi Minh and Mao Tse-tung."[82]

Organic intellectuals, members of the masses, studied and debated the ideas of black power and black colonization throughout the 1960s before traditional intellectuals put those ideas to paper. Harold Cruse, the African American writer and cultural critic, wrote of black alienation and "close rapport" with the spirit of anticolonial self-determination and world revolution in 1962. From the start of the US nation, Cruse recalled, the African American had existed as "a colonial being" in "a condition of domestic colonialism."[83] In 1965 the black psychologist Kenneth Clark published *Dark Ghetto*, which described New York City's Harlem as essentially a colony. Two years later

Stokely Carmichael of the Student Nonviolent Coordinating Committee and the Black Panther Party and the political scientist Charles V. Hamilton published *Black Power*, which codified a systematic black power ideology and made a case for African Americans as "colonial subjects" in a "colonial situation." The distinction between colony and *internal colony* is that the former is external to the colonizing nation-state, while the latter is within the nation-state.

Summary

The Third World liberation movements against imperialism and colonization, as discourses and material conditions, were the antecedents of black power. Black self-determination was the objective of black power. As Stokely Carmichael astutely observed, discursive freedom required escape from "the dictatorship of definition, interpretation and consciousness."[84] Third World liberation from the bondage of colonialism that enslaved bodies and minds was the model for black power, and the BSU- and TWLF-led strike for Third World studies at San Francisco State emerges from that genealogy and history.

In this chapter I refer to the subjects of Third World studies as the field's subject matter—power and the oppressed, and the field's pedagogy—a "Third World curriculum." I describe the field's subject as social power or agency. Self-determination is a key aspect of that agency or ability. I cite the field's focus on the people, the masses, the oppressed, and their deeds. Those too are subjects of Third World studies, as opposed to the elites, the ruling class, the oppressors, and their achievements. Finally I trace the field's origins to the articulations of the Third World Liberation Front at San Francisco State that were diverted into (cultural) nationalisms and (Chicago) ethnic studies. The TWLF's demand for a Third World curriculum is the unfinished business of that student uprising and revolutionary moment in US and world history.

Students chose the name *Third World* and not *national* liberation front, as was the case in Algeria and Vietnam. Race relations and ethnic studies of the Chicago school, civil rights, and inclusion within the nation-state are not the genesis of Third World studies, which is located in human rights and internationalism, as Malcolm X suggested, and in movements for liberation from the bonds of fear and poverty, liberation from physical, spiritual, and intellectual bonds, which have too long stunted the development of humanity's majority, in the stirring words of Sukarno at Bandung. Those are the subjects (and objects) of Third World studies.

TWO

NATIONALISM

The colonial analogy advanced by the black power movement suggests decolonization and the nation-state as the means toward self-determination.[1] In fact nationalism was a prominent feature of Third World decolonization movements and the ideology of black power in the United States. For instance, in 1967 RAM's Max Stanford described his organization as "revolutionary black nationalist." Robert Williams explained, "Black Nationalism is the only common denominator that will solidify our dehumanized and fragmented people."[2] In "Afterword, 1992" Stokely Carmichael, under the name Kwame Ture, describes black power as "an ideology coming from our culture and in which nationalism played its necessary role."[3]

Within the Third World self-determination was associated with the equality of all peoples, ideas derived from Europeans. Speaking before the US Congress on January 8, 1918, President Woodrow Wilson announced his Fourteen Points, which explained the nation's reasons for entering into World War I. Wilson offered principles to guide international relations, including the right of all peoples to self-determination and "national self-determination" for subjugated peoples. Although intellectuals like Hubert Harrison were skeptical of Wilson's self-determination for people of color, self-determination entered into the lexicon of global politics and human rights, and the decolonization struggle conceived of liberation as national self-determination.

That inward turn to the nation contrasted with the global demarcations of the color line and Third World liberation struggles against imperialism worldwide.[4] During World War II, for instance, African American leaders expressed a resurgent internationalism and solidarity with people of color based upon their common condition of subjugation and exploitation along the color line.[5] Walter White, executive director of the National Association for the Advancement of Colored People during the war, testified, "World War II has given to the Negro a sense of kinship with other colored—and also oppressed—peoples of the world" and the realization that "the struggle of the Negro in the United States is part and parcel of the struggle against imperialism and exploitation in India, China, Burma, Africa, the Philippines, Malaya, the West Indies, and South America."[6]

It appears that black power organic intellectuals, while calling themselves and their groups "nationalist," subscribed to a decidedly Third World consciousness and cast, aligning themselves with movements for the liberation of all oppressed peoples. By contrast, it seems that traditional intellectuals of color tended to favor the nation-state and its people as the principal subject matters of their post-1968 ethnic studies. Self-determination authorized their separate, racialized cells of African American, American Indian, Asian American, and Chicana/o and Latina/o studies. At the same time that distinction between organic and traditional intellectuals might have dissolved in the daily struggles for resources, rights, and, ultimately, power in the academy and on the street. Divide and rule is a strategy of the ruling class even as the oppressed can subscribe to that design in pursuit of self-determination as a race and culture while trampling upon the liberties of other oppressed groups. By contrast, a Third World consciousness maintains, agency is not a zero-sum game, and self-determination for the subject-self must not come at the expense of its others.

History has shown that a consciousness of the oppressed without regard to race enabled the postwar creation of the Third World and its non-aligned movement, which descended not from the immediate context of the post–World War II Cold War but from the anticolonial, antiracist struggles that had long preceded the contest between capitalism and communism. In addition that capacious consciousness, that connection between "the struggle of the Negro" in the United States and Third World liberation movements against imperialism worldwide, forms the foundation for Third World studies.

The naming of the Third World nonetheless was an aspect of the Cold War. Albert Sauvy, a French Resistance fighter against Nazi Germany and its collaborators during World War II, wrote in the newspaper *France-Observateur* against the war waged by France in colonized Algeria. In 1952 Sauvy, again in the pages of *France-Observateur*, described the globe as parceled into the First, Second, and Third Worlds, divided by ideologies and economies. The First World, or the West, included Western Europe and the United States joined in market capitalism. The Second World, or the East, revolved around the Soviet Union and its sphere of socialism. The Third World contained the rest, the remaining two-thirds of the planet's peoples in Africa, America, Asia, and "the islands of the sea."[7]

Within the Third World the First and Second Worlds waged wars hot and cold for global dominance. The Third World was enormously rich in resources and labor, but exceedingly poor economically, a result of colonialism, which extracted capital and labor to profit the colonial masters while impoverishing the colonized masses. That material relationship and the racist discourse that supported colonialism were the bases for Sauvy's anticolonial critique and view of the world and the prospects for peace.

The Color Line Revisited

As shown, the intellectual antecedent of Third World studies reaches back to 1900 and W. E. B. Du Bois's articulation of "the problem of the twentieth century" as "the problem of the color line." The occasion was the first Pan-African Conference, which the lawyer and writer Henry Sylvester Williams of Trinidad convened for Africans in Africa and across the African diaspora.[8] Although Williams's purpose was limited to advancing the interests of Africans within the British Empire, the Pan-African Conference called for a more ambitious agenda addressed "to the nations of the world." The document called for the advancement of human progress generally by dismantling white privilege and granting to all of the world's peoples, including those of the "darker races"—black, yellow, and brown—"the largest and broadest opportunity for education and self-development."[9] Antiracism and self-determination for the darker races of the world were the objectives of that first Pan-African Conference.

Nearly a year later in the *Atlantic Monthly* Du Bois reiterated, "The problem of the twentieth century is the problem of the color line; the relation of the darker to the lighter races of men in Asia and Africa, in America and the islands of the sea."[10] In 1906 Du Bois expanded upon that forecast in *Collier's Weekly* by observing, "The color line belts the world." The "Negro problem," he began, "is but a local phase of a world problem." European imperialism and colonization, he explained, drew the global color line; racism was the ideology that justified that appropriation of the lands and labor of the native races. For over a thousand years, through force and fear, Du Bois continued, white races have held dominion over colored races until the Russo-Japanese War (1904–5), in which the Japanese, a colored race, defeated a white nation, breaching the seemingly impregnable color line.[11]

Once the cradles of world civilization, recalled Du Bois, Africa and Asia were conquered, enslaved, exploited, and reduced to European colonies, "slums of the world" and "places of greatest concentration of poverty, disease, and ignorance." The fall of the Roman Empire led to the rise of acquisitive European states that competed for territory, labor, and resources—possessions. Modern colonies were built upon "Negro slavery, Chinese coolies, and doctrines of race inferiority." As a result, Du Bois estimated near the end of World War II, "there will be at least 750,000,000 colored and black folk inhabiting colonies owned by white nations who will have no rights that the white people of the world are bound to respect."[12] Instead "the majority of the inhabitants of earth, who happen for the most part to be colored, must be regarded as having the right and the capacity to share in human progress and to become copartners in that democracy which alone can ensure peace among men."[13]

| | |

On the other side of the color line Charles H. Pearson, a politician in colonial Australia, raised the alarm over "the black and yellow races" in *National Life and Character: A Forecast* (1893). From the empire's periphery Pearson addressed the British metropole: "The day will come, and perhaps is not far distant, when the European observer will look round to see the globe girdled with a continuous zone of the black and yellow races, no longer too weak for aggression or under tutelage, but independent, or practically so." As whites, he warned, "we shall wake to find ourselves elbowed and hustled, and perhaps even thrust aside by peoples whom we looked down upon as servile, and thought of as bound always to minister to our needs."[14] Pearson's book warned against a complacent white supremacy that rested on its laurels, awaiting the decline and eventual extinction of the darker races.

Perhaps more ominous than being elbowed, hustled, and thrust aside was Pearson's prognosis of miscegenation. With their independence, he wrote, Africans and Asians "will then be taken up into the social relations of the white races, will throng the English turf, or the salons of Paris, and will be admitted to intermarriage." The uplift of recumbent races called "the white man's burden" was the source of that development in world history. After all, Pearson noted, "it has been our work to organise and create, to carry peace and law and order over the world, that others may enter in and enjoy." All the while whites fought against whites, "struggling among ourselves for supremacy in a world which we thought of as destined to belong to the Aryan races and to the Christian faith."[15]

Taking up Pearson's dark forecast, Lothrop Stoddard, a Harvard PhD, regretted that unheeded went his warning to the white race over the perils it faced. World War I, the "White Civil War," which was "primarily a struggle between white peoples, who have borne the brunt of the conflict and have suffered most of the losses," weakened white supremacy and stirred nonwhite insurgency. Awaken to a map of the world, he exhorted his fellow whites, wherein "we see a world of which only four-tenths at the most can be considered predominantly white in blood, and the rest of the world being inhabited mainly by the other primary races of mankind—yellows, browns, blacks, and reds," who are increasing more rapidly than whites. Moreover "the colored world, long restive under white political domination, is being welded . . . into a common solidarity of feeling against the dominant white man."[16]

Whites, by contrast, were "forgetting ties of blood and culture, heedless of the growing pressure of the colored world without, locked in a battle to the death." That situation, Stoddard agreed with Du Bois, "is the present status of the world's race-problem."[17] In an earlier book, in fact, Stoddard wrote, like Du Bois, that the conflict of color was "the fundamental problem of the twentieth century."[18]

It is important to consider that the essentializing color line of white and nonwhite emerged in the late nineteenth century at the height of imperialism. Extraterritorial expansion witnessed European nations and peoples, as Pearson and Stoddard regretted, compete with each other in the name of national sovereignty and as separate races. The English race, the Dutch race, the German race were national races, but in their encounter with people of color in the enactment of empire in the Third World, they became the white race. As Germany's Kaiser Wilhelm II had maintained, defense of a common "possession"— Christianity and European civilization—united disparate European races into a single, white race when confronted with a common other and enemy, the "yellow peril."

Race War

Global, regional, and linguistic formations forged solidarities across colonies and nation-states to advance an end to colonialism and white supremacy. The global color line and its essential groupings of white and nonwhite in the imperial encounter supplied the scaffolding for those anticolonial projects. As recounted by the historian Vijay Prashad, the formation of the Third World gained substance in conventions that met across the world from Brussels to Bandung to Cairo, Buenos Aires, Tehran, Belgrade, Havana, and beyond in a breathtaking crisscrossing of the planet.[19]

Having been denied permission to convene in imperial Berlin and Paris, the League against Imperialism and Colonialism held its meeting in Belgium, another colonial power, in 1927. From Africa, America, and Asia the representatives of anti-imperialist organizations came to call for national self-determination. Like the London meeting of the first Pan-African Conference, the League's choice of Brussels was as much directed by the symbolism of anticolonialism in the heart of colonial masters as by necessity. There were few independent Third World nations. As the future president of Indonesia Ahmed Sukarno said, in Brussels delegates "found new strength in their fight for independence," but it was far away, "amidst foreign people, in a foreign country, in a foreign continent."[20]

Six years before the League against Imperialism's meeting in that alien place, the Third Pan-African Congress had assembled in Brussels. There pan-Africanists heard Du Bois declare, "The beginning of wisdom in inter-racial contact is the establishment of political institutions among suppressed peoples. The habit of democracy must be made to encircle the world." By the Sixth Pan-African Congress, held in Manchester, England, in 1945, that "inter-racial contact" had enabled this declaration: "We affirm the right of all colonial peoples to control their own destiny. All colonies must be free from foreign imperialist control, whether political or economic. . . . The object of imperialist Powers is to exploit. By granting the right to colonial peoples to govern themselves that object is defeated."[21]

| | |

Like Europe's First World War, the conflict of color figured prominently in the conduct of World War II. The European theater featured a fratricidal conflict of white against white, wherein Nazi Germany protected superior white genes from contamination and degeneration by "impurities." In the Asian and Pacific theater nonwhites challenged white supremacy and colonialism. The nonwhite struggle for self-determination was twofold: anticolonialism or liberation from the material conditions that oppressed and exploited them, and antiracism or freedom from the discourses that justified and maintained colonialism.

Greater than its victory over the Russians at the century's start, a scholar claimed, Japan's early military successes against European colonial powers in Asia represented "a blow to white prestige" and "heightened the degree of racial self-consciousness" of a world divided between West and East, white and nonwhite.[22] Moreover, as the historian Gerald Horne pointed out, Nazi Germany sustained the idea of white supremacy, while Japan threatened it.[23] A March 1942 commentary in the *Times* (London) took the race relations "problems" approach to Japan's opposition to white dominance: "Japan's attack has produced a very practical revolution in race relations."[24]

Even before the war Japan had championed the cause of peoples under European colonial rule, despite its colonization of Korea in 1910 and expansions into Manchuria and northern China in the 1930s, which mimicked the European formula for national greatness. At the Treaty of Paris (1918–19) and the formation of the League of Nations, Japan proposed an amendment to the League's covenant that would ensure "equal and just treatment in every respect, making no distinction, either in law or in fact, on account of [people's] race or nationality." The colonial powers rejected that challenge to white supremacy, but Japan gained the esteem of Asian and African anticolonialists as the "logical leader," in the words of Du Bois, of "all coloured peoples."[25]

In addition to Japan's military conquests in Asia, the reliance of the colonial powers upon reinforcements supplied by their colonial subjects during World War II spread and hastened the zeal for national self-determination across the colonized world. Britain's prime minister (1957–63) Harold Macmillan recalled, "What the two [world] wars did was to destroy the prestige of the white people. For not only did the yellows and blacks watch them tear each other apart, committing the most frightful crimes and acts of barbarism against each other, but they actually saw them enlisting each of their own yellows and blacks to fight other Europeans, other whites. It was bad enough for the white men to fight each other, but it was worse when they brought in their dependents."[26]

During the war, accordingly, Britain worried over sending black troops from its Caribbean colonies to help defend its colony in India; they might instead join the Indians in the fight against British colonialism. Indian nationalists were divided on the question of defending British colonial India against a Japanese army allegedly fighting to liberate colonized Asia. Jawaharlal Nehru, a leader of the independence movement and the first prime minister of India, remembered that the contradiction heightened for Indian patriots when the British used the Defence of India Act to suppress everyday activities and arrest and imprison Indians without trial: "So instead of the intoxication of the thought of freedom which would unleash our energies and throw us with a nation's enthusiasm into the world struggle, we experienced the aching frustration of its denial. And this denial was accompanied by an arrogance of language, a self-glorification of British rule and policy."[27]

Although sharply divided on the war, the anticolonial Indian National Congress passed on August 8, 1942, the Quit India Resolution, which called British colonialism degrading and enfeebling of India and an offense to world freedom. The next day the British made numerous arrests, and in response acts of mass resistance increased throughout India. "As the war developed," Nehru observed, "it became ever clearer that the western democracies were fighting not for a change but for a perpetuation of the old order," and the Allied and Axis powers shared a common war interest: the preservation of white supremacy and the colonial status quo. Both sides embraced legacies of "empire and racial discrimination," and after the war "the old imperialisms still functioned."[28]

Beyond India's borders anticolonial leaders simultaneously condemned and cheered the Japanese advance. In British, French, and Dutch colonies in Asia, recalled Mahatir Mohamad, Malaysia's prime minister, "most Asians felt inferior to the European colonisers and rarely did we even consider independence a viable option." The colonies were designed "to serve the European demand for raw materials and natural resources" and were thus dependencies. But Japan's expulsion of the British "changed our view of the world," showing that "an Asian race, the Japanese," could defeat whites. And with that reality dawned "a new awakening amongst us that if we wanted to, we could be like the Japanese. We did have the ability to govern our own country and compete with the Europeans on an equal footing." Despite the brutality of and immense suffering under Japanese wartime occupation and the "tremendous disappointment" over the return of the British after the war, the shackles of "mental servitude" had been broken.[29] Similarly Singapore's first prime minister, Lee Kuan Yew, testified that Japan's defeat of the British "completely changed our world," and Singaporean Gay Wan Guay saw that the British "were not superhuman, supermen, as we used to think."[30]

For European colonizers Japan threatened their discursive and material possessions, with which they were slow to part. Prime Minister Winston S. Churchill declared that Pearl Harbor was "a staggering blow" and "our prestige suffered with the loss of Hong Kong," and he called India a nonnegotiable jewel in the British Crown.[31] As he reassured the House of Commons in early 1942 amid widespread, mass resistance to colonialism in India, the Atlantic Charter's provisions were not "applicable to [the] Coloured Races in [the] colonial empire, and . . . [the phrase] 'restoration of sovereignty, self-government and national life' . . . [was] applicable only to the States and the Nations of Europe."[32]

Reporting on that blow to British prestige on the loss of Hong Kong, a US journalist expressed the humiliation of defeat along the color line: "They [the Japanese] paraded us, the hungry, bedraggled two hundred of us, through the crowded Chinese section. We were the perfect picture of the Fall of the White Man in the Far East. A white man lying disemboweled in the dirt, a white woman snatched naked and gang-raped. . . . These pictures delighted the Jap heart." She added, "If you in America could see your own people being marched by those little monkey men with the big bayonets, you would realize what the Japs intend to do to all the white men."[33]

Japan's war intention involved a break from Western dependence, as advocated by intellectuals during the 1930s in the cultural sphere as a flight from bankrupt Western traditions, which had been eagerly pursued since the Meiji Restoration (1868), and a return to Asian values as a source for national greatness. In Japan a new consciousness arising from the ashes of the old was crucial to the nation's survival amid rampant Westernization. That regeneration and pan-Asian solidarity under Japan's lead resisted European imperialism and promised a new dispensation for Asia. Foreign Minister Yosuke Matsuoka, who had been educated in the United States, created the "Greater East Asia Co-Prosperity Sphere" in August 1940, even as Japan was economically dependent upon the West and was engaged in imperial expansion in East Asia. Still the idea of decolonization resonated with Asians widely because, in the words of former US president Herbert Hoover in 1942, "universally, the white man is hated by the Chinese, Malayan, Indian and Japanese alike."[34]

The December 8, 1941, Imperial Rescript outlined Japan's war aims: to ensure Japan's integrity and to remove European colonialism and bring stability to East and Southeast Asia. As Japan's army advanced into Southeast Asia, its generals proclaimed "Asia for Asians," and General Tomoyuki Yamashita announced his intention to sweep away the arrogance of British colonizers and share the "pain and rejoicing with all coloured peoples."[35] As its fortunes on the warfront diminished, Tokyo called a Great East Asia Conference in November 1943 that included representatives from Southeast Asia—Burma, the Philippines, and Thailand. There Prime Minister Hideki Tojo declared that Japan was waging a war against "Anglo-Americans" who sought to perpetuate their colonial hold over Asia, and the conference concluded by urging cooperation based upon principles of coexistence and coprosperity, respect for national sovereignty and cultural diversity, the economic development of all, and the abolition of all systems of racism.[36]

Imperial Japan's hypocrisy in declaring solidarity with "all coloured peoples" was not so distant from the Allies' "universal" Four Freedoms and Atlantic Charter, which conceived of freedom for whites only. With its victory over Russia, Japan posed a genuine challenge, discursively and militarily, to the twentieth century's color line drawn between the essentialized and contrived racialized poles of white and nonwhite. Although allied racially, whites were not homogeneous. As historians have shown, even close friends Britain and the United States held competing interests in the pursuit of the war, and although largely white as a nation in the global arena, the United States was significantly nonwhite in the composition of its people.

If the problem of the twentieth century was the problem of the color line, it was so because both sides of the divide observed and opposed it. Japan's wartime achievement was to capitalize on that partition and the aspirations for freedom among the colonized peoples of Asia and Africa. Although Japan lost the war, a British colonial officer foresaw, it created conditions in Southeast Asia so revolutionary that there would be no easy return to white rule.[37] The mutually constituting shams of white superiority and nonwhite inferiority, along with the colonialism they bred, had been fatally bruised. B. V. A. Roling of the Netherlands, one of the eleven judges presiding over the Tokyo War Crimes Trial, conceded, "It was quite different in Japan [referring to the Tokyo and Nuremberg trials]. The Japanese defended the action of Japan in this Asian land and in the world, to liberate Asia and to change the world. And they had a case, in this respect," whereas "Nuremberg was a clear case of aggression to dominate the European continent."[38]

| | |

Decolonization, the historian Prasenjit Duara declared, was "one of the most important political developments of the twentieth century because it turned the world into the stage of history."[39] Yet there is a tendency within European historiography to deny significance to the anticolonial struggles of the Third World. Such histories credit Europeans with gifting independence to their former colonies and providing them the infrastructures for modern nation-states. They belittle the postcolonial efforts at nation building and reference tribalism, ethnic and religious conflicts, corruption, and ineptitude as some of the consequences of decolonization.[40] A nostalgia for colonialism and the order it imposed over unruly, untutored, and racialized subjects pervades much of those writings. The era of European colonial rule in Asia, one author claimed, was "the most peaceful and stable period the East had ever known"; without the "stabilising" influence of the West, Asia achieved "freedom" and "independence" while sinking into "a morass of debt" and communist insurgencies.[41]

Those defenders of colonialism slight anticolonialism's efficacy along with the racism, which endorsed white expansion and rule. In fact although race forms a crucial aspect of white subjectivity, academic discourses such as international affairs virtually ignore race and racism even as European and US imperialists had few inhibitions about speaking in racist terms. "The greatest influence on racial thinking," the Hungarian sociologist Frank Füredi observed, "was the emergence of resistance to Western domination" and fears of Western decline.[42] The anticolonial, nation-building movement, which long preceded World War II and which white supremacists painted as antiwhite, crested during that war both as discourse and strategies of resistance. Japan and nationalist leaders in Africa and Asia played key roles in that confrontation on both fronts, and they punctuated the contradiction between the West's rhetoric of equality and self-determination and its practice of colonial and neocolonial subjugation.[43]

Bandung

For a brief moment after World War II, in the euphoria of independence struggled for and gained, twenty-nine nations of Asia and Africa assembled in 1955 at Bandung on the island of Java at the invitation of Indonesia's prime minister, Ali Sastroamidjojo. To open the conference President Ahmed Sukarno welcomed the delegates. His nation having just emerged from three hundred years of colonial servitude, Sukarno outlined their task:

> Let us not be bitter about the past, but let us keep our eyes firmly on the future. Let us remember that no blessing of God is so sweet as life and liberty. Let us remember that the stature of all mankind is diminished so long as nations or parts of nations are still unfree.... Let us remember that the highest purpose of man is the liberation of man from his bonds of fear, his bonds of human degradation, his bonds of poverty—the liberation of man from the physical, spiritual and intellectual bonds which have for too long stunted the development of humanity's majority.[44]

US writer Richard Wright rushed to Bandung to witness the proceedings. For posterity he recorded, "Day in and day out these crowds would stand in this tropic sun, staring, listening, applauding; it was the first time in their downtrodden lives that they'd seen so many men of their color, race, and nationality arrayed in such aspects of power, their men keeping order, their Asia and their Africa in control of their destinies." As the conference proceeded Wright observed a growing self-confidence: "They were getting a new sense of themselves, getting used to new roles and new identities. Imperialism was

dead here; and as long as they could maintain their unity, organize and conduct international conferences, there would be no return to imperialism."[45]

Bandung was historic but, in fact, it stood in a long line of such gather-
ings, beginning with the Inter-American Conference of 1899 and Pan-African
Conference of 1900, and others followed it in turn.[46] On September 24, 1946,
as vice premier and foreign minister in the last British colonial government
in India, Jawaharlal Nehru charted a policy that would guide the group called
"the nonaligned nations" that crystallized around Bandung. India, he declared,
"will follow an independent policy, keeping away from the power politics of
groups aligned one against another. She will uphold the principle of freedom
for dependent peoples and will oppose racial discrimination wherever it may
occur. She will work with other peace-loving nations for international cooperation and goodwill without the exploitation of one nation by another."[47]

Despite past precedents, Bandung was, in Sukarno's stirring words, "the
first international conference of colored peoples in the history of mankind,"
and it would be the first articulation of a vision that united the nations of
the Third World and offered to solve the problems created by Europe and its
imperialisms. Asians and Africans, Sukarno contended, "are united by more
important things than those which superficially divide us. We are united, for
instance, by a common detestation of colonialism in whatever form it appears.
We are united by a common detestation of racialism. And we are united by a
common determination to preserve and stabilize peace in the world."[48]

In those ways, Wright noted, Bandung encompassed "the totality of human life on this earth."[49] In their final communiqué from Bandung, the African and Asian representatives declared their commitment to the equality of
all races, the principle of national sovereignty, international cooperation, and
lasting world peace. That declaration is poignant and sobering in the light of
what Wright knew as the Cold War's "international tension with its danger of
an atomic world war." The document concluded with hope and an admonition: "Free from mistrust and fear, and with confidence and goodwill towards
each other, nations should practise tolerance and live together in peace with
one another as good neighbours."[50]

The Nation

The Marxist political philosopher Étienne Balibar observes that the nation
forms a narrative and is a project in the making. The national narrative expresses a design and destiny, which are inventions and illusions but possess
enormous discursive powers given substance by the state and its apparatuses.

The reality, by contrast, is far more complex in that national narratives are not univocal and static; they are multivocal and are sites of constant struggle and contestation. Those relations and outcomes of power produce the national community and its people, and as such they change and have histories.[51]

Central to the constitution of the people, Balibar points out, are language and race. The *nation*, from its etymology "to be born" or "by birth," consists of members related by blood (and hence constituting a race as biologically determined) and, derivative of Roman law, *jus sanguinis*, the right of blood, conveyed national membership and the rights of citizens.[52] Kinship, accordingly, and the patriarchal heterosexual family are foundational to the definition of nationality and crucial for the nation-state and its narration and regulatory regimes. The fiction of race, given force by the state and social practices, forms a "natural" order, and the state's regulation of marriage, birth, inheritance, and the normative family—a "nationalization of the family," in Balibar's apt words—arises from its compelling interest in defining its people or race.[53]

The nation and nationalism reproduces those fictions and features of the national narrative. Further, decolonization might have represented a break from the colonial past, but the formation of Third World nations, the nation-state, introduced another means for domination and exploitation. Neocolonialism succeeded colonialism because the postcolonial state inherited the instruments of economic, political, and cultural dependency installed by the colonial masters.[54] Moreover, the US anthropologists John D. Kelley and Martha Kaplan propose, while not diminishing the struggles of Third World peoples for self-determination, those efforts to establish independent nation-states were extensions of European nation-states and a transition from empire to a new world order of dependent nations.

Most histories and dictionaries, Kelley and Kaplan point out, trace the nation-state to 1918, and they associate its emergence with the development of modernity and President Wilson's articulation of sovereignty as "national self-determination." Locating the nation-state at the start of the twentieth century is questionable, Kelley and Kaplan continue, because European empires, not nation-states, were the dominant features of world power prior to the Great Conflict. Even after World War I and the formation of the League of Nations, the primacy of nation-states was much in doubt and debated.

By contrast, the end of World War II and the establishment of the United Nations in 1945, Kelley and Kaplan posit, marks the start of the nation-state as a primary instrument of international politics. In that regard they cite as appropriate the historian Prasenjit Duara's term for that post-1945 order, a "world-system of states."[55] The UN, formed amid wars and fears of wars, was a means by which to contain the contagion of conflict through legislating and policing. The United States led in that UN formation, and both the United States and UN quickened the pace of decolonization and the rise of new nation-states. US imperialism pursued a strategy of nation formation, open doors, and limited liabilities, Kelley and Kaplan argue, to install a new world order, which it called "multilateralism."[56]

During the 1940s, while installing a hegemon of nations under the UN, the United States planned a global economic restructuring involving the World Bank, the General Agreement on Tariffs and Trade, the International Trade Organization, and the International Monetary Fund. Through those institutions and under the cover of postwar economic recovery, the United States secured economic and political dependency.[57]

Following Kelley and Kaplan's argument, the anticolonial drive for self-determination through the institution of the nation-state removed the Third World from the environs of empire to the custody of a new world order of global capitalism, the UN, and multilateralism. Largely marginal to that turn are the Cold War and its ideologies and economies of First, Second, and Third World. At the center are the long-standing contested hierarchies and complex relations of power along the color line. Although promising freedom, national self-determination was a return to subservience, and while capitalism and juridical and political powers operate transnationally across and without regard to nation-states, the Third World remains transfixed in the quagmire of the patriarchal nation-state.

National Culture

Colonialism, Frantz Fanon argues, denies a people their past. It is in that sense that the fight for a national culture was waged on "a special battlefield" because of its centrality for colonial rule and the anticolonial movement alike. The assumption that European cultures were uncontested while Latin American civilizations required rehabilitation by Europeans exemplified the unequal power relations of that struggle. As a consequence the colonizers' denial of the culture of the colonized requires the recuperation and establishment of a national culture.[58]

In 1959, speaking before the Second Congress of Black Artists and Writers, a pan-African organization, Fanon criticized the notion of a "Negro culture" and of *négritude*, which originated among French-educated intellectuals who proposed a unique "African personality" that flowed through the veins of all Africans. Writers and scholars such as the West African Léopold Senghor and the West Indian Aimé Césaire, the Senegalese historian Cheik Anta Diop, and Alioune Diop, the Senegalese writer and publisher of the journal *Présence Africaine*, were among the central figures in the creation of négritude. Fanon derided those efforts as equivalent to proposing a "European culture" or "Arabic culture"; their singleness denies the diversity within those essentialized, unitary cultures.

Instead, Fanon declared, nation building required a national history and culture, and the struggle for a national culture was a fight for national liberation. National culture involved "the whole body of efforts made by a people in the sphere of thought to describe, justify, and praise the action through which that people has created itself and keeps itself in existence." Not a dead past, national culture is the nation's very heart in that "culture is an expression of national consciousness."[59]

In 1968 the Black Student Union at San Francisco State College listed its curricular goals during the struggle for black studies. Educate for "revolutionary change" and strive for a "socialist society" were among the objectives, but foremost was the rebuilding of a "cultural identity." Influential was Fanon's idea of national culture and its imperative for a people's consciousness and liberation. As Kwame Ture and Charles Hamilton explain in their influential text *Black Power*, cultural integrity is central to self-determination: "No person can be healthy, complete and mature if he must deny a part of himself."[60]

Like the detour taken by decolonization movements in Africa and Asia away from internationalism and toward national sovereignty, the Third World struggles in the United States turned to nationalism and inclusion within the nation as the fullest expression of self-determination.[61] Clearly cultural nationalism was an effective cure to a colonial mentality, but left cold in that warm embrace of nationalism were Native Americans, including American Indians, Chamorros, Hawaiians, Sāmoans, and Tainos, who continued to live as colonized subjects within the nation-state. Insofar as nationalism devolved into claims solely for civil rights, it betrayed Third World liberation and the international human rights freedom movement urged by Malcolm X in 1964.

Indigenous Peoples

Although European colonization of the Third World involved in the first instance the conquest of indigenous peoples, the anticolonial movement, which featured the independent nation-state, failed to account for the self-determination of native peoples. In fact the nation-state absorbed indigenous peoples within its borders and denied them their sovereignty because Third

World nation-states, patterned on the European model and designated by borders fixed by the colonial powers, insisted upon their sovereign rights.[62]

The notion of sovereignty descends from the Peace of Westphalia (1648), which ended recurrent wars and shifting borders by parceling the principle of natural rights into the rights of individuals and the rights of nation-states. Natural law, declared Hugo Grotius (1583–1645), Dutch and a founder of international law, conferred rights to all humans that exceeded the reach of rulers. Westphalia made those rights of rulers and subjects parallel, and the English philosopher Thomas Hobbes (1588–1679) posited the primacy of the nation in that individuals were in a state of nature or chaos prior to joining civil society, which brought order to their lives.

The Swiss diplomat Emmerich de Vattel (1714–69) codified those ideas in his *Law of Nations, or The Principles of Natural Law* (1758). Citizenship is a social contract, an idea introduced by Hobbes, between the individual and state, Vattel wrote, and the state thereby embodies individuals and their rights. Conjoined, the people and state form the nation-state. Exercising their natural rights, nation-states engage in treaty making, which entails respect for the territorial integrity and nonintervention in the internal affairs of other sovereign nation-states.[63]

Vattelian law disadvantages indigenous peoples insofar as they organize themselves into fluid polities and societies and their territories range over national borders and advance and retreat, depending upon the seasons and shifts in their sources of food. Moreover the English philosopher John Locke (1632–1704) held that property rights derived from labor, called "the labor theory of value," and thus to own property men must work the land. Vattelian law and Lockean property rights were influential with the US founding fathers and their conceptions of the nation-state and its rights vis-à-vis indigenous peoples.

The Marshall trilogy of US Supreme Court decisions exemplifies the point. John Marshall was chief justice when the Court ruled on three cases involving the Cherokee "nation" and the state of Georgia. Not only did the Marshall trilogy define the contours of relations between the nation-state and its indigenous peoples; the trilogy forms a foundation for international jurisprudence involving indigenous peoples globally. In *Johnson v. M'Intosh* (1823), the first of the trilogy, the Court subscribed to a limited right of discovery doctrine, which Europeans had claimed since their first encounter with America's native peoples in the late fifteenth century, and the notion that American Indians occupied but did not possess the land. They were thus incapable of transferring land titles, which was the right of the federal government to arrange on their behalf.

Cherokee Nation v. Georgia (1832) followed, in which the Court ruled treaties with independent American Indian "nations" implied their submission to the United States as "wards" and "domestic dependent nations." As such, American Indian peoples did not constitute "foreign states." A year later, in *Worcester v. Georgia* (1833), the Court referred to American Indian polities as "nations" within the US nation-state and imposed limits on the doctrine of the right of discovery.

In accord with Vattelian law, the Marshall trilogy affirmed that American Indians held "natural rights" to land but allowed for its loss through the right of discovery, voluntary cession, and conquest. Moreover, they ruled, treaties imply the nation-state's protectorate over indigenous peoples as wards. Related were the ideas that indigenous peoples occupied but did not possess the land, the concept of vacant land (*terra nullius*),[64] the diminished status of treaties because American Indians were incapable in law, the notion of trusteeships and wards, and the civilizing mission and burden to lift them from savagery to civilization. As the US Indian commissioner Nathaniel G. Taylor explained in his 1868 *Annual Report*, "It is beyond question our most solemn duty to protect and care for, to elevate and civilize them."[65]

That "solemn duty," US scholars Vine Deloria Jr. and Clifford M. Lytle contend, resulted in a unique relationship between the US nation-state and American Indian peoples. Enabled by legal and political instruments, American Indians' self-government within a nation-state distinguishes them from other peoples in the United States and the world. Further, American Indians enjoy federal protection against the states in which they reside in matters such as land use and transfer, water rights, and railroad construction, even as the federal government has sought to diminish Indian autonomy.[66] Federal oversight of Indian "nations" (some have called these internal colonies) and persons rendered them dependents, wards of the US nation-state as domestic dependent nations.

The General Allotment (or Dawes) Act (1887) eroded Indian sovereignty by parceling, buying, and selling reservation land to break up Indian "nations" into property holders and independent farmers. The Indian Citizenship Act (1924) gave US citizenship to Indians born after that year, although still allowing tribal membership. The Indian Reorganization Act (1934) encouraged American Indians to organize as business corporations with by-laws and a constitution for self-government. And "termination," authorized by Congress in 1954, curtailed federal services to and supervision of American Indians, and the social welfare programs of the 1960s, such as President Lyndon B. Johnson's "war on poverty" were designed to treat Indians as individuals and citizens within the nation-state.

After passage of the Dawes Act and 1890, when the military conquest of American Indians was achieved, the federal government pursued the incorporation of Indians into the nation-state like other people of color. The strategy involved privatizing Indian lands and resources and weaning Indians from federal entitlements while retaining Indian entities as domestic dependent nations. Thus through the instruments of assimilation and internal colonization the United States contained indigenous peoples as racialized minorities with claims to civil rights and not as foreign nationals with treaty rights, even as federal social programs cultivated a greater dependency on and hence absorption within the US nation-state.

As a consequence American Indian self-determination expressed itself not within the nation-state as a species of nationalism but in transnational arenas and subjectivities as the world's indigenous peoples before international bodies like the UN and the International Court of Justice (World Court). The North American Indian Brotherhood, for instance, an organization that began in Canada's British Columbia in the 1950s, dispatched a delegation to the UN to seek redress on the basis of human rights. In 1957 the International Labor Organization (ILO), which predated the UN but subsequently became an agency of the UN, adopted Convention 107, which expressed concern over indigenous workers who were particularly vulnerable to labor exploitation. The convention cited self-determination and human rights as arguments for their equal treatment, albeit as citizens within the nation-state.

UN Resolution 1541 (1960) declared decolonization and self-determination to be a basic human right, but it left colonial boundaries and the nation-state intact, leaving indigenous peoples subject to those nation-states. The UN in fact is a union of nation-states, and its charter is respectful of national sovereignty and territorial integrity even as it allows for "equal rights and self-determination of peoples."[67]

In 1974 American Indians in the United States formed the International Treaty Council (ITC), which received nongovernmental organization (NGO) status at the UN. The ITC joined indigenous representatives throughout the Western Hemisphere at the international NGO Conference on Discrimination against Indigenous Populations, held in Geneva in 1977. The conference advanced the transnational subject position as indigenous peoples, widened and deepened their ties across nation-states, and increased their demands on the UN.

In 1989 the ILO amended its Convention 107 by recognizing "the aspirations of [indigenous] peoples to exercise control over their own institutions, ways of life and economic development and to maintain and develop their identities, languages and religions, within the framework of the States in which they live."[68] Still the nation-state remained inviolate, even as the UN declared 1993 the International Year of the World's Indigenous Peoples.

Those efforts by indigenous peoples culminated with the UN Declaration on the Rights of Indigenous Peoples, adopted in 2007. Central to the declaration is the right of self-determination for indigenous peoples. The declaration requires nation-states to honor treaties made with indigenous peoples, to grant environmental and educational rights and the right to be free from discrimination and genocide, and to recognize indigenous laws, traditions, customs, and land rights and land tenure systems. The United States adopted the declaration in 2010 and pledged to support "internal self-determination," defined by the UN as the right of indigenous peoples to negotiate "their political status within the framework of the existing nation-state and [to be] free to pursue their economic, social, and cultural development."[69]

Summary

As Deloria and Lytle point out, the idea of the "American Indian people" is a religious and not a political or economic precept. Their descent, formation, and place in the universe derive from a spiritual understanding of their subjectivities, social relations, and environment. All humans possess rights, and all share sacred obligations toward others and nature. Despite dislocation and dispossession, they observe, American Indians retain spiritual possession of their ancestral lands because social cohesion arises from that identity and identification with the land. Nothing can take that away. Self-government and nationhood are not Indian ideas, they remind us, but are European introductions and impositions, which American Indian peoples deploy to secure a measure of freedom and self-determination.

Indeed, as we have seen, the ideas and applications of sovereignty and the nation-state with its lands (property) and peoples and races (citizens) are European, not Third World or indigenous, precepts and observances. Third World studies understands that Europeans expanded and ruled over the earth discursively and materially at least since the fifteenth century. That imperialism and colonialism built European nation-states and empires from the resources of the Third World. Those mutual processes of European advancement and Third World retardation constituted the world-system, which was simultaneously national and global and demarcated by the color line.

Decolonization struggles in the Third World and the United States pursued mainly national and not global projects to their detriment, creating independent nation-states and national cultures while slighting the pre- and transnational aspects of imperialism and neocolonialism. At the same time Third World nation-states and US. cultural nationalisms were achievements along the color line; they contradicted the old world order of colonialism and racism. Those anticolonial, antiracist movements erred when they, nation-states and cultural nationalism, became ends in themselves.

Some indigenous peoples and their freedom movements reveal alternatives to that national turn. They see sovereignty and nation-states as European ideas and impositions that supply merely a strategic first step toward self-determination; the prevailing social relations make those claims necessary. Their ultimate goal is the (spiritual) bond that defines and unites all peoples of the earth with rights and responsibilities to each other and their environment.

That capacious space of the indigenous world, we should recognize, speaks to the global discourse of anticolonialism and the self-determination and rights of all peoples. The Martinican poet and pan-Africanist and one of Fanon's teachers, Aimé Césaire, in his classic critique of Europe and colonialism, lamented the loss of that universe and worldview. "*I* am talking about societies drained of their essence, cultures trampled underfoot, institutions undermined, lands confiscated, religions smashed, magnificent artistic creations destroyed, extraordinary *possibilities* wiped out," he wrote of the destruction wrought by colonialism. "I am talking about millions of men torn from their gods, their land, their habits, their life—from life, from the dance, from wisdom."[70]

THREE

IMPERIALISM

African American organic intellectuals wrote of imperialism and the colonial condition during the 1960s, echoing Du Bois's articulation of the problem of the twentieth century. As we saw, Third World people in the United States—African, Native, and Asian Americans and Latinx—identified themselves with the Third World anticolonial liberation movements that upended some four hundred years of world history in achieving a degree of self-determination. While nationalists in the Third World and the United States retreated into nation-states as ends in themselves, some Native Americans saw sovereignty as a necessary, temporary strategy and reached past the national to embrace a global, indigenous affiliation for human and not civil rights. Those choices reflected the discursive and material conditions of the 1960s and the post–World War II hegemon of nation-states.

In this chapter I conceive of imperialism as both ideological and material. European taxonomies named, classified, described, and ranked the lands, peoples, and plants and animals of their expansive domain. Those discourses, or ideology and language, served to discipline their wild and unruly subjects, as represented, by installing order where there was disorder, science in place of superstition. They mapped, surveyed, and assigned natures to waters and lands, and they understood the life forms of those lands as determined by their geographies. Humans they saw as undifferentiated features, like the plants and animals, of their environments. Such discourses served to explain and justify the material relations of conquest, colonization, and exploitation as divinely ordered, of superiors over inferiors, and for God and king.

Long before the problem of the twentieth century, however, we find tracings of imperialism's origins in ancient Greece and, during the modern period, in the discourses and material relations that accompanied and emanated from the ascent of science, sovereignty, and capitalism.

Discourses

The power to know and the disciplining of space/time are imperial projects insofar as they claim the mastery of self over others and of humans over their environment.[1] Those ends were on the minds of the ancient Greeks of Ionia, a region in Asia along the west coast of modern-day Turkey. As early as around 600 BC Ionian philosophers sought to break free from religion and superstition with a science based on theory and observation. They conceived of a "cosmos" or order that ruled the universe and physical world, and they believed that substance or matter behaved in predictable ways and described them as "natures." They delineated space as a disk-shaped earth governed by the positions and movements of heavenly bodies, the zodiac. They captured the sun by dividing the year into seasons, and with the sundial they calculated more discrete measures of time.

About 530 BC Pythagoras, an Ionian who migrated to Italy, hypothesized the earth as a globe with an equator, polar extremes, and intermediate temperate zone. Greece was blessed with a temperate climate, while equatorial heat and polar cold cursed those places with conditions impossible of life.

Hippocrates, "the father of medicine," refined those discourses of spatial divides and their natures by advancing the idea of *geographical determinism*. In *On Airs, Waters, and Sites* (ca. 410 BC) Hippocrates explained how the environment shaped human constitutions (bodies) and natures (behaviors). To illustrate that determining power of geography and climate, the father of medicine distinguished Europe from Asia, a parceling of space unlike the classical Greek conception of Asia, Africa, and Europe as a single continent surrounded by water. Thus comprising an island and a center, the "world island" was where order prevailed, while the distant waters signaled superstition and chaos.[2] The world island was a unitary landmass, undifferentiated, and encircled by an undivided ocean.

At a time when Asia was Europe's implacable enemy and other, Hippocrates positioned Europe and Asia as polarities, one set against the other. As oppositions they defined one another; Europe was the self, and Asia was the other, or what Europe was not. The mild and uniform climate of Asia, the father of medicine hypothesized, with its hot and stagnant airs and waters, nurtured lush vegetation but laziness among the people, who appeared yellow, as if suffering from jaundice. "With regard to the lack of spirit and courage among the inhabitants, the chief reason why Asiatics are less warlike and more gentle in character than Europeans is the uniformity of the seasons," he explained. An unchanging climate "engenders slackness, while variation fosters endurance in both body and soul; rest and slackness are food for cowardice, endurance and exertion for bravery." Asians were thus easily governed and ruled by despots. "Courage, endurance, industry and high spirit could not arise in such conditions," Hippocrates concluded, "but pleasure must be supreme."[3]

Europeans, by contrast, experienced frequent and sharp seasonal changes, which in turn favored "the greatest diversity in physique, in character, and in constitution." In Asia, where the land is "rich, soft, and well-watered," the people are "fleshy, ill-articulated, moist, lazy, generally cowardly in character." But in Europe, where the land is "bare, waterless, rough, oppressed by winter's storms and burnt by the sun," there you will find "men who are hard, lean, well-articulated, well-braced, and hairy; such natures will be found energetic, vigilant, stubborn and independent in character and in temper, wild rather than tame, of more than average sharpness and intelligence in the arts, and in war of more than average courage." Hippocrates urged his readers to "take these observations as a standard when drawing all other conclusions, and you will make no mistake."[4] As the truth and norm, geographical determinism attained the status of absolute science.

Observe some of the ideas at work in those Hippocratic conventions. The first is the notion that climates determine constitutions; geographical determinism was and is an influential explanation to our times. The second is the related idea of continents (Europe and Asia) and their separate and distinctive life forms, including humans. Continental varieties, later called races, would descend from that lineage of geographical determinism. Although *race* is not a term employed by Hippocrates, what he described were distinctive peoples, Europeans as set against Asians. Moreover those separate peoples were endowed with attributes that positioned Europeans over Asians, superiors over inferiors. Those qualities of hard, lean, well-articulated, energetic, brave, intelligent, and independent signaled a human variety, Europeans, but also men, while soft, moist, lazy, cowardly, sensuous, and dependent characterized a people, Asians, but also women. In those representations Hippocrates summoned what we now know as race and gender but also sexuality (sensuality), class (rulers and ruled), and nation—the social formation.

By the time of Aristotle (384–322 BC) the idea of the world island was a commonplace, and although he devoted little attention to geography, Aristotle considered the earth in relation to other heavenly bodies in "Meteorologica" and "On the Heavens." Like Pythagoras he believed in a spherical earth located at the center of the universe, and like the philosopher Parmenides (about sixth century BC) he held that there were a torrid and two frigid zones where life was impossible, and between them temperate zones north and south of the equator.[5] Aristotle concurred with and enlarged upon Hippocrates's contention that climate molded human nature and institutions in his disquisition on politics. The cold climate to the north of Greece, the philosopher taught, bred Europeans who are "full of spirit, but wanting in intelligence and skill; and therefore they retain comparative freedom, but have no political organization, and are incapable of ruling over others." Whereas to the east the uniform climate gave birth to Asians who are "intelligent and inventive, but they are wanting in spirit, and therefore they are always in a state of subjection and slavery." In fact, Aristotle maintained, Asians are "by nature slaves" and "do not rebel against a despotic government." The Greek "race," on the other hand, situated between Europeans and Asians, "is likewise intermediate in character, being high-spirited and also intelligent. Hence it continues free, and is the best-governed of any nation, and, if it could be formed into one state, would be able to rule the world."[6]

The empire, both material and discursive, was being created in Aristotle's lifetime by one of his students, Alexander the Great, who crossed the Hellespont in 334 BC with an army of forty thousand men. For the next eleven years Alexander's army advanced eastward across Asia. The expedition pursued the conquest of lands and peoples as well as the disciplining of those subjects by scholars and scientists who were members of Alexander's imperial force. Although a Macedonian, not a Greek, Alexander and the kings of Macedon claimed Greek lineage, and his war against Persia was waged to avenge the sufferings inflicted upon the Greeks during the Persian wars about a century and a half earlier.[7] Turned back from reaching the Ganges only by the threat of mutiny among his own ranks, Alexander fell ill and died in Babylon in 323 BC, leaving behind a divided empire of oft-warring factions and kingdoms that arose from dissension among his generals.

The accumulated observations of plants, animals, lands, and peoples from Alexander's expedition enabled a larger and more detailed apprehension of the world island. Uncertainties of distances and latitudes from Alexander's expedition, however, resulted in erroneous mappings, such as the one drawn by Eratosthenes (ca. 276–196 BC), the "father of systematic geography" and head of Alexandria's immense library. Relying on the centuries-old causal connection between climate and character, Eratosthenes applied the descriptions of Alexander's chroniclers to his mapmaking and placed Ethiopia (Africa) and India on the same latitude because, according to the archive of accumulated knowledge, they shared a similar climate, plants and animals, and black people.[8] The result illustrates the Greek reliance on theory to help organize observation and make it systematic and the persistence and power of certain ideas such as geographical determinism.

After the fall of Rome in the fifth century AD, Europe largely fell under the influence of the Roman Catholic Church. The Middle Ages began in the fifth century and lasted to about the sixteenth. That return to faith was not devoid of reason, despite criticism of the Church as a site of intolerance and superstition by intellectuals of the Enlightenment, the Age of Reason, in the seventeenth and eighteenth centuries. In 1566 a French law professor named Jean Bodin, an opponent of the Church, published *Method for the Easy Comprehension of History*. Human experience, Bodin believed, reveals "universal law," and geography provides for an "easy comprehension" of history.

The universal law of geography, Bodin held, was geographical determinism as inherited from the ancient Greeks. With a wider apprehension of the world than the ancient Greeks had, Bodin modified their latitudes of life by dividing the earth into a sparsely populated polar zone, a thickly settled and developed temperate zone, and a tropical band. Each zone, he maintained, had its own place as assigned by the environment and geography,[9] and, as in Plato's republic, the whole functioned to create universal harmony, unity amid diversity in a "republic of the world."[10] The center of his analysis, like the ancient Greeks, remained the temperate zone and its superior peoples. With the voyages to Asia led by Portugal and Spain well under way, Bodin knew of America, the "new world," and of the tropics and equatorial band, which, despite the "incredible heat," supported human life.[11] Still, like Eratosthenes, Bodin held erroneously that Africans and Indians inhabited the same latitude and were thus black by "seed." In his understanding of "seed" Bodin followed Hippocrates, who noted that healthy seed produced healthy children, and Plato's admonition, "the best men must have sex with the best women as frequently as possible" to produce offspring of "the highest possible quality."[12]

Geographical determinism, Bodin believed, endowed men in cooler climates with "inner warmth," which sparked energy and enabled robust activity, whereas Africans in hot climates were devoid of "internal heat" and were thus lazy, although bearing work and heat patiently. The climate and celestial bodies, however, failed to determine completely human behavior, which can overcome those laws of nature through divine aid and continued self-discipline. Further, while the environment shapes human constitutions and physiques together with the habits of the mind, the "inborn nature of each race" of body type, intellect, and natures is also "in the blood" and "from blood."[13] That idea of "seed" and "blood" and their determining role in shaping bodies and behaviors is the fallacy of *biological determinism*. Bodin embraced, accordingly, both geographical determinism and its parallel, biological determinism, and both notions originate with the ancient Greeks.

In the words of a recent study of the modern idea of race, Bodin in his search for universal law produced "a history of mankind divided up into peoples and dispositions arranged according to astrological and astronomical influences, climate, language, geographical location."[14] Those groupings, loosely marked by "the inborn nature of each race," would achieve greater solidity as "races" by the scientific classifiers of the eighteenth century.

Called the "father of modern taxonomy," the Swedish physician and scientist Carl Linnaeus (1707–78) published his treatise, *Systema naturae* (1735), and its expanded editions that established the science of classification. The Linnaean system of nomenclature involves aggregations based upon similarities and differences. A group thus shares certain characteristics that differentiate it from other groups. Linnaeus grouped humans into four varieties based on the four continents—Europe, Asia, Africa, and America—and skin color. In the first edition of *Systema naturae* he named those varieties European (white), Asian (brown), African (black), and American (red). Linnaeus changed the Asian skin color from brown to yellow in his tenth edition and added temperaments derived from antiquity, involving humors or bodily fluids that allegedly determined natures. Those attributions suggest both geographical and biological determinism, along with a hierarchy of an ideal and departures from that standard.

Human varieties in the Linnaean system were differentiated by color, posture, and temperament. Ruled by the bodily fluid blood, Europeans were white, muscular, and sanguine, or optimistic. Asians, determined by black bile, had a yellow tinge, stood stiffly, and were melancholic. Africans, ruled by phlegm, had a black color and were relaxed (slack) and phlegmatic, slow and without much energy. Yellow bile caused Americans (Indians) to have a red skin color, an upright posture, and a choleric, or irritable and unpredictable, temperament. Those Linnaean notions identify and assign desirable and undesirable traits and racial stereotypes familiar to us today.

A student of Linnaeus, Johann Friedrich Blumenbach, called the "father of physical anthropology," published his dissertation, *On the Natural Varieties of*

Mankind, in 1775. In that edition Blumenbach described, like his teacher, four "varieties" of humans—European, Asian, African, and American—together with the factors that produced those groupings: climate, mode of life, and hybridity. Climate, Blumenbach held, can alter body shape and therewith culture, though humans and animals can move to unfamiliar climate zones and change their physiques. Likewise mode of life and hybridity can yield new body forms. Differentiation, however, has its limits, the anatomist cautioned, and despite "the unity of the human species" there remain four "mere varieties" separated by "the structure of the human body."[15]

Europeans, Asians, Africans, and Americans, Blumenbach noted, differ in "bodily constitution, stature, and colour," and those features are due "almost entirely to climate alone." Thus, following Hippocrates, "in hot countries bodies become drier and heavier; in cold and wet ones softer, more full of juice and spongy." Where the climate is mild, as in Asia, people are smaller and less fierce, and Africans have black skin color because of the climate, temperature, soil, and mode of life. That idea of geographical determinism, Blumenbach acknowledged, "is the old opinion of Aristotle, Alexander, Strabo, and others." But Africans can lose their blackness by moving to northern Europe, where their skin will become brown; conversely white Spaniards living in the "torrid zone" have "degenerated" to the color of the soil. Those examples point to changes induced by the environment but not to the creation of entirely new species.[16]

Blumenbach departed from Linnaeus in his third edition, issued in 1795, by positing five principal human "varieties": Caucasian (European), Mongolian (Asian), Ethiopian (African), American (Indian), and Malay. The third edition also highlighted a concept first introduced in the earlier version, the notion of "degeneration" as seen in skin color, hair texture, stature, bodily proportion, and skull shape caused by diet, mode of life, hybridity, and, above all, climate, which was "almost infinite" in its power over bodies. Climate has "the greatest and most permanent influence over national colour," Blumenbach declared, and skin color is the most reliable indicator of human variety because, "although it sometimes deceives, [skin color] still is a much more constant character, and more generally transmitted than the others." Thus Caucasians are white, Mongolians yellow or "olive-tinge," Americans copper or "dark orange," Malays tawny, and Ethiopians tawny black to "pitchy blackness." In the "torrid zone" abundant heat and carbon induce the liver to produce an excess of bile, and consequently "the temperament of most inhabitants of tropical countries is choleric and prone to anger."[17]

Unlike Bodin, whose historical schema of progress and stagnation relied upon a near mystical quality of blood, Blumenbach catalogued differences on the basis of his measurements of skulls and cranial capacities, teeth, breasts, penises, hands, feet, and statures.[18] The result was a scientific nomenclature and classification of human types, which supplied a foundation for the studies that followed. Notably, by citing degeneration as the process involved in differentiation, Blumenbach established a hierarchy among his five varieties of humanity. As he explained, his use of the word Caucasian to denote the former "European" derived from the Caucasus Mountains because that area produced "the most beautiful race of men, I mean the Georgian."[19]

All others represented degenerations from that ideal type, like the African of Bodin's description, who was "very keen and lustful" and "small, curly-haired, black, flat-nosed, blubber-lipped, and bald, with white teeth and black eyes."[20] The hair of Blumenbach's Caucasian was soft, long, and undulating, whereas Mongolian and American hair was black, stiff, straight, and scanty.[21] Furthermore, despite a recognition of the essential unity of humans as a single species and the ties between varieties that "run together," Blumenbach offered a history, an evolution of human types distinguished by physical and behavioral characteristics that were transmitted through reproduction and formed correspondences with mappings of climates and constitutions.[22]

For many European Enlightenment thinkers, geography and history were the critical engines of civilization and progress. Change was enabled by an apprehension of history and its laws, as expounded upon by Bodin. Conversely peoples without history were those mired in stasis and bondage. Contemporaries of Blumenbach, the eighteenth-century German philosophers Kant and Hegel, enlarged upon those ideas of Eurocentrism and white supremacy. Hegel wrote that "historical peoples" could not be found in the frigid or torrid zones and that the "true theatre of history" was enacted only in the temperate zone, notably in its northern part, where "free movement" was possible.[23] Kant claimed that in "hot countries the human being ... does not ... reach the perfection of those in the temperate zones. Humanity is at its perfection in the race of the whites." In addition "the inhabitant of the temperate parts of the world, above all the central part, has a more beautiful body, works harder, is more jocular, more controlled in his passions, more intelligent than any other race of people in the world."[24] In that judgment Kant joined the ancient lineage of geographical determinists.

By the nineteenth century, after three hundred years of European imperial expansion into the tropical band, or Third World, Arthur de Gobineau could write with confidence *The Inequality of Human Races*, a four-volume treatise (1853–55). In that work, expanding upon Blumenbach's theory of degeneration and Bodin's of blood, Gobineau's primary concern was the pollution of white blood by inferior elements. The problem, he observed, arose from the distribution by whites of the yellow and black races, "weaker" and "backward" strains, from the tropics to the temperate zone and indeed to all corners of the globe because of their utility as workers.

Although their labor is indispensable to their masters, Gobineau worried that their physical proximity and intimacies would inevitably produce a "mixture of blood." As a result the "primordial race-unit is so broken up and swamped by the influx of foreign elements" that it no longer has "the same intrinsic value as it had before, because it has no longer the same blood in its veins, continual adulterations having gradually affected the quality of that blood." Like civilizations that have collapsed because of barbarian invasions, whites faced decline and extinction through the introduction of impurities, which erode their inner constitutions.[25]

Gobineau and many of his contemporaries were more impressed by the power of blood than that of climate or social institutions, which played roles in but failed to account for racial inequality.[26] In his scheme society and geography form nondetermining environments in which humans operate and to which they respond, explaining how "inferior" peoples like Hawaiians could mimic but not fully apprehend civilization, and North American Indians could live in a temperate and resource-rich land for centuries but fail to advance to a high state, as he defined it, of civilization.[27]

Gobineau accordingly parted company with the geographic determinism of his forebears and proposed just three races based upon skin color—white, yellow, and black—with all others derivatives of those primary groups. He believed in the unity of all humans, like Blumenbach, but placed whites at the apex and yellows and blacks as "degenerations" from that ideal. "I . . . have no hesitation in regarding the white race as superior to all others in beauty," Gobineau stated categorically. "Thus the human groups are unequal in beauty; and this inequality is rational, logical, permanent, and indestructible." Accordingly there was "irreconcilable antagonism between different races," and "innate repulsion" was the main motive force of history, directing its course.[28]

| | |

It is important to remember that those imperial discourses were not left unchallenged. Particularly striking are instances when the oppressed, the objects of the imperial sciences join in the conversation, employing the language and ideology of science to refute its assumptions and teachings. Such was the case of Anténor Firmin, an African in the diaspora, a Haitian attorney, and an anthropologist who published a point-by-point rebuttal of Gobineau's racist text. Born three years before *The Inequality of Human Races* was published, Firmin answered with *De l'égalité des races humaines* (The Equality of Human Races) in 1885.

Educated in Haiti, the world's first black republic, which had won its independence from France in 1804, and while serving in its diplomatic corps in Paris from 1884 to 1888, Firmin observed the proceedings of the Paris Anthropological Society, a group Paul Broca founded in 1859. Broca was a professor of clinical surgery and is the father of craniometry, the science of cranial measurements to determine intelligence. "In general," Broca wrote in 1861, "the brain is larger in mature adults than in the elderly, in men than in women, in eminent men than in men of mediocre talent, in superior races than in inferior races."[29] Those associations of gender, race, age, and ability exemplify the multiple, intersecting categories of power expressed in the social formation.

Firmin was eager to debate the racist discourse he heard in the society's chambers, but as a mere observer and nonmember he was denied that opportunity. He found his voice in his book, *The Equality of the Human Races* (English version, 2000). In this remarkable treatise, Firmin critiqued Broca's craniometry and more broadly anthropometry, the hallmark of nineteenth-century anthropology and the science of measurement pioneered by Blumenbach and physical anthropology. Firmin began his exposition with the discipline of anthropology as a whole, which he defined as the study of humans in their entirety.

All humans, Firmin held, possessed the same intellectual and moral qualities and shortcomings without distinction, having descended from a common ancestor. He argued for the essential unity of the human species. Moreover, while conceding racial differences, he stressed the mutable as opposed to permanent biological boundaries of racial types and questioned the myth of pure races. Hybridity, he pointed out, blurred the divisions among races, and climate and geography factored into the equation of human variation.

Rather than threatening decline through degeneration and race mixture, Firmin observed, Africans influenced the rise and ascent of ancient Greece and Rome and, accordingly, the birth of European civilization. Ancient Egypt was an African civilization, contrary to racists who claimed Hamites, an invented race and offshoot of Europeans, were the real originators of Egyptian civilization because black Africans allegedly were incapable of developing large-scale societies, polities, and economies. That theft of ancient Egypt from Africa and its annexation to whiteness and "Mediterranean civilization," together with Egypt's importance to Greek and Roman civilizations, would engage racialist discourse from the nineteenth to the twenty-first century.[30]

Firmin's position on ancient Egypt was a cornerstone of négritude, the pan-African cultural movement derided by Fanon in his address advocating the need for national culture. Like Firmin, many of négritude's leaders were Africans from the francophone Caribbean. A common black subjectivity and the colonial condition united Africans across the diaspora, négritude proponents held, and a correct understanding of African culture and history, beginning with ancient Egypt, worked to dismantle French colonialism and hegemony. Négritude discourse forged a pan-African consciousness, and Firmin was among the black intellectuals who organized the first Pan-African Congress in London in 1900. *The Equality of the Human Races* was an opening salvo in the decolonization struggle, Fanon's important critique of an African personality notwithstanding, and an emphatic corrective to the problem of the twentieth century.

| | |

It is no coincidence that the cartographies of human varieties arose during the period of European expansion and imposition of imperial order over the world. Ideas of an active, invasive Greece and an inert, receptive Asia accompanied Alexander's military conquest of Asia and Asians. Discourses propelled and justified the material conditions of expansion and empire. Taxonomies assembled, described, and ranked the physical world and all of its life forms, including humans, and the power to know eventuated into the power to materialize, blanketing the earth and indeed the universe. As human impositions over nature and European taxonomies of non-European peoples, discourses exercised imperial power. They produced hierarchies of merit and worth, disciplined and exerted mastery over imagined primitive, perverse subjects, and imposed regimes of order, explanation, and prediction—the hallmarks of science. That discursive conquest was and is an imperial project, emanating from the self to self's others to center and champion Europe by marginalizing and diminishing the Third World.

Material Conditions

European global expansion beginning in the fifteenth century can best be described as *imperialism*, and imperialism as a phase of capitalism. That expansion of nation-states beyond their limits was classified and defended as extraterritorial extensions of national sovereignty. That is, conquests and colonial possessions constituted the lands and peoples of the acquisitive, imperial nation-state. In his classic text on imperialism, the English writer and economist J. A. Hobson observed that while the relationship between imperialism and nationalism was complicated, colonialism was clearly an extension of nationalism.[31] Conflicts like the First and Second World Wars and the Cold War were thus waged to retain those sovereign estates even after the end of formal colonialism.

There is disagreement over the exact phase of capitalism during which that European extraterritorial spread occurred. Some, like Hobson and Lenin, who drew generously from Hobson,[32] hold that imperialism takes place only during the stage of monopoly capitalism, which is generally seen as the coming together of industrial and financial (banking) capitalism to form monopolies. Others believe imperialism is a product of industrial capitalism in its search for resources and new markets. Still others use the term *imperialism* to describe capitalism's expansion during the period of mercantile (trade) capitalism, which preceded industrial capitalism. As I use it in this text, *imperialism* refers to capitalism's expansion beginning in the fifteenth century with Europe's search for Asia.

Mercantile capitalism was a creation of ocean worlds that linked land with water across and upon which commerce flowed, resulting in complex mixes of material and ideological exchanges and coercions as well as hybrid peoples, languages, and subjectivities. Europeans, Asians, and Africans converged on the Mediterranean world, while the Atlantic world involved Europeans, Africans, and Americans (indigenous peoples of America). Asians were prominent features of European ocean worlds and the modern world-system in that European expansion and commerce were predicated upon securing the goods of Asia. In that sense Asia was the object of European imperialism.

The Mediterranean Sea connected Europe, Asia, and Africa, linking them in commercial traffic and linguistic, religious, and cultural exchanges and impositions. Some scholars place the origins of the modern world-system in that Mediterranean world with the onset of trade begun by Asians. (Asia and Asians, the Orient and Orientals, as established by the ancient Greeks, were lands and peoples to their east.) Preeminent traders, the Phoenicians spread from modern-day Lebanon to Africa's Mediterranean coast around 1500 BC. They were a maritime people, carrying wood, slaves, glass, and dye, and their trading culture lasted for over a thousand years. About 500 BC Greek traders established colonies along Africa's Mediterranean coast extending eastward to the Red Sea, and when Rome ruled the Mediterranean world, products from India reached that Roman sea as early as the first century BC. Long after Rome's fall, from the eleventh to fifteenth centuries, Italian city-states like Venice, Genoa, Florence, and Milan emerged to control the Asian commerce in the Mediterranean, marking the start of what many consider to be the beginnings of mercantile or trade-based capitalism and the modern world-system.

The Atlantic world eclipsed the Mediterranean with the rise of the Iberian states, which bypassed the Italian city-states in the fifteenth century and moved the traffic from the Mediterranean to the Atlantic. On islands off the African coast, Spain transplanted sugar, which had entered the Mediterranean from Asia. The sugarcane plant was probably domesticated in New Guinea, and from that Pacific Island spread around 8000 BC to China and India, where sugar production was highly developed. By the eighth century AD sugar plantations appeared on the eastern shores of the Mediterranean, and crops like sugarcane, rice, sorghum, cotton, citrus fruits, and plantains accompanied the spread of Islam into the Mediterranean world.

Merchants from Venice and Genoa built plantations to produce sugar in the Mediterranean on islands like Crete and Cyprus. Plantations involved large tracts of land, foreign conquerors and landowners, imported laborers, and production of a single crop for export. Those plantations accompanied the expansion of Spain, Portugal, and other European nations into the Atlantic, and they supplied the tropical products Europeans desired. Europe, the apex of the Atlantic trade triangle, sent its manufactures to Africa, the second corner of the trade triangle, to capture and purchase enslaved laborers; European ships transported their human chattel to plantations in America and the Caribbean islands, which formed the third corner of the triangle; they returned to Europe laden with the sugar, rum, cotton, and other goods produced by American Indian and African laborers.

The Atlantic world accordingly was built on extractive, exploitative relationships, not a trade-based system of exchanges; conquered lands and enslaved peoples generated the wealth that enriched Europe even as the process impoverished Africa and America. That violent and exploitative Atlantic world supplied the means by which Portugal and Spain achieved their destiny in Asia.

According to standard narratives of US history, Atlantic civilization is the wellspring of national formation and constitution. Herein assumed is the European cast of the nation-state. That is, the United States is essentially and centrally a European state and people, ignoring the Black Atlantic and African diaspora and its mixtures and hybridities.[33] In that historical narrative of nation the Atlantic world is the familiar self, while the Pacific world is the alien other. Despite those representations of oppositions, the Atlantic world splashed into the Pacific world precisely because of Europe's search for Asia to plunder its treasury, and America was an accident of that ancient pursuit.

By the fifteenth century a few Europeans had crossed the Eurasian continent to reach the Pacific's shore. Still China and India remained fabulous in European accounts and imaginations largely because of their resources, mainly raw silk from China, which fed the expanding textile industries of northern Italy, but also spices and slaves from India. A possible consequence of that traffic with Asia was the Black Death, the bubonic plague of the first half of the fourteenth century, which decimated many European cities. In addition to that pandemic, wars, like the Hundred Years' War (1337–1453), waged mainly for the French throne, destroyed much of the countryside and significantly reduced and dislocated the population. Europe clearly was not in a position of global dominance.

Asia was the senior partner in the east-west traffic beginning with ancient Greece and Rome up to at least the sixteenth century. Asians controlled the products desired by Europeans, and they managed the trade's nature, volume, and prices. Thus, for instance, in 1428, when the sultan in the city of Alexandria raised the price of pepper by more than 60 percent, it caused the price to rise in Europe and reduced the profits enjoyed by Venetian merchants involved in the commodity. Dependent upon and susceptible to the controls over the lands to their east, Europeans sought out new avenues to escape those gatekeepers and gain direct access to Asia's goods.

Positioned at the western end of the Eurasian continent, the people who became the Portuguese and Spanish were at a disadvantage vis-à-vis the Italian city-states that had capitalized on their location in the overland trade with Asia in the Mediterranean world. However, their perch on the Atlantic's shore conferred an advantage in charting a route to China and India by sea, circling around the landed middlemen to Europe's east. It had been known to Europeans since the ancient Greeks, who had hypothesized the world as a disk and later as a sphere, that Asia could be reached across the Atlantic or by sailing around Africa to the Indian Ocean world of Africans, Arabs, and Indians.

For hundreds of years to about the fifteenth century AD, Muslim caravans from West African kingdoms like Mali, Ghana, and Songhai had transported gold, ivory, and slaves to the Mediterranean's southern rim. That trans-Saharan trade had supplied most of the gold held by Europeans, who in turn traded it for Asian silks, spices, and slaves. Led by its Arab and Jewish merchants, Catalonia, situated on the Mediterranean bordering present-day Spain and France, prospered from that commerce, but the Catalans could not surpass Venice and Genoa in the Asian trade. Like the Genoese, the Catalans tried in the fourteenth century to reach Asia by sailing around Africa, but they failed. In 1469 Catalonia became a part of Spain with the marriage of King Ferdinand II of Aragón and Queen Isabella of Castile, and the Catalan project of finding a route to Asia became a national object of Spain.

It was Portugal that took up the ambitious business of circumnavigating Africa for the Asian trade. The project began with Portugal's wars against Africans, called "Moors" ("dark people")—really Berbers, Arabs, and West Africans who had invaded and occupied much of the Iberian Peninsula starting in 711 AD. For seven hundred years the Africans ruled until the Portuguese and Spanish succeeded in the "reconquest" of the peninsula in the fifteenth century. Shortly after the Portuguese conquered the African city of Ceuta (1415), which was a terminus of the trans-Saharan gold caravans, Prince Henry assumed the task of leading the Portuguese effort to get to Asia around Africa. After his death the fall of Granada in 1492 marked the end of Muslim rule in Iberia.

The young prince assembled geographers and astronomers and books, charts, and maps at his headquarters at Sagres on the southern tip of Portugal, and from there he sent expeditions to the West African coast. Based upon that body of information, Henry amassed details of winds, currents, tides, and sailing directions to aid the next voyages, and with that accumulated knowledge his captains reached Africa south of the Sahara. There, in 1441, the Portuguese traded for African slaves. The prospect of a lucrative traffic in slaves and gold lured agents from Venice and other Italian trading cities to Sagres. Over the next five years Henry imported about a thousand African slaves, whose sales helped to support his enterprise, and he formed a company with Italian shareholders to generate more income for his expeditions.

Prince Henry, called "the Navigator," died in 1460 before realizing his dream of reaching Asia, but his successors eventually succeeded when Bartolomeu Dias rounded the Cape of Good Hope at the southern tip of Africa in 1487 and finally in 1498, when Vasco da Gama arrived at Calicut on the southwest coast of India with the help of a Gujarati (Indian) pilot he had captured on the East African coast. That Portuguese success, the Atlantic world's invasive entrance into the Indian Ocean world, was not Portugal's achievement alone, having been underwritten in large part by the enslavement and sale of thousands of Africans and aided by African and Asian sailors and seamen who steered the Portuguese vessels through unfamiliar waters and contrary winds and currents.

The triumphant da Gama, when faced with Indians reluctant to give away their trade, shelled Calicut and took Indian hostages for his full cargo of spices, which, upon his return to Portugal in 1499, paid for his expedition six hundred times over and reaped a 3,000 percent profit. He returned to Calicut in 1502 and again bombarded the town and sank the anchored ships of his competitors, Indians and Arabs. The Portuguese proceeded to select Goa as their base to effectuate, with their superior sea power, the demise of the Indian Ocean world and a monopoly over the Asian trade. By the sixteenth century the Portuguese controlled the sea-lanes, and they spread from India and Ceylon to Indonesia and Macao, China.

To capture the Asian spice trade and with it initiate a reconfiguration of European power relations was on the mind of Portugal's chief architect of its Asian commercial empire, Alfonso de Albuquerque. Named viceroy of the Indies in 1508, Albuquerque planned and executed the capture of Malacca, a key trade city on the Malay Peninsula, in 1511. "The first aim is the great service . . . to our Lord in casting out of this country and quenching the fire of the sect of Mohammed," he wrote in anticipation of the battle. "And the other is the service we shall render to the king," which was the taking of the city that is "the source of all the spiceries and drugs which the Moors carry every year." Upon capturing Malacca he boasted, "Cairo and Mecca will be entirely ruined, and Venice will receive no spiceries unless her merchants go and buy them in Portugal."[34] A man of his word, Albuquerque slaughtered all of Malacca's Muslims and other "heathens," Hindus and Buddhists, for "our Lord" and the king, and used torture to win converts to his Christianity.

Meanwhile the Portuguese demonstrated a way of generating the income necessary for the Asian trade. On their island possessions off the African coast, including Madeira and the Azores, the Portuguese imported African slaves to grow and produce on plantations of sugar and wheat, which they sold to Italy and Spain. During a fifty-year period, from 1450 to 1500, some 150,000 African slaves filled the holds of Portuguese ships bound for those island plantations and for sale on the European continent. In that way Africa purchased Portugal's Asian goods with enslaved African laborers who served European masters, extracting "green gold" on plantations built on expropriated land. In addition Portuguese manufactures undermined African producers, and enslaved Africans resulted in a net loss of labor for Africa. Portugal's producers gained new markets in Africa, and its plantations profited from their exports to Europe, financing the commerce with Asia.

Before sailing for Spain, Christopher Columbus, a Genoese, first petitioned Portugal to outfit an expedition to sail westward to Asia. The Portuguese king had no interest in Columbus's proposal because his sailors had already progressed far down the African coast; returns from slave sales made those voyages viable. Spain instead sponsored Columbus, and therewith renewed an enmity and a rivalry between the two nations. The rivalry was resolved to the satisfaction of Spain but not Portugal by Pope Alexander, a Spaniard, in Rome. The pope, disregarding the people of Africa and "Asia" (America), assigned Africa to Portugal and Columbus's "India," which he had "discovered" in 1492, to Spain. Two years later the Treaty of Tordesillas extended the line for Portugal across the Atlantic to Brazil, but Spain assumed rights to lands west of the line.

As early as 1497 other European powers, like England and France, ignored that global, papal division and pursued colonization of lands they also believed to be Asia. But their efforts were mainly confined to what became known as North America and islands of the Caribbean. Spain retained most of the initiative in colonizing America, a continent named for a trafficker in human chattel, Amerigo Vespucci, who, like Columbus, captured and sold American Indians as plunder. Spaniards called the people *indios* or "Indians" because Columbus had believed them to be natives of India. In their global expansions the Spaniards used "indios" broadly to designate native peoples wherever they encountered them in America, the Pacific Islands, and Asia.

While the Portuguese landed in India proper, the Spaniards soon learned that their lands were not a part of Asia but a "new world," as was described by Pietro Martir de Anghiera in his 1493 account of Columbus's achievement, *De Orbe Novo* (Of the New World). On his second voyage Columbus established settlers on Hispaniola, which later became Haiti and the Dominican Republic. He forced the Indians to forsake their food cultivation to dig for gold, an order that led to famine, revolts, harsh reprisals, and many deaths. On his third crossing, in 1496, Columbus transported back to Spain 550 Taino Indians, 350 of whom survived the transatlantic middle passage to be sold as slaves to defray the costs of his expedition.

Spanish conquerors captured Mexico, with the aid of native allies, in 1521, and Peru in 1533. From Mexico City the representative of the Spanish crown ruled "New Spain," which covered much of the American continent and the islands of the Caribbean. The Spaniards brought diseases like smallpox and measles that infected and spread quickly among the people of the islands and then the continent, killing millions in what some called "the great dying." Another introduction, malaria, infiltrated the tropical and coastal lowlands and worked its deadly dealings. Slave raiding, yet another contagion, destroyed villages and decimated populations by the hundreds of thousands. In Mesoamerica alone the pre-Spanish population was an estimated 25 million, but by 1650 it fell to 1.5 million.

Extracting gold and silver from the earth's veins drove the Spaniards' brutal mission of expansion and conquest in America, which built a great empire. Over a 150-year period beginning in 1503, gold from Colombia alone increased the entire European supply by about 20 percent. Silver, however, was the bullion that kept afloat the Spanish Empire, and during the period 1503–1660 more than 7 million pounds of silver from America reached Spain. Silver mining in Mexico, Bolivia, and Peru required hundreds of thousands of Indian workers and tens of thousands of pack animals and led to countless deaths in the mines, along the roads, and during the smelting process from mercury poison and silicosis. Besides flowing from New Spain to Spain, silver found its way from Acapulco, Mexico, to Manila in the Philippines.

The Manila galleon trade, begun in 1565, finally connected Spain with Asia proper. It was American silver, extracted by Indians, that purchased the goods so coveted by the Spaniards. In the Philippines American silver bought Chinese silks, satins, and porcelain along with Southeast Asian spices that were transported back to New Spain and, from there, to Spain and Europe. The trade brought Chinese and Spanish merchants to Manila, which grew into an urban trade hub supported by the agricultural production of Filipino farmers in the rural hinterland. In one exceptional year, 1597, more American silver went to Manila than to Seville, and from 1570 to 1780 an estimated 4,000 to 5,000 tons of silver were delivered into Asian hands. The galleon trade ended in 1815 during the Mexican War of Independence, but its influence was transformative in Asia, America, and Europe. This included the introduction of American Indian crops—maize, potatoes, beans, squash, and pineapples—into Asia, which changed Asian diets and economies.

The Manila-Acapulco galleon trade was so lucrative that its competitors, merchants in Spain, petitioned the king to limit the number of ships to two each year. To compensate, galleon traders increased the size of their ships to 1,700 to 2,000 tons, built of Philippine hardwoods capable of carrying up to a thousand passengers. Scores of Filipinos died from the forced labor imposed by the Spaniards to build those galleons.

Moving from Asia to America, among the loads of textiles, spices, porcelain, and furniture on board the Spanish galleons were Asians, mainly Filipinos and Chinese and possibly, because of the richly hybrid Southeast Asian waters around the Philippines, South Asians and Arabs, who for hundreds of years had negotiated those islands and seas. Those Asians worked on board the galleons, and Spanish masters enslaved some of them for sale in New Spain until 1700, when the practice ended. Spaniards also took Filipina concubines to America, where they produced mestizos, who, along with galleon-deserting Asian seamen, blended into Mexico's Indian population. Called "indios" by their Spaniard colonizers, Asians and American Indians alike were of the subject class, and a century later, in 1810 to 1821, when Mexico rose up in rebellion against Spain, hundreds of Mexican Filipinos joined the struggle for freedom as military commanders, like Ramon Fabie, and as soldiers.

Summary

European expansion involved the disciplining of what Europeans perceived to be a world in chaos. European sciences systematically named, classified, and described all of the earth's lands and peoples, and through conquest Europeans exploited the abundance of those distant, largely tropical shores. They extracted precious metals using American Indian and African labor, exchanged the gold and silver to obtain Asian products, and deployed African, Asian, and Pacific Islander labor in the Atlantic and Pacific worlds to farm vast plantations of spices, tea, sugar, and other tropical produce. Imposition of an imperial order enabled that systematic exploitation of the world called the world-system that led to European development and its reciprocal, Third World underdevelopment.

Those Portuguese and Spanish initiatives in the Atlantic world at the end of the fifteenth century were not trade in the usual sense. As Spain's viceroy in Peru observed in 1736, the colonial economy was not built on trade or exchange between partners because the colonizers held a monopoly over the means of production and economic relations operated within a closed system. Instead he likened the Spanish Empire's extraction of America's wealth to an "inheritance." The English, Dutch, and French soon joined that Spanish model by establishing outposts along the coasts of Africa, America, and Asia to defend and advance their national interests. Their ships stopped at those ports to replenish their water and food supplies and to replace their crew, many of whom died from diseases or deserted. Powerful trade monopolies, like the English and Dutch East India companies, were formed and behaved like nation-states, with their private navies, armies, and bureaucrats, imposing imperial order within their domains.

European nations staked out and claimed African, American, Asian, and Pacific Islander lands and established settler colonies to profit the imperial powers. Following the practice of encouraging expeditions to generate income to cover their expenses, European expansionists required of their settlers economic self-sufficiency and material returns. Those settler colonies, tropical plantations, and the exploitation of natural resources using bound, mainly nonwhite labor produced European empires. As such, Africa, America, Asia, and the islands of the sea made Europe. By the eighteenth century the rapacious Atlantic world encircled the entire globe, consisting of a European core and outlying peripheries and movements of capital from the margins to the centers. With the advent of imperial order, both material and discursive, fierce blew the winds of that world-system.

FOUR

WORLD-SYSTEM

Like most definitions of imperialism, *world-systems theory* purports to explain the career of capitalism and its appropriation of land and labor starting in the fifteenth century. World-systems are plural because, although self-contained as operating systems, several can coexist at the same time, and they rise, change, and fall in different places over time. But the world-system is also singular in that each consists of a core and its periphery and their relations. The system's core is a place of high capital concentration, while areas of low capital concentration compose its periphery. In fact I subscribe to the idea of a single world-system because its social formation, the locations and articulations of power, while multiple and variable over space/time, remain at the macro level consistent and constant.

From the fifteenth through the nineteenth century Europe was the world-system's core, while Africa, America, and Asia—the Third World—were its peripheries. That spatial binary is connected and reciprocal in that capital or value flows from the periphery to the core, resulting in the core's enrichment and development and the periphery's impoverishment and underdevelopment. Conquest, colonization, and migrant labor structure those processes, relations, and movements, making them systematic and dynamic. Moreover resistance to incorporation and anticolonial struggles have challenged and altered the modern world-system.

The US sociologist Immanuel Wallerstein theorized the modern world-system. In developing the idea he cites three sources influential in his thinking.[1] First, in the 1950s scholars in the Third

World conceived of the core and the periphery in their writings, articulating what became known as *dependency theory*. European mercantile capitalism in the age of expansion was an unequal exchange that produced profits for the core and poverty and hence dependency in the periphery. The second inspiration for world-systems theory, Wallerstein recounts, was the *Annales* group in France, led by the historians Lucien Febvre and Marc Bloch. In 1929 Febvre and Bloch launched the scholarly journal *Annales d'histoire économique et sociale*, or simply *Annales*, which became a leading proponent of economic and social history. After World War II Fernand Braudel extended *Annales* history, or history in totality, to even wider geographical spaces and longer historical times, veering away from national, episodic histories. Braudel's histories examined the longue durée in the Mediterranean world and in the career of capitalism and civilization. The third, an experiential source for the idea of the world-system was the 1968 student strikes in the United States, Europe, Mexico, and Japan. More immediate for Wallerstein was the 1968 student strike at Columbia University, where he taught and which he supported. All of those strikes were critical of global capitalism and US and European imperialism and its wars in the Third World.[2]

Wallerstein's world-systems theory, in sum, emerges from Third World dependency theory, the capacious space and time of the *Annales* school, and the student-led protests against capitalism and imperialism in the Third World.

Dependency

The world-system's core, as we have seen, dispatched expeditions to plunder the resources of its others in the periphery. Ships conveyed laborers and products from Africa, America, and Asia to Europe and its colonies, and plantations anchored an empire of plants cultivated by workers, enslaved and indentured, who were transported from Europe, Africa, and Asia. Factories in the European core hummed, processing raw materials like silk and cotton into textiles and cloth and sugar and molasses into rum and sweets, and those products were sold at home and abroad, transforming the nature of capitalism from a mercantile or trade economy to one based on industries and manufacturing.

Gain and development, however, were uneven. In the core, as Hobson suggested, only certain classes and businesses profited from imperialism. Those included banking and especially finance capitalism, together with the army and navy and the manufacturers of ships, armaments, and military supplies. In fact, Hobson argued, imperialism was bad for the national economy as a whole, and those who benefited from extraterritorial expansion were, in his apt phrase, "parasites of patriotism."[3] Disparate development in the core emerges in the clearly demarcated class structure and pockets of poverty and plenty, places of underdevelopment and capital concentration in rural and urban settings alike.

That asymmetrical spatial dimension of imperialism and capitalism in the core was mirrored in the periphery. Andre Gunder Frank, a German- and US-educated sociologist who pioneered dependency theory in Latin America, notes how capitalist relations in the periphery resembled those in the core. In the case of Chile, the process of Indian incorporation under Spanish colonialism began with military conquest and the deliberate destruction of indigenous economies and their absorption into capitalism. Key in that transformation was the discourse of racism that assigned Indians to a lower state and explained their subjugation, exploitation, and assimilation in the language of progress, uplift, and the triumph of science over superstition.[4] Hobson makes a similar point in his discussion of imperialism and race. As tropical peoples, he writes of that discourse, the "lower races" were lazy and backward, conditioned as they were by the hot, stale climate, and thus had to be forcibly conditioned or "seasoned" into the dignity of labor.[5]

Instead of being mired in a state of nature, Frank explains, Indian poverty was intentional and structured by capitalism's expropriation of their land and labor, resulting in the development of underdevelopment. In Chile local centers connived to remove masses of peasants from their land, consolidate ownership of large tracts of land in the hands of a few, and employ workers rendered landless to produce surpluses for landowners, bankers, and merchants. The wealth, generated by not indolent but productive laborers, flowed from those rural peripheries to urban centers in Chile and from thence to the parasitic, colonial power, Spain. Their indigenous subsistence economy destroyed at the local level, Indian producers were coerced into becoming wage workers and consumers in global relations of the capitalist economy and world-system.[6]

Frank and others, especially in Latin American studies, like the Brazilian sociologist Fernando Henrique Cardoso,[7] described that process by which former colonies of Spain, Portugal, and other European nations enriched the core while impoverishing the peripheries, rendering them dependent upon their colonial masters. Dependency theory derived from and informed those studies of imperial systems and relations. *Dependency*, as I employ the term, is a discourse and condition of economic, political, and social subordination following conquest and incorporation, at first produced by segregation and, later, by assimilation.[8]

The social formation of race, gender, sexuality, class, and nation segregates by inventing and policing discrete binaries and hierarchies of white and non-white, man and woman, straight and queer, capitalist and worker, and citizen and alien. Separation ensures the purity and vigor of the superior stock and culture, claims the discourse of segregation, and social supremacy is justified by the supposed uplift and eventual absorption of inferior peoples and classes. Even after the end of legal segregation, other instruments, such as schools, churches, asylums, and prisons and discourses, perpetuate dependency through assimilation and a process of coercion and consent called *hegemony*. Under hegemony, as Antonio Gramsci describes it, dependent subjects comply with their subordination and reliance upon the ruling class.

Gramsci's important concept of hegemony derives from his concern with political consciousness and the mobilization of the masses for revolution. Gramsci was born in 1891 on the island of Sardinia off the Italian coast. His first cause was Sardinian nationalism, which arose in resistance to the island's colonial relationship with the mainland. While a student at Turin University, he became a socialist and adopted from his teacher Antonio Labriola the "philosophy of praxis." Ideology has a material existence, the philosophy of praxis held, and ideology organizes action and is materialized in practice. Gramsci joined the Italian Communist Party and became its general secretary in 1924, for which he was arrested and imprisoned for over seven years. His imprisonment broke him physically, and he died just three years after his release.

During his time in prison, however, Gramsci secretly wrote and smuggled to the outside some 2,848 handwritten pages of text that became his *Prison Notebooks*. A complex set of writings engaging numerous subjects, *Prison Notebooks* reveals his evolving notion of hegemony.[9] First conceived as a tool of the proletariat to mobilize the rural peasantry for revolution, hegemony was later deployed by Gramsci as an instrument of the state and capitalism to induce consensus and a genuine national popular will.[10] Gramsci's hegemony is not a simple imposition of the superior over inferior classes, nor is it the Marxian idea of "false consciousness" or a misapprehension of class identifications and interests. Hegemony involves complex relations of power and struggles and is thus mobile and indeterminate. Ideology is the terrain "on which men move, acquire consciousness of their position, struggle."[11] Ideology, then, is a battlefield on which wars of position are waged.

Subjects are produced by ideology, Gramsci begins, showing how ideas are embodied and become materialized (philosophy of praxis). Intellectuals, organic (of the masses) and traditional (of the dominant class), produce ideology, which structure subjects through various apparatuses of the state and the ruling class, including laws, schools, churches, the media, and even architecture (buildings) and street names—the entirety of civil society. But subjects can withdraw from the struggle and achieve a passive consensus or agreement of acquiescence under the ruling order, or they can actively engage the discourse to achieve an expansive hegemony or a genuine national consensus and will. Either way, as agents, subjects perceive the dominant social relations and the nation-state as expressive of their self- and class interests and thus submit to the prevailing power relations and to their own subordination.

Unlike Marxists, who believe in the irreducible, singular, and determining force of the means and relations of production, Gramsci conceived of a more complex and contested ensemble of social, political, and military powers articulated through ideology percolating through the whole of society to produce and preserve economic and political relations and moral and intellectual unity (consensus). In this Gramscian world, power is expressed by social forces linked with the material forces of production, by political forces or group consciousness and organization, and by police and military forces that can coerce and prove decisive. The hegemonic or ruling class, then, is the class that articulates the subjectivities and interests of the entire nation-state or society by means of ideology and ideological struggles.

Louis Althusser, a Marxist philosopher born in 1918 in the French colony of Algeria, refined and introduced rigor to Gramsci's idea of hegemony. Like Gramsci, Althusser believed that ideology in the creation of subjects is not simply imposed as a coercive power over subject classes but is negotiated and struggled over before reaching a consensus. Apparatuses like language, social codes and conventions, the family, and society offer the masses a sense of identity and security. Ideology thus interpellates or produces subjects within social contexts that give them meaning through identification with and positioning within a social order.[12]

In that articulation of coercion and consent, Albert Memmi holds that there exists a "relentless reciprocity" in the relationship between the colonizer and the colonized.[13] Some understand that bond as shared, blurring the distinction and relations of power between the colonizer and the colonized. I disagree with that contention, as I stress in my critique of postcolonialism in chapter 9. But Memmi correctly, I believe, describes the complexity of colonization and dependency, Gramsci's hegemony. Subjugation, as Gramsci and Althusser observe, begins with subjectivity or consciousness as articulated and expressed through language and ideology. Memmi poignantly reflects upon the multiple valences of language, the colonial language imposed on colonial subjects by France.

Growing up a Jew in North African Tunisia, Memmi spoke a Judeo-Arabic dialect of Tunis, "a crippled language reinforced by Hebrew, Italian and French words," he wrote. Arabs barely understood his mother tongue, and everyone else ignored it completely. Only within the confines of Tunis's Jewish ghetto was his language useful, Memmi confessed, but it was woefully inadequate in "the political, technical and intellectual universe which I was yearning to conquer." It was in the colonizer's schools that he received "the gift of French. It was an intimidating present, exacting and difficult to handle; it was also the language of the colonizer. But this superbly sophisticated instrument could express everything and opened every door. One's cultural attainments, intellectual prestige and social success were all measured by one's assurance in the use of the conqueror's language."[14]

Herein Memmi acknowledges the simultaneous colonizing and liberating aspects of the French language. Of course the colonizer's tongue functioned well within the colonizer's world; at the same time, as Sartre pointed out, French assimilation created "ex-natives" and pliant colonial subjects. Speaking the colonizer's tongue, however, enabled participation in and the possible subversion of the colonizer's discourses and powers. In addition speaking and writing in a "broken" version of the colonizer's language can mock, undermine, and produce creole languages that can destabilize the ruling order while mobilizing counterdiscourses and anticolonial movements.[15]

Hawaiians "broke" English in their makeshift, trade language, at times called *hapa haole* (half-foreign) pidgin, which formed a basis for plantation pidgin English. Overseers on the sugar plantations deployed pidgin as the language of command to order and discipline workers, while the masses, the working class spoke pidgin to cut across the divides of race and ethnicity and to compose a "local" subjectivity in opposition to haole (foreign) and global dominance.[16] The complexity of plantation pidgin English arises from its mobility and differences among speakers of Hawaiian, Chinese, Japanese, Korean, Filipino, Portuguese, and Puerto Rican. Each group added their traces to the language, which varied in vocabulary, sentence structure, and pronunciation.[17]

By the early twentieth century, with the birth of a second generation of plantation pidgin English speakers, the language was formalized into Hawai'i Creole, with distinctive rules, vocabulary, and grammar. Called simply pidgin, Hawai'i Creole was the first language of the home, workplace, and street and policed only by its practitioners.[18] As the African writer and cultural critic Ngũgĩ wa Thiong'o explains of language and its agency in developing consciousness, "It is an ever-continuing struggle to seize back their [colonized people's] creative initiative in history through a real control of all the means of communal self-definition in time and space. The choice of language and the use to which language is put is central to a people's definition of themselves in relation to their natural and social environments, indeed in relation to the entire universe."[19]

When the Nigerian writer Amos Tutuola submitted his work that became *The Palm-Wine Drinkard* in 1952, the English poet Dylan Thomas welcomed the text as "written in young English."[20] In fact Tutuola's London publisher, Faber and Faber, saw the book's value more as an anthropological artifact than as a work of literature. While paternal colonizers might have been amused by Tutuola's "young" language, some African critics found his "broken English" offensive because it confirmed the racist assumption of primitive, undeveloped, and incapable African subjects.[21] Other scholars see the writer Tutuola as indigenizing and hybridizing English and creating an "interlanguage," or third space between the colonizer's tongue and, in this instance, an African language and culture. In effect Tutuola's text represents a new syncretic, anti-imperialist language and literature.[22] While Memmi might have found liberation in mastering the colonizer's language, an unsettling achievement insofar as the colonized gains entry into the colonizer's discourse, Hawaiian pidgin and Tutuola's hybrid English resist incorporation in the interstices and contradictions of language and culture.

| | |

Exposing imperialism and capitalism and their discourses, then, are world-systems and dependency theories, and crucial to those ideas is the Third World. Wallerstein credits Third World intellectuals critical of imperialism and capitalism's expansion into the Third World as sources for his world-systems theory. Although of the First World and educated at the University of Chicago, the dependency theorist Frank admits that when he took a faculty position in Chile he had to unlearn what he had learned in the United States. Chicago laissez-faire capitalist economic theory, he writes, failed to explain adequately the actual conditions he found in the Third World.[23]

Frank lived and worked in the midst of a revolution, the democratic election of a Marxist president, Salvador Allende, in 1970. Three years later Allende's efforts to democratize the capitalist economy and reverse neocolonialism led to a military coup that was aided by the US Central Intelligence Agency. That coup ended nearly forty-one years of Chilean democracy and installed the brutal military dictatorship of Augusto Pinochet, which lasted until 1990. Following Allende's death, Frank fled to Europe, but his political identification remained with the people of Chile and the Third World. Like Gramsci's philosophy of praxis, Frank writes of the imperative for intellectuals to join the masses in revolutionary struggles against dependency as advanced by the nation-state and global capitalism.

Conquest

A crucial element of the imperial compass and world-system is *colonialism*, which I have defined as the discursive and material subjugation of extraterritorial spaces and their life forms, including lands and waters and all of their properties. Seaborne expansion required landings, places to replace and replenish crews and supplies of fresh water, fruits, and vegetables, which were necessary for survival. Those pacific harbors became strategic, militarized centers to defend the sea-lanes from imperial competitors. As such they were at once tranquil waters and sites of danger. Dotting Africa's coastline and its offshore islands were those militarized zones that faced the sea, but also the interior, where the African masses presented opportunities while posing threats to the permanence of those often tenuous outposts of expansionism.

European powers classified those imperial landings as their property and extensions of national sovereignty, despite the legitimate claims of the indigenous peoples. From those footholds Europeans marched into the interiors, mapping and annexing foreign lands and peoples in the act of conquest. Andrea Smith, a scholar of American Indian studies, likens that conquest by European men to rape—rape of the land and women.[24] Rape, she notes, is an act of violence and an exertion of power over one's other. The lands of indigenous peoples, commonly called "virgin soil," seemingly invited European men's violation and possession; in fact, as we have seen, Locke held that land became property only after it had been worked and made to produce. In America, Spanish conquerors often saw native women as like the soil, inviting their dominion. That rape, Smith recounts, characterized the process of European subordination and exploitation, and it represented racial, gender, and sexual violence: "The history of sexual violence and genocide among Native women illustrates how gender violence functions as a tool for racism and colonialism among women of color in general."[25]

Prior to Smith's study of sexual violence and genocide, the US historian Richard Trexler traced the pattern of gendered violence and the installation of political order in the European conquest of America. Compulsory heterosexuality, Trexler noted, as a prerequisite for patriarchal state formation, manifested itself as gender and sexual violence against American Indians as conquered peoples, as women, as aliens, and as queers (in particular, those called *berdache,* or "two-spirited," multigendered persons). Conquest was thereby justified by the necessity of replacing disorder and deviance with normalcy and order. Those figures of subordination in America, Trexler recounts, followed from a genealogy of punitive (re)gendering in the ancient Mediterranean world and medieval Spain, where homosexual violence, rape, castration, and evisceration were rituals of humiliation and paths to nation building. In addition those acts of conquest reduced subordinates to the states of property and dependency.[26]

Conquest, as Smith and Trexler gesture toward, and colonization involved the totality of the social formation. Discursive and material powers exerted their authority over racialized, gendered, sexualized, classed, and nationalized lands and peoples. While one in general features and functions, extraterritorial colonies were of two main varieties: extractive colonies and settler colonies. *Extractive colonies,* sometimes called "classical" colonies, were installed by colonial powers to extract the colony's natural resources, including minerals, timber, furs, and whales, and to export products grown often on vast plantations. Extractive colonies typically had small numbers of Europeans managing large numbers of Third World peoples, and their principal function, as in all colonies, was to generate wealth for the colonizing power. Accordingly the legal, political, and economic structures, the infrastructure of roads, bridges, railways, ports, and towns, and the military presence were all designed to reduce costs and increase profits. Europeans served their nation-state and employers, and their stay in the colony was typically temporary and only for the duration of their contracts.

Settler colonies, by contrast, consisted of European settlers who saw their presence as permanent and as serving their interests as opposed to those who sent them. The colonies were often in the temperate zone, such as Canada, the United States, South Africa, and Australia and New Zealand, which was more conducive to European life. Settlers established and patrolled borders, at times erecting literal fences, between the more numerous population and themselves and sought to remove indigenous peoples from their claims. Within the colony white settlers thus constituted the majority, and nonwhites the minority and aliens. Because they held interests often at odds with their imperial nation-state, settlers frequently clashed with the colonial power, which they came to see as meddlesome and even repressive. Rebellion, when successful, resulted in independent settler colonial states.

In general the colonial powers and investment companies aimed to squeeze as much profit as they could for themselves while securing their colonies against the prospect of native and settler rebellion. In Spanish America, for instance, the Crown reserved to itself the rights to Indian land and labor. The Crown thereby limited settler gains in New Spain by taxing Indians and their labor and instituting the *encomienda* system, by which the Crown issued to settlers temporary land grants. In 1542 the Crown abolished Indian slavery, thereby reducing settler control over Indian bodies and labor even as African slavery continued and grew.

The Cape Colony at the southern tip of the African continent began in 1652 as a refreshment station. The Dutch East India Company (Vereenigde Oostindische Compagnie, VOC), one of the two largest and most influential corporations in the world at the time, established the outpost. Formed in 1602, the VOC was a chartered, shareholding company with the powers of a nation-state to wage war with its own standing army and navy, promulgate and execute laws, negotiate treaties, mint money, and implant colonies. As its name describes, the VOC held a monopoly over the Dutch trade with Asia.

As a temporary landing the Cape Colony was bordered by a hedge to establish the colony's land claim and to segregate the Dutch from the vastly more numerous indigenous African inhabitants. At the same time, the Dutch traded with Africans for goods, imported African and Asian slaves, and produced mixed-race children, and Dutch farmers and their slaves cultivated fruits and vegetables for the colony and to supply passing ships. Those farmers (*boers*) in time attempted to escape the colony's strictures, crossed its borders to migrate into the interior, and became *trekboers* (migrant farmers). In the process the trekboers became white settlers, holding land as property, extending European claims along the southern African frontier, and waging wars of removal and extinction against Africans. It was that process that the US sociologist and race relations proponent Robert Park called, as noted earlier, the African problem.

In America company controls over employees, as in the Cape Colony, led to discontent and rebellion. The English Company established Jamestown in 1607 to earn returns for its shareholders on their investment. The company accordingly directed the first settlers to find gold and silver and cut a path to the Pacific Ocean and Asia. Neither proved feasible, so the company's directors, seeking profits, turned to trade with the Indians and the cultivation of export crops. Tobacco, a gift of American Indian horticulturalists, became the Virginia Colony's principal export commodity, but its cultivation required greater numbers of workers, mainly European indentures and, later, African slaves, and consumed increasing acreage of fertile lands.[27]

Along that expanding frontier colonists, white and black, free and bound, chafed under the colonial government's monopoly over the trade with Indians and its policy that restricted expansion beyond the colony's borders. That unhappiness, as we will see in chapter 8, crystallized into Bacon's Rebellion (1675–76), led by a patrician landowner, Nathaniel Bacon, involving white and black landowners, indentures, and slaves. As a united class of frontiersmen, the rebels sought freedom from the colonial rulers and land from American Indians. After the rebellion's end, because of the potency of the class alliance exhibited in the movement, the colonial rulers declared landownership to be restricted to white men and citizens (race, gender, class, and nation), reducing the possibility of another white-black class coalition against imperial rule. Hereby landholding or the right to real property, a key feature of capitalism, signaled manhood, whiteness, freedom, ownership, and citizenship.

Migrant Labor

Even as colonies anchored the world-system, *migrant labor* was a product and vital element of that world-system. Places of underdevelopment do not merely supply natural resources but also offer pools of cheap labor, which colonizers transport to plantations and factories in the periphery and core, wherever such labor is needed. In the empire of plants, enslaved American Indian and African workers and indentured Asian laborers cultivated the sugar, cotton, tobacco, and tropical fruits that enriched the core. The laborers were selected by race, ethnicity, gender, and age for efficiency and cost reductions. For most manual labor young men were preferred over children and the aged, and for sailing, whaling, mining, construction, and agricultural tasks men were preferred over women. Women and children supplied cheap labor for plantations, and women were recruited for and labored in industries like canneries and garment factories and reproduced the next generation of workers. The expulsion of migrants in "repatriation" drives signaled the end of their utility to their employers.

Whether in the periphery or the core, when the cost of labor increases, capital generally seeks cheaper but just as efficient labor. Often that labor was found in the Third World after European capitalism and colonialism had undermined the bases of self-sufficient economies and native industries, producing markets for their goods and exacerbating displacement and unemployment among the periphery's peoples. In addition coercion through forced labor, military service, and taxes required colonized subjects to enter into capitalism. Foreign goods, which dominated the market economy, had to be purchased with cash and colonial taxes paid in the colonizer's currency.

Wages from labor were the means by which to survive in that new world order.

The United States, at first as a periphery and later as a core, illustrates the deployment of migrant labor. As noted, the Virginia Colony was established in 1607 by the London Company to turn a profit on the initial investment. As John Smith, who emerged as the colony's leader, confessed, the religious conversion of the native peoples was simply an excuse for conquest "when all their aim was profit."[28] Despite that motive of gain, the colony floundered even as the London investors poured more money and settlers into the project. After tobacco, procured from Indians, addicted a generation of European men, its successful cultivation helped to stabilize for a time the financial life of the Jamestown colony. By 1624 the colony exported 200,000 pounds of the "jovial" or "vile and stinking" weed, depending on one's relation to the smoke, and its cultivation required ever expanding fields and larger pools of laborers recruited mainly as indentured servants from Europe's castoffs.

European indentures, men and women, signed contracts, and ship captains sold them upon arrival. An estimated 25 percent of them died en route to America largely because of unsanitary conditions on ships. Terms included free passage along with housing and meals in return for labor. Indentures varied from periods of four to seven years, and the conditions of labor were often exceedingly harsh. Physical and psychological abuse by masters was common. Rape was routine, and courts, controlled by the master class, frequently deprived mothers of their illegitimate children and fined them severely for lost days during pregnancy and childbirth. Reproduction for that indentured class and gender was a matter of the master's property and labor rights. The period of indenture, however, unlike for slavery, was limited, although not all indentures actually gained their freedom to become landowners. Most succumbed to diseases and the afflictions of work and punishment. Those men who survived, upon gaining their freedom, received money, tools, and even a piece of land, and, as whites, men and women became members of the colony.

Africans, familiar laborers in Europe's Atlantic world, worked as servants alongside European indentures in Virginia's tobacco plantations beginning in 1619. At first Virginia's planters preferred indentures to slaves, and for over fifty years European servants outnumbered Africans by a three to one margin. By the 1670s the supply of servants from Europe diminished and grew expensive, while the flow from Africa was increasingly larger and cheaper. Those supply and cost factors made the colony more dependent upon African migrant labor, both free and bound. That, along with the rising demand for laborers in the tobacco fields, soon resulted in African migrants exceeding the number of white indentures and fortified the related ideas of white freedom and black bondage.

When Britain and the United States made the African slave trade illegal in the early nineteenth century, British planters began the experiment of replacing African slaves with Asian indentured laborers. Nonwhites, Africans and Asians, from areas of underdevelopment were generally cheaper than whites, and they could be super-exploited on the basis of race, gender, and citizenship. Marked as inferior peoples, Africans and Asians were also aliens without the rights of property and citizenship. Bans on mixing policed the lines of segregation, and nonwhites in white settler society could be easily spotted and put into their assigned places. Additionally white privilege discouraged border crossings and thereby reduced incentives for solidarity of race or class.

The transatlantic commerce of enslaved Africans grew from 275,000 sent to Europe and America between 1451 and 1600 to over a million in the seventeenth century, and then to over 6 million in the following century, due mainly to the boom in sugar and tobacco production in America's plantations. The traffic was a human catastrophe for those enslaved and a windfall for planters and merchants and helped to retard Africa and advance Europe and the United States.

Indentured labor, a form of bound labor, characterized Asian and Pacific Islander migration. European settlers in Mauritius in the Indian Ocean drew indentures from India, and by the end of the eighteenth century South Asian workers, contracted for periods of two to three years, were in most major ports throughout Southeast Asia. The end of the African slave trade in the Atlantic world led to a "new system of slavery," as labeled by the British imperial historian Hugh Tinker, devised for Asians and Pacific Islanders as replacements for enslaved Africans. South Asian indentures labored in cane fields in Fiji and South Africa; Chinese contract workers served in tropical plantations, South African mines, and guano deposits along Peru's coastal islands; and traffickers captured Melanesians and Polynesians and sold them to planters in Australia and Peru. Labor recruiters procured Hawaiians to work in Peru, where many of them perished from diseases and unforgiving conditions.

That recruitment of Hawaiians to work in Peru in the early nineteenth century followed a practice begun decades earlier by ship captains who relied upon Hawaiian sailing skills and labor. Over a two-year period beginning in 1845, nearly two thousand Hawaiians served on foreign ships, and by 1850 that total reached four thousand, or almost one-fifth of the Hawaiian kingdom's population. To benefit from that labor migration and limit the loss, the kingdom imposed a poll tax on foreign employers of Hawaiians who by midcentury were toiling on ships and on land from Tahiti and Peru in the south to the Pacific Northwest and Alaska in the north. Hawaiians served in the Mexican Navy and worked on Russian holdings along the West Coast.

By 1830 Hawaiians composed the majority of crews on US ships on the West Coast, and they were also found in the Atlantic and its port cities. When in 1854 American Indian and African slavery was abolished in Peru, the nation's planters recruited Chinese, and later, during a brief ban on Chinese indentured labor, they sent ships to capture Polynesian workers. The slaver *Adelante*, with its barred hatches and compartments and swivel guns to sweep the deck, returned to Callao, Peru, in 1862 with 253 Polynesian captives whose sale reaped their owners a profit of $40,000, a 400 percent return. Men sold for $200 each, women $150, and children $100.

For those ill-gotten gains Pacific Islanders were hunted down and captured, marched to the beach in chains to waiting ships, thrust into crowded, unsanitary ships' holds, and sold to the highest bidder on shore. Along the way many died from the raids and introduced diseases, ranging from 24 percent of one island's total population to 79 percent of another's. Rapa Nui (Easter Island) had an estimated population of 4,126 in 1862 but lost 1,386 to labor raids and about 1,000 to disease, and thus endured a 58 percent population decrease. Moreover the island's social order was devastated by the loss of its leaders and learned old people, who were the repositories of history, law, and culture.

British sugar planters in the Caribbean grafted their need for labor onto the empire's circuits in the Indian and Pacific oceans. In India, a British colony since about 1800, the recruitment system involved both British colonizers and South Asian accomplices who contracted recruiters to scour the Indian countryside in search of indentures. Working through local bosses or headmen, recruiters offered cash advances as enticements to recruits who were in debt or trouble. The British colonizers privatized land in India to encourage agricultural production for export, and the ensuing land grab concentrated wealth and displaced peasants, making them ideal hired hands and migrant workers. Over a million South Asians served masters on tropical plantations, and about half a million labored in America, where, in our time, they make up significant proportions of the populations of Guyana, Trinidad, and Jamaica.

China too became a prime source for migrant labor, especially after its defeat by Britain in the Opium War (1842), whereby Hong Kong became British territory until 1997. European entrepreneurs, working through Chinese brokers in Macao, Singapore, and Penang, tapped into China's pools of labor, which were mainly Chinese but also included Vietnamese and Filipinos. Village leaders identified recruits; some signed or were deceived into signing indenture contracts, which bound them to employers for a period of years, while others received credit for their transpacific passage from creditors who controlled their movements and the terms of employment. Reduced to commodities, this human traffic was called "pig-dealing" by the Chinese, and the transaction was described as the buying and selling of pigs. Nearly all of those destined for America came from Guangdong Province, clustering around the British and Portuguese enclaves of Hong Kong and Macao. About 125,000 went to Cuba, 100,000 to Peru, 18,000 to the British West Indies, and the remainder to Panama and Costa Rica, the Dutch and French West Indies, Brazil, and Chile. An estimated 46,000 Chinese indentures went to Hawai'i, and primarily via the credit-ticket some 200,000 made the passage to California.

Coolies were an invention of Europeans, beginning with the Portuguese, who used the term to mean Asian laborers, but by the nineteenth century the word specified an Indian or Chinese indentured worker bound for sugar plantations in America to replace enslaved Africans. Coolies were thereby the means to recoup the loss of labor incurred by the emancipation of slaves, and they signified freedom over bondage, yet the coolie trade, with its roots in slavery and its abuses, continued to haunt that human traffic. Despite investigations, hearings, and regulations by the British government, the planters exercised control over their investments, and laws criminalized resistance by indentures as violations of civil contracts. Moreover coercion was a central feature of the coolie trade, which involved kidnappings, debt servitude, ships outfitted as prisons, and rapes, floggings, and corporal punishment.

In the 1850s one out of six South Asians bound for the Caribbean died before making landfall, and of the first group of 396 South Asian indentures taken to British Guiana in 1838, one-fourth failed to survive the period of their five-year contract and only sixty chose to remain in the colony. The mortality rate for Chinese indentures during the second half of the nineteenth century was between 12 and 30 percent—higher than the middle passage of the Atlantic African slave trade. Some ships reached as high as 50 percent. Conditions on board the ships and the length of the crossing—three to four months from India and four to eight months from China—might have accounted for those staggering figures. While nearly all of the Chinese were men, South Asian indentures included men, women, and children; women were susceptible to rape, and children to malnutrition and disease. For example, over half of the 324 South Asian coolies from Calcutta on board the *Salsette* bound for Trinidad in 1858 died, and according to court papers, a woman on a different ship died en route after having been gang-raped by the crew.

Asian coolies and African slaves shared similar points of origin, the Third

World, and destination, the plantations of the New World. Within the expanding world-system they were migrant laborers in service to mercantile and industrial capitalism in field and factory made eminently exploitable by the discourses and materializations of race, gender, sexuality, class, and nation—the social formation.

Summary

Capitalism's expansion, whether driven by the desire for commerce, the search for new markets, the need for resources and labor, or investment and military interests, installed the modern world-system. Discourses directed and justified that global imperial order, and conquests of waters, lands, peoples, and nature enriched the core with material extractions from the periphery. Like rape, those conquests were exertions of power for possession and subjugation. Dependency was a condition deliberately crafted by the colonizers, and hegemony subdued both the mind and the body of the colonized. Contentment, however, was not total or forever, even as the processes of conquest, colonization, and dependency were uneven and resisted. The colonizer's tongue induced dependency, but it also sharpened capacities to escape, destabilize, and engage.

Colonies dotted the periphery, and the means of production, including raw materials and laborers, flowed on the currents generated by the world-system. Unlike the white settlers who established European and, later, their own claims, migrant laborers from Africa, America, and Asia were tools, indeed property of the master class and were not intended for incorporation into the settler colony and nation-state. They were aliens, like the indigenous peoples, segregated and excluded from membership and civil and human rights on the bases of race, gender, sexuality, class, and nation. But over time and with the settler occupation complete, the colonizers faced the vexing question of their conquests and their absorption into the nation. As described by Gramsci and Althusser, the apparatuses of the state were central to that assimilation, including consciousness and education.

FIVE

EDUCATION

Student activists of the Third World Liberation Front knew that their strike for educational transformation was essential for the liberation of their minds and bodies from the chains of colonialism. They read Frantz Fanon and agreed that their generation's mission was anticolonialism through revolution. As we have seen, the fight for a national culture, Fanon foresaw, was on a special battlefield, and he described that contest as nothing less than the creation of a people. In fact, he pointedly observed, denied a history and culture, the people—the subjects of Third World studies—would cease to exist. A national culture was an expression of "national consciousness."[1]

According to intellectuals like Gramsci and Althusser, as we have seen, consciousness is crucial to the interpellation of self and its location in society. Consciousness is also an indispensable aspect of education in a work widely cited by post-1968 ethnic studies proponents titled *Pedagogy of the Oppressed* (1972) written by the Brazilian educator Paulo Freire. Even as subject matter can liberate students, Freire contended, the teaching method should free students and teachers from the "circle of certainty" that characterizes schooling for colonialism.

That positivism or regime of truth underwrites colonial education, and it involves teacher bankers who deposit knowledge into student ciphers. That banking concept of education, Freire declared, was bankrupt and must be replaced with a liberating pedagogy of dialogue among equals.[2] Instead of teacher-subject and student-object, a pedagogy of the oppressed humanizes teachers and students alike by disrupting the binary and hierarchy of teacher-colonizer and student-colonized. From a process of mutual, dialogic teaching and learning will emerge consciousness and intervention, critical independent thinking and action (praxis), recalling Gramsci. Consciousness formation, Freire believed, is a constant, revolutionary struggle for self-determination and change that creates subjects (as opposed to objects) and thus agents of history, rendering them "truly human."[3] We are hereby reminded of Fanon's anticolonial project of a new humanity, a new humanism.[4]

American Education

Third World Liberation Front students were aware that schooling in the United States served the ruling class. They understood that the subject matter of the curriculum featured the ideology and language, history, culture, and achievements of the powerful and slighted the agency of people separated from power. Third World studies, they believed, possessed the potential to transform education and thereby society. Like Gramsci and Althusser, they saw the schools as apparatuses of the state that produced subjects destined to rule and objects schooled to serve. They understood that education can colonize, but it can also liberate. A Third World curriculum and pedagogy of the oppressed can plant the seeds of consciousness and revolutionary change.

In 1968 Third World students noted that California's public higher education mirrored and produced the relations of power. Community colleges composed the state's lowest tier; above that was the California state system; and at the top was the University of California system. Students of color populated the lower two levels, while whites and children of the elite predominated in the highest tier. At the two-year community colleges students generally received vocational training and earned associate degrees, while the four-year state system offered bachelor's degrees; for advanced studies and degrees, students had to attend the University of California. Employment patterns followed the three-tier educational hierarchy, from manual technical labor for community college graduates to middle-level professional jobs for California state graduates to management and advanced degrees in business, education, engineering, law, medicine, and the arts and sciences for University of California graduates.

| | |

Founded as an English settler colony in the seventeenth century, the United States installed an educational system designed for rule. Like those who arrived in Plymouth Colony in 1630 under the leadership of John Winthrop, the Puritans were highly educated, and they predominated at many English colleges, including Oxford and Cambridge. Determined to build "a city upon a hill" that would serve as an exemplar of godly governance, the Puritans established Harvard College in 1636 to train a cadre of clergy and teachers to school the masses. Intellectuals, as Gramsci observed, shape ideology and consciousness, producing rulers and subjects. In 1642 the Puritans founded a tax-supported school system to train children to read, learn the principles of religion, and comply with the law. Those educational goals—literacy, values, and a pliant citizenry—remain fundamental to schooling in the United States.

White women were generally excluded from the clergy and teaching, but the postcolonial nation, from 1790 to 1820, established a number of female academies to train women to take their place in the new republic as "republican mothers" and "daughters of Columbia." These were white, middle-class women who, as mothers, bore the responsibility of nurturing the next generation of leaders. Education for those privileged women nonetheless was designed for "the gentler sex" because philosophy, mathematics, and science might overtax their limited mental capacities, resulting in illness or deviant, manly women. Herein we see the workings of race, gender, sexuality, class, and nation.

Blacks, both men and women, were broadly seen as chattel and as such were widely excluded from education and, especially under slavery, literacy. In fact education might lead to transgressions and rebellion. That strategy of racialized and gendered distinctions and segregation would change to a strategy of inclusion and assimilation when the US social formation required the labor and citizenry of white women and African Americans.

Native Americans supply an example of education's powers in nation building through the processes of segregation and assimilation. Although a violent act of colonization, education of native peoples was often couched in the language of redemption and uplift from a state of savagery to an exalted plane of civilization. In 1793 Congress allocated $20,000 for American Indian education, and in 1816 missionaries founded the Foreign Mission School in Cornwall, Connecticut, "a school for the education of heathen youth." The intention was to train native youth as ministers, teachers, interpreters, and physicians to minister to their people and "promote Christianity and civilization."[5] The original Puritan mission of literacy, religion, and loyal citizens pervades the Foreign Mission School's aims of advancing Christianity and civilization. The curriculum was directed at molding useful citizens whose busy hands in domestic service and agriculture, not thinking minds, best served the nation and common good.

Among the Foreign Mission School's students in 1818 were six Hawaiians, two Society Islanders, two Malays, and eleven American Indians, mainly Cherokees and Choctaws. In 1824 Miles Mackey, a Choctaw student, described in a poem he wrote "a school compos'd of foreign youth" for the purpose of "propagating gospel truth." In 1825 the school enrolled six Hawaiians, four Chinese, fourteen American Indians, a Portuguese from the Azores, and a Jew from England.[6] For the school's masters, "foreign" and "heathen" youth were a motley mix of those of a darker hue.

The students' 1822 lesson book, *The Missionary Spelling Book, and Reader*, offers a glimpse of their indoctrination. Lessons began with vocabulary sets, including parts of the body, household objects, nature and time, and relationships and work. By lesson 12 students recited phrases like "I am very well," "She is sick," "He is a Christian," and "Our bodies must die." Building on those blocks, the destiny of all flesh is the subject of lesson 19:

> We shall all die.
> When our bodies die, our souls will go away from this world.
> Angels will come, and take the souls of good men up to heaven.
> They will see God. . . .
> There they will be happy, and will live forever.
> The souls of wicked men will go to hell.
> There they will dwell with devils, and will be miserable forever.[7]

The Cornwall Foreign Mission School's sponsor was the American Board of Commissioners for Foreign Missions, which trained Hawaiians and in 1819 sent its first contingent of missionaries to Hawai'i. Prior to that expedition, US missionaries ministered primarily to American Indians and whites along the western frontier, which for the young nation demarcated a "domestic" from a "foreign" territory. Among the fifth company of missionaries dispatched by the American Board to Hawai'i were the Reverend Richard Armstrong and his wife, Clarissa Chapman, who sailed from New Bedford, Massachusetts, and arrived in Honolulu on May 17, 1832, after an ocean voyage of 173 days. On the occasion of her eightieth birthday, Clarissa Chapman Armstrong recalled her labors among Pacific Islanders as "a life amongst the heathens with the privilege of uplifting dark, degraded humanity" and a work dedicated to "children of nature, with no knowledge of civilization whatever and given over to animal lusts and selfish degradation."[8]

Richard Armstrong retired from mission work in 1847 to assume the post of minister of public instruction in the Hawaiian kingdom. In that office he was responsible for "private and public morals" and introduced "American education,"[9] which stressed agriculture for boys and homemaking for girls. Missionaries favored that same design of manual and industrial education—racialized, gendered, and sexualized—in their work among American Indians. Armstrong's curriculum, like the Puritan educational ideal, proposed to nurture a "mental and moral culture" in which Christianity, civilization, and industry might prosper. His system of education followed the original design for education in America and became the standard schooling for Native Americans; it was indeed American education.

Their son, Samuel Chapman Armstrong, learned from his father and took that educational model designed for Native Americans and applied it in his work among African Americans and American Indians in the postbellum US South. He established the Hampton Normal and Agricultural Institute in Virginia in 1868 under the aegis of the American Missionary Association. Hampton's purpose was to train African American teachers to spread the good word of Christianity and civilization to the recently emancipated slaves. Armstrong's gospel directed African Americans to defer their dreams of freedom and remain contentedly in their assigned place: agricultural labor for men and domestic work for women. Hawaiians and African Americans, "darkies" in Armstrong's choice language, composed a single, "undeveloped race," an infantile race at the "dawn of civilization." Later Hampton admitted American Indians into its educational mission. Because of their state and mental capacities, like women and children, Hawaiians, African Americans, and American Indians had to be patiently and slowly nurtured into civilization. The Hampton idea that equality must await conversion from a primitive to a civilized people secured nonwhite subservience and advanced white supremacy. It was also thoroughly American.

One of Armstrong's star pupils was Booker T. Washington, who, in 1881, founded Tuskegee Normal and Industrial Institute in Alabama. Patterned on Hampton, Tuskegee promoted industrial education and "the dignity, the beauty and civilizing power of intelligent labor with the hand." The stress was on manual, not mental work. "My race in this country can never cease to be grateful to General Armstrong for all that he did for my people and for American civilization," Washington gushed of his master teacher. Hampton's educators and curriculum offered him "parental care" and made him "all that

African American students examine Louis Firetail (Sioux, Crow Creek), who poses as a museum artifact. Hampton Institute, late 1890s. Photo by Frances Benjamin Johnston. Courtesy of the Library of Congress.

I am."[10] As was described by Gramsci's hegemony, Washington took comfort and found satisfaction in paternalism's embrace as extended by Armstrong and Hampton.

In his popular autobiography, *Up from Slavery* (1901), Washington describes his role in educating American Indians at Hampton. Deemed less civilized than blacks, American Indians were taught to follow the African American pattern. Washington served as "house father" to young, "perfectly ignorant" Indians, living with, disciplining, and serving as a role model for them. African American students, Washington recalled, assisted Indian students with English and the acquisition of "civilized habits." In reality Hampton collaborated with the US government in its expansionist campaign to conquer and rule over "rebellious" Indian nations in the West. Hampton's American Indian pupils, taken mainly from chiefly families, were hostages of imperialism and war. Like their kinfolk, many of those children died in Indian boarding schools, on battlefields far from their ancestral homes.

"The Indian question will never be settled till you make the Indian blister his hands," Armstrong declared in support of Hampton's manual labor education. "No people ever emerged from barbarism that did not emerge through labor." Richard Henry Pratt, like Armstrong a commander of African American troops during the Civil War, agreed with Hampton's educational aim of "civilizing" American Indians. In charge of some 150 Arapaho, Cheyenne, Comanche, and Kiowa prisoners of war in Florida, Pratt sent seventeen of them to Armstrong and Hampton in 1878. "A great general has said that the only good Indian is a dead one," Pratt agreed, with one modification: "that all the Indian there is in the race should be dead. Kill the Indian in him, and save the man." Armstrong rephrased that solution to "the Indian question": it is cheaper to civilize Indians than to exterminate them.[11] Education was the weapon of choice to kill the Indian.

With federal aid, in 1879 Pratt founded the Carlisle Indian Industrial School at Carlisle Barracks, Pennsylvania. Carlisle was the start of an archipelago of Indian boarding schools littered throughout Indian country. Estelle Reel, the first woman in US history requiring Senate confirmation for her appointment, served as superintendent of Indian schools from 1898 to 1910. Her *Uniform Course of Study* (1901), according to a press release, mirrored her belief in "what Booker T. Washington is doing for the negro," and she adopted "many of the Tuskegee methods for Indian schools."[12] Her curricular influence extended beyond the 250 Indian boarding schools under her supervision on the continent, spreading to US colonial possessions abroad to Puerto Rico and the Philippines.

The incorporation of Native Americans—American Indians and Hawaiians—into the nation required their gradual uplift and assimilation. American education, involving Christianity, civilization, and manual labor, tutored Native Americans in Cornwall and Hawai'i and from that precedent African Americans and American Indians at Hampton. Tuskegee descended from Hampton, which sired Carlisle, and all three institutions gave rise to Reel's *Uniform Course of Study* for American Indians in the United States and related colonized subjects, called *indios* by the Spanish conquistadors, in Puerto Rico and the Philippines. That genealogy of American education reveals its hegemonic power as an imperial and colonial project.

The inclusion of white women and the white working-class masses into US public education accompanied the nineteenth-century transformation in the social formation produced by the industrialization of the Northeast and the nation's transition from mercantile to industrial capitalism. In Massachusetts Horace Mann (1796–1859), a politician and educational reformer, regularized school hours and instituted grade levels and a standardized curriculum. Mann championed universal public education as essential for shaping useful citizens.

Teacher training for men and women began in 1837, and for the first time in US history school attendance became the rule rather than the exception for white children from five to nineteen years old. There was regional disparity, however; in New England 81 percent of white children attended school, but a mere 15 percent in the South. Industrialists, popularly called "robber barons," like Andrew Carnegie and John D. Rockefeller created foundations to support public libraries and higher education, and the number of colleges and universities and students leaped fourfold between 1850 and 1910. The need for skilled labor and scientific and technological breakthroughs spurred the expansion.

Meanwhile segregated and inferior schools relegated African Americans to service and agricultural work in the North and South, and "Mexican" and "Oriental" schools in the West schooled children into subservience and thus utility for the ruling class. Those segregated schools and the inequality they produced and sustained bred resistance, culminating with the US Supreme Court's *Brown v. Board of Education* (1954) decision that rendered illegal public school segregation. Leading up to and foundational for the *Brown* decision, seen mainly as an African American achievement, were Asian and Mexican American demands for educational equity.

In 1884 the white principal of California's Spring Valley Primary School refused to admit eight-year-old Mamie Tape. A US citizen by birth, Mamie was the daughter of Chinese migrants Joseph and Mary McGladery Tape. Mamie's parents sued for their daughter's admission, citing the equal protection clause of the Fourteenth Amendment (1868). The court agreed with the Tapes and declared, "To deny a child, born of Chinese parents in this State, entrance to the public schools" is "a violation of the law of the state and the Constitution of the United States." In reaction California passed legislation to provide segregated Oriental schools for Asian children, which satisfied the equal protection clause according to the Supreme Court's *Plessy v. Ferguson* (1896) decision that was the pillar upholding racial segregation. Separate was equal, *Plessy* declared. Mary Tape disagreed. In her letter dated April 8, 1885, she assured the board of education that her demand for equality was "more American" than the "race prejudice" of school segregation.

In 1924 Martha Lum was barred from enrolling at Rosedale Consolidated High School in Mississippi because, although a US citizen, she was of Chinese ancestry. In *Gong Lum v. Rice* (1927) the US Supreme Court unanimously ruled that Martha Lum must attend "a colored school" for children "of the brown, yellow or black races." School segregation, the Court declared, fell within state powers and did not violate the Constitution's equal protection clause. It was thoroughly American: superior schools for whites and inferior schools for nonwhites. Although *Gong Lum* failed to desegregate the public schools, the case provided a precedent for *Brown* and constitutes an aspect of the struggle and movement for civil rights.

Like Mamie Tape, a California public school denied entry to Sylvia, Gonzalo, and Jerome Méndez on the basis of their race. The children, the Westminster Main School maintained in 1943, must attend the segregated Mexican school a few blocks away. Three years later the children's parents (their mother was Puerto Rican) and other Mexican Americans joined in a lawsuit against school segregation in *Méndez v. Westminster* (1946–47). As Felicitas Méndez, the mother, testified in court, "We always tell our children they are Americans, and we thought that they shouldn't be segregated like that, they shouldn't be treated the way they are."

David C. Marcus, the plaintiffs' lawyer, presented the challenge as a violation of the Fourteenth Amendment's equal protection clause. Mexican Americans were US citizens and whites as provided by the Treaty of Guadalupe Hidalgo (1848) that ended the war on Mexico, Marcus argued, and they were thus entitled to attend the white public schools. While California's statutes allowed segregated schools for nonwhite children, *Méndez* contended that Mexican American children, as US citizens and whites, should not be forced to attend inferior Mexican schools. Senior District Judge Paul J. McCormick of the Ninth Federal District Court rendered the decision in favor of the petitioners on February 18, 1946. That finding was affirmed on appeal in 1947.

The National Association for the Advancement of Colored People (NAACP) and the Japanese American Citizens League (JACL) joined the *Méndez* appellate case as *amici curiae* and offered their arguments in briefs for the proceedings. The NAACP saw *Méndez* as a prelude for what would later become its legal challenge to Jim Crow schools, and one of its attorneys involved in *Méndez* was its lead attorney in the *Brown* case, Thurgood Marshall. Judge McCormick's finding that "equal protection of the laws . . . is not provided by furnishing in separate schools the same technical facilities, text books and courses of instruction . . . [rather] a paramount requisite in the American system of public education is social equality," anticipated the language of the future Supreme Court chief justice Earl Warren, who was California's governor during *Méndez*. In *Brown v. Board of Education* some eight years after *Méndez* the Court unanimously agreed: "Separate educational facilities are inherently unequal."

The JACL, having just experienced the wartime detention of Japanese Americans, warned against the dangers of singling out a class of people. (During the war the Méndez family lived on a farm leased from Japanese Americans who had been forcibly removed to a concentration camp in Arizona.) If discrimination against Mexican American children is established "on the basis of ancestry only," the JACL brief noted, "then who can tell what minority group will be next on the road to persecution. If we learned one lesson from the horrors of Nazism, it is that no minority group, and in fact, no person is safe, once the State, through its instrumentalities, can arbitrarily discriminate against any person or group." That cooperation between the JACL and the NAACP in the *Méndez* case led to greater solidarities in the fight against restrictive housing covenants and school segregation in the 1950s, right up to *Brown*, in which Japanese Americans were the only nonwhite group to participate in the case as an *amicus curiae*.

| | |

Even as the widening of US public and higher education in the late nineteenth and early twentieth century accommodated the needs of a rapidly expanding industrial capitalism, their narrowing followed the democratizing and diversifying of the nation through civil rights struggles and immigration reform. Pivotal in that regard were the Civil Rights Act (1964) and Immigration Act (1965); the former outlawed discrimination on the bases of race, color, religion, sex, or national origin in voting, public education, and accommodations, while the latter ended the racist immigration quotas imposed since the 1920s. Among their results were greater freedom for those excluded from the full promise of equality under the law and vastly larger numbers of Asian and Latinx immigrants.

Those openings prompted a white, middle-class backlash evidenced in the "Reagan revolution" launched during Ronald Reagan's presidency (1981–89) and based on the rhetoric of reducing government and state-initiated social reform programs and a faith in supply-side economics that restructured taxes to favor the wealthy. Those acts pushed back against the massive New Deal programs of President Franklin D. Roosevelt (1933–45) and the Great Society policies, including civil rights and antipoverty programs, of President Lyndon B. Johnson (1963–69). The demands for a Third World curriculum were made during the Johnson administration, and the drive to reverse and absorb Third World gains in higher education came during the Reagan years. Defenders of the faith resolved to return to the traditional and core values of American education by singing the praises, without apology, of the dominant majority and so-called natural good.

Natural Good

The battle to reclaim US higher education, sometimes called the canon or culture wars,[13] can be dated to the publication of Allan Bloom's *Closing of the American Mind* (1987). In that hugely popular, best-selling broadside, Bloom, a University of Chicago classicist, railed against what he called the new orthodoxy of equality and relativism. Those ideas, he wrote, produced a "drab diversity" and parochialism, an ethnocentrism and indifference. Instead of an opening, they induced a closing of the American academy and mind. Minorities, in their demands for tolerance and separateness, were destructive of the "natural" and "common" good; minorities in fact were in general "bad things," a view held by the founding fathers. Black power advocates were divisive and disrespectful of the Constitution; they were not defenders of reason and the universal rights of men. Higher education, in its capitulation to demagogic radicals, failed democracy and impoverished students. The university's politicized curriculum of relativism and openness led to "civil strife," a "weakness of conviction," and a citizenry devoid of "moral passion" for democracy.

Instead, Bloom urged, the university must return to education's foundations that establish "a moral goal," recalling the Puritan ideal. American education should produce a "democratic man" with a "democratic personality." It should create "unity and sameness" by accepting "natural rights" wherein distinctions of race, class, and religion disappear and assimilation substitutes old worldviews for new and promotes "a tendency, if not a necessity, to homogenize nature." In place of minorities, education should favor the "dominant majority" and its "sense of superiority." After all, Bloom reasoned, Western civilization has given the United States "a dominant culture with its traditions, its literature, its tastes, its special claim to know and supervise the language, and its Protestant religions." Prejudice is good, intoned Bloom. Without prejudice there is emptiness. Error is the enemy, not prejudice.[14]

In his response the University of California historian Lawrence W. Levine accuses Bloom of inventing a topsy-turvy world in which openness is closure and democratization is fascism.[15] Apologists like Bloom, he writes, display a naïve nostalgia for a mythic past wherein higher education stood in splendid isolation from its social contexts and the unadulterated pursuit of universal truth and beauty prevailed. Those days of paradise lost never existed. In fact before the civil rights and feminist movements higher education was narrowly designed, and parochialism was the rule. The equation of civilization with the West and claims of Western civilization's superiority are "nation-building myths" that avoid "dangerous quests for the complicated truth." Attacks such as those initiated by Bloom are hyperbolic, skewed, and doctrinaire—attributes they accuse their opponents of possessing. The university is not the enemy, Levine concludes, nor is it separate from its social contexts and times. The conflicts in higher education mirror the divisions in US society. To understand that unfolding history of struggles and change is to comprehend the process that leads to an apprehension of the self.[16]

Punctuating the attack on post-1968 ethnic studies in higher education was Dinesh D'Souza's widely referenced *Illiberal Education* (1991). D'Souza, a South Asian American, gained notoriety as editor of the *Dartmouth Review*, which mocked the college affirmative action program, "unqualified" black students, and an African American music professor. Ethnic and women's studies, writes D'Souza, have led a "victim's revolution on campus," in which their entitlements derive from their claimed status as victims of racism and patriarchy. Liberal campus administrators, in compensation, award those victims a privileged place in the university. In fact that victim's revolution, following Bloom's account, has mastered and transformed US higher education.

Witness the changes in admissions, the curriculum, and student life, D'Souza points out. Affirmative action or "preferential treatment" programs have recruited to campus masses of unqualified nonwhites, "mainly blacks and Hispanics," with records inferior to Asians. Western civilization has been "diluted or displaced" and substituted for required courses in ethnic and women's studies and non-Western cultures. Special services cater to blacks, women, and gays; campus rules impose "censorship" on speech deemed offensive to those protected groups; ethnic student organizations thrive under multiculturalism and diversity; and charges of racism, sexual harassment, and homophobia draw criticism and punishment.

Waged in the name of Third World anticolonialism, D'Souza correctly observes, the campus revolution is not limited to higher education but is directed at US society as a whole. The university is simply the chosen site of battle. Consider, he warns, the changing demography of the United States sparked by waves of Asian and Latinx immigrants. The nation is rapidly becoming multiracial, multicultural, imposing demands and pressures on the American core and Western civilization. Higher education reflects those social divides, D'Souza points out, dominated as it is by a generation of radicals from the 1960s.[17]

The US culture wars of the 1980s and 1990s featured calls from the right for a return to whiteness and European values to reclaim and restore the nation from people of color and the radical left. The 1965 Immigration Act opened wide the gates to Asians and Latinx, and their steep increase through migration and reproduction led to the darkening of the people's complexion. If left unchecked, some warned, by 2040 nonwhites will form the majority and whites the minority in the United States. In higher education (post-1968) ethnic studies, women's and queer studies, and poststructuralism and relativism have undermined the founding contract and rational order. Seen in that light, (post-1968) ethnic studies and its allied fields are threats to the nation's integrity. As people of color, as women, as queers, they divide what was a single whole. Yet as autonomous groups they could preclude coalitions and hence a united front, and they could be celebrated as creating a colorful, multicultural nation. Self-determination can undermine colonialism and simultaneously buttress divide-and-rule and a drab, disempowering multiculturalism.

Summary

American education, at least since the Puritans, was designed to inculcate civic virtue to produce a pliant, useful citizenry. At first that brand of education was limited to propertied white men who were the only category of persons with the full rights of citizenship. Those educated white men were to lead the masses as clerics and teachers. Later elite white women were included in women's education as mothers of citizens and, in the twentieth century, as citizens with voting and civil rights. Nonwhites were neither free nor citizens before the nineteenth century, and as such were largely excluded from education. Only after their inclusion within the nation-state were nonwhites subject to that education, albeit in segregated, inferior schools, where they were tutored into civility and utility.

Education for the masses, including white immigrants and workers, arose from the growth of manufacturing industries and agriculture during the nineteenth century. Still private schools and higher education remained bastions of the elite, while the subservient classes largely populated public schools and junior colleges. Education sought assimilation for nonwhites; "kill the Indian in him" to save him for Christianity, civilization, and manual labor. By the time of the Third World Liberation Front's strike, the curriculum, with its exclusions and inclusions, mirrored those objects of American education.

"As the dark world rises," wrote Malcolm X, "the white world declines," and from his vantage he reported, "The dark world is on the rise."[18] Malcolm X made that observation in a speech delivered on January 24, 1965, about a month before his assassination. African Americans are not a minority, he declared, because they are united in struggle with the Third World people of the earth in their challenges to white supremacy. Black contributions to Western civilization "under the tutelage of the white man" were false; they endorsed and reinforced black subjugation. White masters tried to deny and make light of African history, language and culture, and systems of belief. They invented races and placed them on a scale of superior and inferior to justify conquest and colonialism. The rise of the dark world, Malcolm X noted, like Fanon's imperative for a "national consciousness," involved the nonnegotiable claim to a name, language, and history.

Like Carter Woodson, Eldridge Cleaver, a leader of the Black Panther Party, wrote, "We understand that those who control the mind can control the body." American education is the means by which the ruling class subjugates to exploit. By contrast, Cleaver observed, a liberating education as embraced by black studies can inspire and nurture a "revolutionary consciousness" to upend and reconstitute US society. But there is a danger in compartmentalizing our struggle, he insightfully pointed out, because education is implicated in the economy and politics of the nation-state and as such is a single aspect of the overall relations of power. Thus, of necessity, "we are revolutionaries, and as revolutionaries, our goal is the transformation of the American social order."[19]

SIX

SUBJECTIFICATION

Liberation, Freire teaches us, begins with consciousness in articulation with society, or the social formation. Creation of the subject-self, subjectification, works against objectification, the production of the colonized-object. Moreover consciousness and an affiliation with the oppressed intervene in the regimes of positivism and colonization as exhibited in the banking concept of education. Unlike the hegemonic instruments that strive to separate the self from society, Freire's subjects engage the social through consciousness and agency and in the struggle become "truly human."

The US sociologist C. Wright Mills, in an essay on "intellectual craftsmanship," advises intellectuals to keep a daily journal of their activities and ideas. Those can become files to spark the "sociological imagination," which enables comprehension of "the larger historical scene in terms of its meaning for the inner life." Our predicament, Mills writes, is the trap of daily life that can easily occupy the totality of our consciousness and activity and our need to rely upon that very experience to plot our escape from the personal and immediate. Reason, "the advance guard in any field of learning," will allow us the possibility of progressing past that befuddlement by installing discipline and systematic thinking to give direction to our search for meaning, "to make a difference in the quality of human life in our time." Further, "scholarship is a choice of how to live as well as a choice of career" because our work mirrors our character.[1]

Much like Gramsci, Foucault explains the strategy of power to divide and rule, whether Freire's self from society or Mills's personal from the political, in topographical terms. Power, Foucault observes in *Power/Knowledge* (1980), constitutes subjects through a process of division, an isolation of self from others and society. That separation is institutionalized in the form of prisons, hospitals, and asylums wherein are confined those deemed unfit or unwell. Segregation, however, is simply one of a complex, shifting ensemble of relations because power expresses itself through heterogeneous elements such as the state, laws, science, philosophy, morals, architecture, and so forth. Those elements change over place and time to fulfill specific, shifting purposes and needs. Power is thus relational; it circulates and is never localized; it is not a commodity; it is deployed, not possessed. Individuals are mere vehicles of power. Power's strategy of segregation is mirrored in taxonomy and the structuring of knowledge into discrete disciplines (discourses) to attain finality as closed, self-contained systems. The coherence they offer emerges from and typifies the rise of rationality, science, modernism,[2] and *humanism*.

Humanism

Fanon advanced a "new humanism" to differentiate it from the European Enlightenment's humanism begun by Descartes's (1596–1650) formulation "I think, therefore I am." That founding principle of humanism expresses a decidedly optimistic appraisal of the human condition, which previously, under the Roman Catholic Church and secular science, was considered to be subject to the powers of divine will and cosmic forces. By contrast the Cartesian representation conceived of autonomous human subjects with the power to call into existence the self, "I am," through the self's mind, "I think." Central to existence thus were humans with agency, the ability to shape their own destinies, and not forces beyond their control. That profound anthropocentrism distinguished humans and their faculties as paramount within the natural order.

Humanism, moreover, created and accommodated divides and hierarchies beyond the human center and nonhuman periphery. The science of taxonomy, as we have seen, separated and ranked humankind as polarities of white and nonwhite, man and woman. Therein the center's peripheries might approach but could not attain the truly human side of the conjured and imposed border. Those others lacked the agency possessed by white men only. Kant and Hegel, two influential Enlightenment thinkers, affirmed that belief in white men's perfection because they alone possessed freedom and the ability to make history. European humanistic discourses, in fact and contrary to their alleged universalism, advanced and installed the divides of imperialism and the modern world-system. Surely Fanon could not have favored that species of humanism.

Influential in disrupting the Cartesian formulation were the works of Marx (1818–83) and Freud (1856–1939) that questioned the complete autonomy of the human subject. Marx argued that one's class position or location within the relations of production shaped consciousness, while Freud uncovered the unconscious dimensions of the self, inaccessible to thought. Marx pointed to the social context as central in the constitution of the self, while Freud identified the inner workings of the subliminal within the human mind. Marx's idea of "false consciousness," an identification and affiliation of workers with the ruling class, was modified by Althusser. As we saw, Althusser, following Gramsci, describes ideology as the vehicle through which the state and its apparatuses achieve hegemony; not simply imposed, thus, the power to rule is acquired through ideological agreement and consensus. Moreover ideology can be fragmentary and contradictory, allowing for contestation and change.

Consciousness and "human nature" as science or biology underwent further scrutiny. Questions of language and discourse as pivotal in producing the human subject were especially influential in loosening the grip of humanism's positivism. The Swiss linguist Ferdinand de Saussure (1857–1913) explained how language is the means by which humans constitute and articulate themselves and their world. Without language the Cartesian formulation of "I think" is impossible. Nothing exists outside of language. A short leap from that insight is the idea that language structures consciousness and the subject. Relevant in that context of subject formation is Saussure's idea that language operates within a social context and is accordingly a relational rather than a solitary expression. In those ways Saussure established linguistic structuralism and, many believe, structuralism itself. Briefly, *structuralism* in social science is the theory that society is organized around social structures and their interrelations.

The French psychoanalyst Jacques Lacan (1901–81) was, like Saussure, a structuralist, but he influenced many key intellectuals foundational to post- or antistructuralism. Lacan found that Freud's unconscious behaves like a language, and in the same way that language produces meaning the subject is produced through language in a process called *subjectification*. For Lacan, accordingly, coming into language is of primary importance in the constitution of the subject-self. Language, however, does not emerge from within but from the Other; it is, following Saussure, relational. While a child's mother occupies a position of alterity or otherness, the child's father is the dominant Other because the mother signifies lack or absence (a castrated other), while the father signifies presence and authority. Language, a symbolic order whose locus is power, is accordingly located in the phallus, Lacan maintains. Subjectification thus involves a submission to the discipline and rules of language and an apprehension of gender and its hierarchy.[3] Although Lacan persists in Freudian myths of gender and sexuality, his articulation of language and power remains valuable to Third World studies in which power and its relations are the principal objects of analyses.

Poststructuralists descend from those interventions on humanism's sovereign subjects, from Marx and Freud to Lacan. Foucault extends the insights by Gramsci and Althusser on how subjects are interpellated or produced through ideology and apparatuses of the state. Foucault describes subjects as effects and aspects of *discourse*, which he understands as language and ideology. There are no sovereign subjects with agency over their consciousness. Subjects are produced through discourse. As we will see, subjectification and not identity formation is the analytical category for Third World studies.

Identity versus Subjectivity

The search for subjectivity, called derisively "identity politics," has come to describe and trivialize the movement for Third World studies. College students coming of age, the misrepresentation recounts, were privileged, even spoiled youth in anguish over their racial, gender, and sexual identities. Those came to a boil in the 1960s free speech and free love movements fueled by rock music and a culture of drugs. Youthful rebellion sought freedoms from parental and societal constraints, and promiscuity thrived in the fluidity of intellectual relativism as hypothesized by Allan Bloom. Queer, Third World, and women's studies, the story goes, emerge as residues of the victims' revolution and identity politics described by Dinesh D'Souza.

Set amid stereotypes and demeaning depictions and words that wound,[4] by contrast, the emphatic declaration "Black is beautiful" is a step forward on the long road to healing bruised and battered minds. Self-hatred is a consequence of the colonial condition, and loving oneself can constitute an anticolonial affirmation of human dignity and self-determination. Skin lighteners, hair straighteners, breast and butt augmentations, and eyelid surgeries are symptoms of deeper maladies, and those racial markers afflict more severely women and queers of color because of patriarchy and heterosexism. Erasures and caricatures in textbooks, the school curriculum, and national narratives prompt demands for accurate depictions and the voices of those not heard within the nation-state. Those acts of recovery—the reconstitution of a people and culture—were not mere identity politics or the tantrums of immature children; as Fanon points out, they were building blocks toward revolution.

Despite that radical Third World idea and project, the turn from the social to the self, including the national turn involving the divides of race, gender, sexuality, and nation, paralleled the move away from Third World consciousness to European humanism's "I am." Even as Chicago sociology's ethnic studies dulled the edge of Third World studies, social science described that search for the self as a return to identity—organic, biological, and developmental. Influential were the psychosocial stages of Freud in the work of Erik Erikson (1902–94). In tandem with Freud's infant (trust), toddler (autonomy), child (initiative), puberty (industry), teen (questioning), young adult (intimacy), middle age (midlife crisis), and old age (wisdom), Erikson posited a "normal" growth chart from conformity (child) to rebellion (youth) to resolution (adult). Attached to biology and age, those human behaviors are naturalized and universalized.

Assimilation, Chicago sociologists held and as we have seen, tracked a natural history of how immigrants became Americans. Like psychosocial development, assimilation moved in stages from contact to conflict, accommodation, and finally assimilation, according to Robert Park. The US sociologist Milton Gordon enlarged on Park's ethnic cycle by distinguishing between culture or patterned behavior and social structure or institutions. In his definitive book on assimilation, *Assimilation in American Life*, published in 1964, Gordon describes the stages of assimilation as progress toward invisibility and absorption within the Anglo-Saxon core. Contact induces immigrants to adopt the dominant culture, Gordon writes, which then leads to admission into host institutions; those stages progress from "acculturation" to "structural assimilation." Intermarriage, which Gordon calls "amalgamation," follows together with identification with the core group, which then results in an absence of prejudice and discrimination; those stages mark movement from "identificational assimilation" to "attitude" and "behavior receptional assimilation." Gordon's final stage is "civic assimilation," when there are no value or power conflicts between the former immigrant and core groups.

Race and immigration are traumas that can disturb the "natural" progression of development, including assimilation, and lead to mental health "pathologies" and "personality disorders." The "problem" with the Negro and Oriental, Park declared, is not their inability to assimilate but their racial badges, which isolate and mark them for prejudice. The "tragic mulatto" exhibits signs of marginality when facing rejection from both sides of the black-white racial divide. Immigrants remain mired in the old country, while the second generation possesses an almost pathetic desire to assimilate into the new. Even as they reject their parents, second-generation immigrants face rejection from the host group. Thus they remain, as coined by Park, marginal men.

Minority racial identity accordingly is not simply a matter of individual human growth but is additionally a relational, social process. The Minority Identity Development model, for instance, explains racial identity as life stages but also as a consequence of physical appearance, racism, socioeconomic status, and cognition. The nonwhite child begins life at the conformity stage but at the next stage encounters dissonance or inconsistencies between the rhetoric of equality and the practice of racism. From dissonance the young person enters a rebellion and immersion stage and actively seeks minority group membership, and as an adult, the nonwhite person reaches a synergetic stage of articulation.

Erikson's "identity crisis" during the stage of youthful rebellion is the formative moment of identity politics. Seeking identification as and with people of color, women, and queers results in marginalization from the majority group. Further, having to prove their genuine affiliation with the oppressed, activists take radical positions as "race men," feminists, and queers, alienating themselves even more from the normative whole. Those choices, some identity models suggest, are self-destructive, disrupt the natural order, and divide the nation-state because they are self-serving and ultimately antisocial. The charge that post-1968 ethnic studies threatens the good order of the nation resonates with that variety of identity politics.

In those biological models of human development, deviations from the norm constitute unnatural and even pathological conditions. Central to that assumption is the normative, white, heterosexual, middle-class, citizen man, and degenerations from that standard invite racism, sexism, homophobia, exclusion laws, poverty, and personality disorders. The victims of oppression thereby bear the blame for their alienation. It is also important to recognize in those portrayals of identity how departures from the natural order of things represent illnesses. I remember the college I attended in California during the 1960s having a handbook of student conduct in which interracial dating was forbidden. When a couple, an Asian man and white woman, chose to violate that rule, they were called in for spiritual and psychological counseling as if interracial dating were a violation of nature and god and a mental disorder.

Subjectivity offers a poststructuralist understanding of consciousness contrary to the naturalism of identity and human growth. By queering the subject, we interrogate the normative design, and by thinking of race, gender, and sexuality as performances, we come to understand the social construction of biology and nature.[5] If identity is a stage of psychosocial development and a positivist science derivative of humanism's "I think, therefore I am," then subjectivity is the indeterminate, unfolding creation of consciousness in negotiation with the social and can be expressed as "I think I am." The subject-self is uncertain and in process and in relation to the regimes of space/time. Age, birth order, and generation can matter as well as contexts such as a temple, club, school, or police station. Those spatial and temporal factors can bring to the fore race and gender, for instance, while suppressing sexuality and class. Also the times in which we live, say, the 1960s versus the 2010s and their contrasting social formations, can alter and anchor our mobile subject positions. Locating the subject within that indeterminate flux is a complex if not impossible proposition. Still, per Freire and Mills, we must position the subject-self within the social formation to be "truly human." Our liberation depends upon that apprehension.

Voice

Related to the power of consciousness and subjectivity is *voice*, which is an articulation of consciousness and subject position. Third World studies began as an insertion of presence in a wasteland of absences. The field was critical of the master narratives, discourses that refused to listen to and distorted the voices of Third World peoples. Often, even when heard, Europeans spoke for the masses of the Third World. As Marx famously observed in *The Eighteenth Brumaire of Louis Bonaparte* (1852), "They [the peasant masses] cannot speak for themselves, they must be represented."[6] Devoid of history or movement, without agency, Marx held, peasants could not speak for themselves as a class. That criterion for voice, the ability to make history, silenced peasant masses as well as denizens of the Third World, as Hegel alleged. Those acts of omission and (mis)representation are purposeful exertions of power designed to maintain the social relations.

Subjectivity, or the sociological imagination, Mills reminds us, is retarded and advanced by *experience*. According to the Welsh cultural and literary critic Raymond Williams, experience involves the whole consciousness or being, including the personal, subjective, and emotional. Experience, Williams writes, is subjectivity or the conscious apprehension of a state or condition.[7] Within religious experience that state involves the inner, personal self, and it assumes not only the status of truth but the most authentic, indisputable kind of truth.

Originating from within, religious experience cannot be denied from without. As a consequence some believe in the primacy of experience, while others, because of its subjective quality, reject experience as an unreliable, unverifiable source of evidence. While Mills contends experience is the necessary condition affecting reason and analyses, the US historian Joan W. Scott offers a powerful critique of experience and its truth claims.

Experience, Scott observes, has been a key instrument in the political contest over voice and historical agency. The social movements of the 1960s and 1970s were replete with demands for visibility, breaking the silence or giving voice, and rendering historical what had been hidden from history's purview. Such political possibilities for social change are both exhilarating and frightening because they point toward the prospects for liberation and the responsibilities of historical representation. But the arguments of those insurgents resemble rather than depart from the methodologies of the dominant class. Conventional histories, Scott notes, cite documentary evidence in support of its claims to truth or what really happened. Similarly the new social history of women, blacks, and queers deploys experiential evidence to sustain its claims to veracity and worth. Even as many conventional historians hold written records as the final determinant of historical truth, some new social historians see experience as incontestable because they emanate from the subject-self and consciousness.

Such historians of difference, whether of race, gender, or sexuality, naturalize and assume distinctions even as they allege a homogeneity and hence solidarity as queers, women, and blacks: "The evidence of experience then becomes evidence for the fact of difference, rather than a way of exploring how difference is established, how it operates, how and in what ways it constitutes subjects who see and act in the world."[8] Instead, argues Scott, like written documents, experience as written (such as diaries, memoirs, oral history transcriptions, and testimonies) or recorded (like oral histories) must be subjected to interrogation. All documents bear the imprint of their author, their context, and their intended readers or listeners. Difference and experience are social constructions and require deconstruction. Absent that acknowledgment, experience adduced as uncontested evidence reproduces rather than refutes discourses of oppression and hegemonic systems involving sexuality, gender, and race.

"Experience is a subject's history," concludes Scott. "Language is the site of history's enactment. Historical explanation cannot, therefore, separate the two."[9] Besides appealing for the literary within the "science" of history, Scott therewith warns against assuming the unmediated relationship between words (language) and history, or the material conditions. All categories of analyses, including the historian, she maintains, must be taken as contextual, contingent, and contested. We must, she argues, insist on the discursive nature of experience and the politics of its construction because experience is always contested and is thus political, and the process of its creation accordingly requires interrogation.

In addition to that important question of historical methodology posed by Scott, the Third World literary critic Gayatri Spivak points out that voice is a matter of epistemology. "Can the subaltern speak?" she asks in a celebrated essay. Poststructuralists like Foucault, Spivak relates, while critical of positivism, hold essentialist notions of Third World peoples and the oppressed. The West is the assumed, unexamined subject, and despite being deaf to the voices of the *subaltern*, a Gramscian term referencing the oppressed, the West, including Marx, exercises the power to represent them. Those discourses are implicated, Spivak observes, in the West's imperialism, and they are thus colonial projects intended to subdue and rule over Third World peoples. In those conversations white men speak to white men about nonwhite men and women. They are acts of "epistemic violence," following Foucault's terminology. Existing outside the circle of power and discourse, then, the subaltern cannot speak.

But can the subaltern find his or her voice in representation? Of course, as Spivak correctly notes, imperial (mis)representations of colonial subjects fail to register the voices of the oppressed. The Continental philosopher Linda Martín Alcoff discusses that predicament and responsibility of scholars as the "problem of speaking for others." That problem begins with the demand by post-1968 ethnic and women's studies for self-representation, for self-determination based upon the assumption that one's subject position is unique and valued. Moreover, as Scott reminds, speaking from that subject position privileges that articulation as primary and authentic. To complicate matters, subjects can be members of single and multiple social groups for which they might claim to speak. It is impossible, Alcoff contends, to disentangle "speaking for others" and "speaking about others" because both are representations of others. At the same time, self-representation is a representation and as such is a construction, and refusing to speak for or about others can result in paralysis.

Scholars, Alcoff argues, must speak for and about others to nurture a critical consciousness and promote social change. A retreat into silence is not liberating and, in fact, advances disempowerment. Further, to speak only for oneself falls back to the old liberal humanism and individualism that isolate the self from society as if one is not constituted by or related to others. To guide our speaking for others nonetheless, Alcoff suggests, following Foucault, adopting some "rituals" of speaking that consider the speaker's subject position and the relations between the text or utterance and its address or the text's listeners. Those factors can affect the significance and afterlife of the text. For instance, in general and because of their hierarchical subject positions and discursive contexts, a teacher's opinion outweighs a student's, a white man commands greater authority than a black woman, and Western philosophy carries more weight than its African counterpart. Those illustrate how speech is related to politics and power.

Alcoff's rituals of speaking are dialogic, following Freire; they engage the other in a conversation. Speakers must not silence others, and listening is as important as or more important than speaking. Speakers must interrogate their subject positions and discursive contexts and recognize the contingent and contested ground of the engagement. Those who purport to speak for others must accept responsibility for their actions, and they must account for the potential and actual effects of their representations. Finally, those rituals of speech arise from the possibility of the subaltern uttering a "counter sentence," in Spivak's words, that can speak against the colonizer's discourse and imperial project. While the subaltern cannot speak within the conversations of the West, speaking for others in their language and ideology can liberate.

Within Third World studies there are many examples of self-utterances that instead illustrate the practice of giving voice to and about others. Perhaps foremost for those who came of age during the 1960s was *Black Elk Speaks* (1932), an account of the Oglala Lakota sacred man, Black Elk, "as told through" John G. Neihardt, a white writer and poet. "My friend," begins Neihardt's narration, "I am going to tell you the story of my life, as you wish." It is important to note Black Elk told his story because Neihardt sought him out. Black Elk located his telling as an old, frail man with failing vision: "I can see it all as from a lonely hilltop, I know it is a story of a mighty vision given to a man too weak to use it; of a holy tree that should have flourished in a people's heart with flowers and singing birds, and now is withered; and of a people's dream that died in bloody snow."[10]

Listening to Black Elk speak, Neihardt remembered, was "like half seeing, half sensing a strange and beautiful landscape by brief flashes of sheet lightning." The context of Neihardt's visit was his search not for the "facts" about the "messianic craze" among Plains Indians of the 1880s but for "something to be experienced" through intimate conversations with participants in the "craze." In fact the 1880s stirring among American Indians was really a revolutionary, mass movement premised upon cultural revival and renewal to

Big Foot, a Sioux leader, lies frozen in bloody snow at the site of the Wounded Knee massacre, 1890. Department of the Army. Courtesy of the National Archives and Records Administration.

counter the dispossession by and forced assimilation of the white invaders. Black Elk's narration can be read as a text of rebellion, having arisen within the context of Neihardt's research on the late nineteenth-century insurgency and Black Elk's intention to speak "not for myself, but for my people . . . make my people live!" Resuscitation, Black Elk knew, was imperative when "there is no center . . . [and] the sacred tree is dead." Despite the text's power, attested to by generations of readers, *Black Elk Speaks* is Neihardt's written representation of Black Elk's oral narration complicated by the contexts and times of that telling. Black Elk might have crafted this version for his audience. Indeed Neihardt wrote truthfully when he described Black Elk's speech as fleeting moments of sight and sense illuminated by flashes of lightning.[11] In addition to the question of language (Black Elk speaking in English), there is the problem of an oral, living conversation between Black Elk and Neihardt reduced by Neihardt to the static, written form.[12]

Testimonios are another variety of speech put to paper and are, like *Black Elk Speaks*, commonly read as the genuine voices of the speakers. Perhaps the best known is *I, Rigoberta Menchú: An Indian Woman in Guatemala* (1984) by the Nobel Peace Prize laureate.[13] A testimonio is a narrative told in the first person to an interlocutor who records, transcribes, and edits the account. In that way the process transforms a living, oral testimony into words on paper.[14] Testimonios thus are translations, mediated texts. At the same time they give voice to subalterns who speak back against the "othering" discourse of colonial texts that objectify colonial subjects. Testimonios thereby resist erasure and appropriation, and because they, unlike biography and autobiography, speak for the people and not the self alone, they represent "a collective self engaged in struggle."[15] As a genre testimonios skirt the margins of the spoken and written word and question the very idea of literature as written texts produced by a single author and as expressions of the elite. Contrarily testimonios are quintessentially voices of women and the oppressed even as they privilege personal experience and can mask the multiplicity of mass struggles.[16]

In *Let Me Speak!* the Bolivian Domitila Barrios de Chungara draws authority from the collective and not the self and declares through her translator, "I don't want anyone at any moment to interpret the story I'm about to tell as something that is only personal. Because I think that my life is related to my people. What happened to me could have happened to hundreds of people in my country." Her subject-self, Domitila points out, exists in relation to and for her people. "I don't just want to tell a personal story. I want to talk about my people. I want to testify about all the experience we've acquired during so many years of struggle in Bolivia. It's for them that I agreed that what I am going to tell be written down."[17] Testimonios, Domitila reminds us, are multivocal (they derive from and speak for a community) and bespeak liberation through struggle.

| | | |

As written texts, those voices nonetheless are *translations* of the original form, and translations carry the following meanings. The Roman orator Cicero in 46 BC advocated the tethering of texts to rhetorical models, to have translation serve the purposes of speech, of free style to convey the full force of language.[18] In 1813 the German philosopher Friedrich Schleiermacher lectured to the Berlin Academy of Sciences on the ideal translator, who creates an "image" to produce a sense of foreignness because to the home-staying reader, the text is in a foreign tongue. That distancing, that othering, he hoped, would in turn create and enhance a German language, literature, and nationalism.[19]

Walter Benjamin, the German literary critic and philosopher, argued in a 1923 essay for the autonomy of translations as texts in their own right, derivative but also possessing the integrity of a work of signification.[20] While to the postcolonial critic Spivak translation is "a simple miming of the responsibility to the trace of the other in the self."[21] Part of that responsibility, Spivak states, is the learning of other languages, and yet the translation, as an intimate act of reading, bears a mere "trace of the other" because the self produces it. In that way, concludes the translation theorist Lawrence Venuti, translation is a form of imperialism, and reveals "the imperialistic impulse that may well be indissoluble from translation."[22] If Venuti is correct, we must, as Spivak holds, read in the language of the masses and not translations to truly hear their voices.

Summary

Identity politics, as charged by critics of post-1968 ethnic studies, is not the breeding ground for Third World studies. Subjectification understands the subject not as humanism's "I am" but as complex subjects in formation and in constant engagement with society. That recognition emerges not from a trivial, youthful search for identities but from profound acts of power or agency. Self-determination by the oppressed against the forces of colonial, hegemonic discourses and material conditions is the objective of subjectification; the agency of the subject-self drives the movement for Third World liberation. In that confrontation Third World studies faces a daunting if not impossible task of dismantling the master's house while speaking in the language and ideology of the master and ruling class. That predicament, like creating consciousness in the colonizers' tongue and hearing the subaltern speak through interlocutors and translations, is exemplified in the theory of racial formation.

SEVEN

RACIAL FORMATION

Audre Lorde, the black, lesbian Third World feminist, notably reminded us that "the master's tools will never dismantle the master's house." The context of that speech was a 1979 (white) feminist conference at New York University that left out Third World women's voices from the general concerns of women as a whole, such as culture, existentialism, the erotic, and theory, and relegated them to the margins of issues involving women of color. There was, Lorde observed, no attempt at respect, mutuality, and interdependence across the differences of race, sexuality, and class, which create not a divide but a common ground. The conference, she pointed out, addressed the needs of "acceptable women," not those who stand outside that circle: the poor, black, lesbian, and elderly. Survival nonetheless is not an academic skill, Lorde prodded her largely university audience, and the master's tools will never dismantle the master's house. Those tools might allow us to beat him at his own game, but only temporarily and superficially and not fundamentally or permanently.

Lorde's contention merits our serious consideration. To engage the imperial discourses means to speak in the language and ideology of the colonizer. Fanon's liberating "new humanism" is encumbered with the humanism of Europe's Enlightenment and its consort, imperialism. Despite the enabling freedoms gained by Albert Memmi in leaving his crippled, inadequate North African tongue for the precision of the French language, the colonizer's instruments, as we understand from Lacan, interpellated his consciousness. Moreover, in speaking against the dominant discourses we are constrained by the extant order of language and ideology; to counter that world we are disciplined by that prior state. A countersentence, by definition, addresses the original sentence even as it seeks to oppose it. A two-part struggle, liberation requires a dismantling of the master's house with his tools and the creation of alternate languages and ideologies—discourses—not derivative of the master's world.

The Theory

In their 1986 book US sociologists Michael Omi and Howard Winant inform us their theory of racial formation engages mainstream sociological discourse. Their countertheory accordingly converses principally with US sociology and its cult of ethnicity that had dominated the discipline for most of the twentieth century. Racial formation arose within that context of US national culture but also within the disciplinary formation of US sociology as a reaction to the then dominant idea of ethnicity as advanced by the Chicago school of sociology.[1] As we saw, Robert Park and his colleagues and students, in their focus on the urban frontier and the process by which European immigrants were assimilated into American life, tried to distinguish themselves from the race relations approach pioneered by sociologists such as George Fitzhugh, Henry Hughes, William Graham Sumner, and Lester Frank Ward.[2] Those founders of US sociology understood race as a natural state and racial hierarchies as permanent and necessary for social order; by contrast, attempts at mixture, called "miscegenation" in 1864, and challenges to white supremacy constituted social "problems" caused by "problem minorities."[3] Although intent on breaking away from US sociology's founders, Park was not immune from the influences of his intellectual forebears. Because of their racial badges, Park believed that African and Asian Americans were unassimilable; "The chief obstacle to assimilation of the Negro and Oriental are not mental but physical traits," he explained. Recall Park's "Negro problem" and "Oriental problem."[4] The "problem" of the twentieth century, Du Bois wryly mused.

Racial formation, as coined by Omi and Winant, has deservedly captured the field of post-1968 ethnic studies. I find especially brilliant their choice of the term *formation*. As a historian of Africa trained during the 1970s, I understood formations from French and British structural-functionalist anthropology and from Marxism as advanced by structuralists like Maurice Godelier and Louis Althusser, among others. Moreover I was taken by the notion of "social formation" from my studies of precolonial African economies and their modes and relations of production, and the equation of "society" with "social formation" with a preference for the latter by some Marxist African historians because of the movement and articulation implied by formation as social history in process. Within that tradition I understand Omi and Winant to name and articulate *racial formation* as an idea and practice in the making.

As such, Omi and Winant state, racial formation is the "process by which social, economic and political forces determine the content and importance of racial categories, and by which they are in turn shaped by racial meanings."[5] The formation is in process and, contrary to sociological theory, which reifies race, reduces it to ethnicity or culture, and cites its declining significance, race is a central, irreducible axis of social relations. In fact they point to the "naturalness" and ubiquity of race as evidence for its prominence and assert that racial identity forms "often without obvious teaching or conscious inculcation" such that racial identity is associated with human nature from looks to tastes, temperament, intelligence, sexuality, music, sports, and food. Racial identity and ideology are "too essential, too integral to the maintenance of the US social order" so that they appear to be "permanent" features of US culture.[6] Although Omi and Winant know race to be a social construction in formation, they approach the biological model insofar as they partner race with human nature and hypothesize its permanence. Perhaps, in responding to sociology's cult of ethnicity and diminishing of race, they overstate their case.

At the same time, Omi and Winant write, racial meanings are contested ceaselessly and are thus in motion and subject to change. That process they call "racialization" to stress that race is made or constructed and its content and importance change over place and time. Further, race is not, as some Marxists hold, an epiphenomenon or a superstructure, nor is it false consciousness, Omi and Winant maintain. Race is a fundamental organizing principle of social relations at both the individual or micro level and the societal or macro level. Racial meanings and their significance turn on those mutually constituting relations between the self and society, and that process implicates social, economic, and political forces.

| | |

In a parallel disciplinary intervention, the social and political philosopher Charles W. Mills scores philosophy and normative liberal theory broadly for their virtual silence on race, a failure constituting an "episteme of ignorance." Not merely complicit with the acts of racialized slavery, imperialism, and genocide, that absence underwrites the "racial contract," a normative, unacknowledged agreement of white supremacy and nonwhite subservience. In that way "whiteness is not really a color at all, but a set of power relations." The racial contract accordingly is a discourse as well as a political and historical reality that explains and justifies white exploitation of and violence toward nonwhite peoples. Personhood for whites derives from subpersonhood for nonwhites, and insofar as whites benefit from the racial contract, writes Mills, they are signatories to that transaction.[7]

| | |

Racial formation theory, while grounded in US sociology, has been influential across many disciplines because of its explanatory value and, as the model predicts, the enduring quality of race and racism. In addition racial formation theory reflects contemporary social science discourse. The theory's insistence on context, change, and variation corresponds with the turn to postmodern and poststructuralist theories that arose following World War II. Despite its utility for explaining the condition of nonwhites in the United States, racial formation theory begins with and pivots on the discourse and materialization of whiteness. That is, as its negation, nonwhiteness depends on the definition and quality of whiteness. Critical race theory, an application of racial formation theory in legal discourse, illustrates that focus on whiteness in US history and jurisprudence. Recall that the law, as an instrument of the nation-state, is a crucial apparatus that interpellates subjectivities, including racialized (and gendered, sexualized, classed, and nationalized) bodies.

Whiteness

From our understanding of the nation-state, we recognize the state's interest in defining its people, race, citizens. As we know, the United States was conceived as a settler colony of imperial England, and its colonial and postcolonial pasts form continuities of that founding proposition and project. As a settler colony and settler nation-state, the United States restricted its people, race, citizens to free white persons, linking freedom with whiteness and manhood. Whiteness was the requirement for membership and privileges in the US social formation, and laws and their applications were the principal means of specifying and policing the borders of whiteness. Consequently the wages of whiteness and their eradication are the analytical and political concerns of critical white studies and a progressive wing of legal studies called critical race theory.[8] To avoid confusion keep in mind that critical race theory descends and departs from its forebears, which I trace to critical legal studies and critical theory.

Critical Theory

Third World studies, while committed to devising and deploying languages and ideologies not derived from the master's toolkit, descends from the discourses and practices of the ruling class. This entire book on the theories that inform Third World studies, including social formation theory, attests to the verity of that lineage. Critical theory is another such ancestral figure in our intellectual genealogy. *Critical theory* emerges as a critique of society and culture as understood by structuralism, materialism, and positivism. Following the optimism of the nineteenth century and its faith in science, capitalism, and human progress, critical theorists in the following century perceived social structures, including the nation-state and its apparatuses, and culture or patterned behavior as largely oppressive. Human liberation, they held, required freedom from the powers that held them under subjection. Those powers included ideology and language.

A neo-Marxist strand of critical theory centers around the Frankfurt School, which is associated with intellectuals at the Institute for Social Research at Goethe University in Frankfurt. Founded as a Marxist research center and employing mainly social scientists, the Frankfurt School was critical of orthodox Marxism even as it deployed Marxist theory to undermine capitalism and advance socialism. Although members of the Frankfurt School are far from uniform, several key ideas hold them together; among these are that dialectics, contradictions, and indeterminacies are inherent to the human condition and that ideologies shape consciousness and understandings of self and society. While traditional theory justifies and supports capitalism's control and exploitation of people, a Frankfurt School founder charged, critical theory is aimed at social change and emancipation from the forces and devices that enslave humanity.[9]

A second, related strand of critical theory arises from literary criticism as a form of hermeneutics or interpretation of texts. Like self and society, texts are not self-evident or transparent; as representations they are constructed and mediated. Literary criticism accordingly entails the *deconstruction* of those texts, revealing the complexities, contingencies, and contradictions in them. Although resisted by deconstruction's founding figure, Jacques Derrida,[10] *poststructuralism* flows from his skepticism of reason and absolute truth, essentialisms, taxonomies, oppositions, and hierarchies. Poststructuralism is antistructuralism; if structuralism arranges self and society along binary oppositions, poststructuralism interrogates and rejects those structures—white/nonwhite, man/woman, straight/queer, and so forth—that divide and discipline. A strategy to break those binaries employed by a variety of poststructuralism is to show how binaries are related and form continuities; there is no opposition, and hierarchies are reversed such that the self is dependent upon its other.

Critical theory's two strands occupy European thought from the 1920s to our present time. In the United States *critical legal studies* inherited critical theory's explication of power, ideology, discourse, and the material conditions. Marxism, the Frankfurt School, deconstruction, and poststructuralism remain influential in critical legal studies. Critical legal studies holds that power, not legal principles or precedents, is the guiding interest of law and its applications, and the deconstruction of legal texts demonstrates the arbitrary and inconsistent, contingent and indeterminate aspects of legal discourse and rulings. The law and legal system, critical legal theorists explain, name, classify, and value persons and groups over others, revealing power and the accumulation of rights and resources at the expense of the oppressed.

In the United States during the 1960s *critical race theory* departed from critical legal studies for its failure to account for race and racism.[11] As in critical theory and critical legal studies, critical race theorists focus on power and its articulations, but unlike their precursors, they highlight the racial formation. In addition to that critique of critical theory and critical legal studies, critical race theorists score liberalism in legal studies for subscribing to notions of allegedly color-blind and race-neutral laws and language. Like sociology's declining significance of race thesis, color-blind and race-neutral legal discourse contends the civil rights movement has removed the debilities of race through civil rights acts that ensure equality in voting rights, housing, and employment. Those laws, the discourse claims, actualized Martin Luther King Jr.'s dream of an America in which a person is judged not by the color of his skin but by the content of his character. The law thus is color-blind.

Critical race theorists emphatically disagree.[12] Like racial formation theory, critical race theory recognizes that racism is thoroughly ingrained in the fabric of US society. Individual and institutional racism is pervasive in the dominant order, and those structures of power are based upon white supremacy and privilege and nonwhite subservience and marginalization. The tradition of law serves the interests of whites and adversely affects people of color, as revealed in the everyday lives of the oppressed. Consequently a practice in critical race theory is to cite those experiences as evidence attesting to the reality of racism. To express those voices, storytelling narrates and affirms the presence, persistence, and effects of racial oppression. Additionally, in their response to liberals, critical race theorists depict civil rights gains not as concessions to US people of color but to burnish the US image as an exemplary democracy for Third World consumption during the Cold War.

In addition to adopting novel forms of evidence, critical race theory embraces interdisciplinary work, unlike legal scholarship, which converses mainly within legal discourse. Critical race theory is catholic in its method and theory and is especially attentive to social science, assimilating its insights into legal discourse. Prominent critical race theorists like Kimberlé Crenshaw modify racial formation theory with *intersectionality*, accounting for the interlocking systems of oppression, and in the matter of subjectivity they reject essentialisms of race, gender, and sexuality and acknowledge the diverse and multiple forces at work shaping the subject-self. In accord with their commitment to unifying theory with practice, critical race theorists see the political in the personal, participate in freedom movements, expose and take into account their subject positions in their scholarship, and engage students in critical pedagogy, recalling Freire's call for a dialogic pedagogy.

White by Law

If whiteness and its powers can be apprehended, critical race theorists like Ian Haney-López write, then white privilege can be disavowed.[13] In that US law constructs race, Haney-López explains, the law is both an ideology and a method of control. But the law is not singular, and it comprises a complex, incoherent ensemble of practices, actors, institutions, and ideas that are interdependent but rarely in sync with each other as in a system. Institutions such as Congress and the courts, along with actors who populate them such as politicians, judges, attorneys, petitioners, and juries, are all related though independent of each other. In that way the practice of law is multiply constituted and contains contradictions, is contingent, has no necessary direction, and is not normatively good or bad. So while the law is primarily a coercive system, its interpretations, enforcements, and outcomes are indeterminate.

With those caveats in mind, Haney-López proceeds to describe how the law participates in producing race. US law, he writes, creates races and hierarchies and racial meanings based upon physical appearances, natures, and cultures. The law segregates those racial categories to maintain differences and award privileges and poverties, and the law establishes material conditions that signify race, such as the alien Asian and white citizen. As a part of society the law reflects social powers and their distribution and choices; conversely, as ideology the law shapes people's thinking and behavior. Abstract law can produce palpable, real effects in the lives and life chances of its subjects. Despite the Supreme Court's current skepticism of race such that allegations involving race are subject to "strict scrutiny" and must show a compelling state interest, Haney-López wrote in 1996, the Court still recognizes racial classifications and race-based laws, showing the undiminished capacity and centrality of race.

US legal history shows how whiteness is a human construction in the "racial prerequisite cases," Haney-López explains. The prerequisite for naturalization, and with it citizenship, was set by the 1790 Naturalization Act that specified "free white persons" as the necessary condition for naturalization and citizenship. At the center of postbellum debates concerning race were Asians, Hawaiians, and Mexicans who challenged the definitions of whiteness and Asians who were denied naturalization and stood outside the circle of citizenship, African Americans having acquired that title with adoption of the Fourteenth Amendment (1868).

Amid virulent anti-Asianism in the second half of the nineteenth century, the fifty-two racial prerequisite cases began with *In re Ah Yup* (1878), a federal district court ruling that denied naturalization to Chinese because they were not white according to Johann Blumenbach and as was held by popular opinion. The Court's tortured reasoning, Haney-López points out, reveals there was little judicial precedent to determine whiteness. The challenges, although continuing to 1952, came to a head in the Supreme Court decisions *Takao Ozawa v. United States* (1922) and *United States v. Bhagat Singh Thind* (1923).

In *Ozawa* the Court ruled that the category white excludes American Indians and Negroes and refers to the class of people called Caucasian as popularly understood. Ozawa, a Japanese man, was "not Caucasian and therefore belongs entirely outside the zone on the negative side." In *Thind* the Court refined its definition of Caucasian because Thind, a South Asian man, claimed social science affirmed that people from India belonged to the Indo-European linguistic family and were Caucasians. Rather, the Court declared, "white" and "Caucasian" are terms "of common speech and not of scientific origin." So while "the blond Scandinavian" and "the brown Hindu" (as the Court incorrectly called Thind, who was of the Sikh faith) might have shared a common ancestor "in the dim reaches of antiquity," the Court conceded, "the average man knows perfectly well that there are unmistakable and profound differences between them today." As the framers of the 1790 Act understood it, "free white persons" are "words of common speech, to be interpreted in accordance with the understanding of the common man."

In ruling against Ozawa, who had claimed whiteness was defined by culture, cultural practices, and loyalty to the nation-state, the Court argued that race is not culture and that nonwhites inherited dispossession, being entirely outside the zone of whiteness on the negative side. And while science might have named and classified races as Thind contended, the Court dismissed that history and discourse because race is a matter of contemporary expression by the ordinary man. Those astonishing admissions by the Supreme Court confirm the positions held by racial formation and critical race theories that race is a social construction and that privilege accrues through the category of whiteness.

White privilege, Haney-López explains, involves invisibility or not having to be burdened by race. Whiteness is naturalized, while nonwhiteness is racialized; the former is the standard and norm, while the latter is deviant and inferior. The white subject position, hence, is normativity, privilege, and domination. Correspondingly the nonwhite subject position is marginality (deviance), disadvantage, and subordination. Insofar as it is a binary, white/nonwhite breaks down under third and multiple categories that deny polarities. Because Asian disrupts the black/white binary of race, the category "Asian" inspired the invention of nonwhite or the negation of whiteness and thus an empty, dependent category of whiteness.

Later, during the twentieth century, the "model minority" idea assimilated Asians into whiteness, and now in the twenty-first century racial "diversity" is reserved for blacks only, deracinating and placing in limbo Asians, Latinx, and Native Americans. As we recall from San Francisco State in 1968, administrators and faculty positioned African Americans as a race and American Indians, Asians, and Latinx as cultural or ethnic groups. With those moves white/nonwhite falls by the wayside, and the black/white binary of race prevails.

We should observe that all of the prerequisite cases involve challenges to the category of whiteness. Despite sharing the alienations of nonwhiteness, Asians, Native Americans, and Mexicans generally resisted the strategy of pursuing rights within the US nation-state as blacks. While racialism played a role in that choice, blackness was also defined by blood and geography, namely a native of Africa. Whiteness, on the other hand, is an elastic category that includes culture, language, religion, and class position.[14] Courts ruled variously on cases involving Asians from Turkey, Lebanon, Syria, and India, sometimes classifying them as whites and at other times as nonwhites. Even those from the continent of Africa along its northern shores of the Mediterranean Sea oscillated between whiteness and nonwhiteness. Those ambiguities are reflected in the decennial US census.

The Census

Mandated by Article 1 of the US Constitution to ascertain "all persons" for representation in the nation-state, the census not only enumerates; it produces citizens and subjects. As Benedict Anderson observed in his much-celebrated book on the making of a nation and people, the census, the map, and the museum produce the national consciousness.[15] Those instruments, Anderson writes, implicate the power of numbers for taxation, military service, and immigration, the power of the grid to mark the boundaries of the sovereign nation-state, and the power over memory to articulate and memorialize the national inheritance.[16] Article 1 specifies that representation and direct taxes are to be apportioned according to the nation's numbers, specifically the "Number of free Persons, including those bound to Service for a Term of Years, and excluding Indians not taxed, three fifths of all other Persons."

Accordingly, following the language of Article 1 and as expressed in the first census, of 1790, "free Persons" that included indentures were classified as "white"; Indians not taxed were nonpersons and thus not enumerated; and "all other Persons" were African Americans, counted as three-fifths of a person and as colored persons or nonwhites. Generally, "other" persons referenced nonwhites who were "other" than white. Beginning in 1790 and continuing to the latest census (2010), the category "white" remains constant; white is the originating point of all persons and citizens, the privileged, protected category. Even European indentures, although not free, were counted as full persons because they were *potentially* free because of their whiteness; whites, as a race, were free persons by definition.

In the language of the 1790 census, all persons were classed as "free white," "slave," or "all other free." The latter two were "three-fifths of all other Persons."[17] From 1790 to 1840 the "free white" and "slave" classes remained, while "all other free" in 1800 and 1810 became "all other free, except untaxed Indians," which then changed to "free colored" in 1820, 1830, and 1840. Note the use of the term *other* to designate nonwhite. To distinguish citizenship among whites, the 1820, 1830, and 1840 censuses had a category for "foreigners," or whites not yet naturalized.

Changes in the nonwhite category reflected the varying complexion of the nation because of imperialism, conquest, migration, and miscegenation. In 1850, with the annexation of Mexico's territories, Mexicans were folded into the census as whites, as was provided for by the Treaty of Guadalupe-Hidalgo (1848). In 1850 the census differentiated between black and mulatto, indicating race mixing and anxieties over the "contamination" of white blood by black. The 1860 census was the last enumeration of "slave" because emancipation in that decade eliminated the category, and it counted for the first time "civilized Indians." In 1870 "Chinese or Mongolian" appeared in the national census, and in 1890 "Japanese," marking the labor migration of Asians and the need to track those aliens. (California's census counted Chinese in 1860 and Japanese in 1870, reflecting the prominence of Asians in that state long before they emerged as a concern in the national consciousness.)

The 1890 census counted all Indians on and off reservations, and it expanded its determination of blackness (and whiteness) during the era of Jim Crow and segregation. The census used blood quantum to define *black* as having three-fourths African blood; *mulatto*, three- to five-eighths African blood; *quadroon*, one-fourth African blood; and *octoroon*, one-eighth African blood. We see the one-drop rule for African Americans began in 1662. The federal government also applied blood quantum to Indians. The Dawes Act (1887), as we learned, tried to dissolve Indian nations by treating Indians as individuals rather than as foreign nations, and it led to a commission and tribal rolls based on blood quantum and the issuing of a Certificate of Degree of Indian Blood by the Bureau of Indian Affairs. Thereby the state and not Indians determined their subjectivities.

The 1900 census introduced "Negro or of Negro descent" for blacks but returned to "black" and "mulatto" in 1910 and 1920. During the Great Depression the 1930 census accounted for Mexicans as a separate category by removing them from the classification "white." Identification of Mexicans was helpful for the US government's expulsion program, which, from 1929 to 1939, displaced an estimated 500,000 to a million Mexicans and Mexican Americans to Mexico. William Doak, head of the Labor Department that managed the program, declared that the intention of the forced "repatriation" was to hasten the day "when our population shall be more homogeneous." Mexicans turned white again in the 1940 census, where they remained until 1970, when the term *Hispanic* first appears. Considered an ethnic and not a racial term by the Census Bureau, *Hispanic* referred to people who spoke Spanish, had a Spanish surname, or self-identified as Hispanic. Contrarily many people from the Caribbean, Mexico, and Central and South America prefer the term *Latina/o* to differentiate America from its colonizer, Spain. Latinx were made in America, not Spain. *Hispanic* also neglects other European colonizers in America, such as Portugal, Britain, the Netherlands, and France.

The 1930 census, besides racializing Mexicans, added Filipino, Hindu (again a misnomer), and Korean, indicating their arrival in the United States as migrant laborers and the need to track them, indeed all Asians, with the

Mexican mother, June 1935, California. Photo by Dorothea Lange. Documenting the
Great Depression for the Farm Security Administration, Lange captioned this photo,
"Sometimes I tell my children that I would like to go to Mexico, but they tell me 'We don't
want to go, we belong here.'" Lange's quote can be read as her commentary on the forcible
expulsions of Mexicans during the 1930s. Farm Security Administration. Courtesy of the
Library of Congress.

onset of laws that excluded them: Chinese, 1882 Exclusion Act; Japanese, 1908 Gentlemen's Agreement; South Asians (Hindu), 1917 Barred Zone; Filipino, 1934 Tydings-McDuffie Act. The Filipino Repatriation Act (1935) encouraged Filipinos, like Mexicans during the same period, to vacate the United States for their place of birth. Organized as a race, unlike "Hispanics," "Asians and Pacific Islanders" was used in the 1980 and 1990 censuses, and has been separated into "Asian" and "Native Hawaiian and Other Pacific Islander" since 2000.

The census mirrors the nation's imperialism in its expanding category "colored" that began in 1820 with "free colored," a descendant of "all other free" of the first (1790) census. A footnote to "colored" in the 1890 census indicated the term included Negro, Chinese, Japanese, and civilized Indian. By 1920, following the late nineteenth-century expansion of the United States overseas, the footnote to "colored" expanded the term to cover Negro, Indian, Chinese, Japanese, Filipino, Hindu (South Asian), Korean, Hawaiian, Malay, Siamese, and Maori. As in US law, the census produced the binary of white/citizen and "colored" or nonwhite/alien. "Mexican" and later "Latina/o" troubled and continues to haunt the census, which is considering for 2020 whether the category is a race or an ethnic grouping. While Mexicans might have been classed as white by the census, they were treated as "colored" in segregated schools, residences, and jobs.

Even as "colored" varied in the census following the course of imperialism, "white" was and is a changing race and discourse. For instance, the 2000 census defines *white* as "any of the original peoples of Europe, the Middle East, or North Africa." That annexation of Asia and Africa to Europe violates the continental definitions of race established by the science of taxonomy. That bloating of the category, the census explains, follows common belief and not science, but presents an odd mix of "Irish, German, Italian, Lebanese, Near Easterner, Arab, or Polish," not to mention Algerian, Egyptian, Libyan, Moroccan, Tunisian, Palestinian, and Saudi, as members of the white race. That elastic quality of whiteness takes place in the midst of nonwhite gains fueled by unprecedented numbers of Asians and Latinx migrating to the United States following the 1965 Immigration Act that ended racist immigration quotas. That demographic shift might concern some whites, but the change has not resulted in a proportionate transfer of power. The US census produces race (and citizenship) and confirms what the courts have historically ruled: white and nonwhite are not scientific concepts but categories of privilege and rights as determined by whites.

Critical White Studies

A new field has emerged from the realization of the necessity for racializing whiteness. As an invisible category indicative of power, whiteness incurs privileges. We in Third World studies thus must racialize whiteness. I cite as the founding document for critical white studies "The Souls of White Folk" from Du Bois's *Darkwater* (1920). In that essay Du Bois historicizes whiteness, observing that the white race was created in the nineteenth and twentieth centuries.[18] Whiteness was made in empire and thrives on colored oppression. That is, Du Bois explains, robust Europe is wealthy because the Third World is poor. The labor of colored folk amassed that fortune for Europe. Moreover, Du Bois notes, whiteness is a creation of nonwhiteness; the process, while oppositional, is linked and reciprocal. Finally, although whites appear oblivious to those ties, nonwhites know whites intimately because their survival depends upon that apprehension. I know the souls of white folk, Du Bois exclaims, "I see their souls undressed" and "I see the working of their entrails."[19] Colored folk live with and work for white folk within their homes and businesses, and they speak the language and learn the ideology of their oppressors.

In describing the souls of white folk, Du Bois outlines the major themes of *critical white studies*, which emerged as an interdisciplinary field during the second half of the twentieth century.[20] Whiteness has a history, he points out in *Darkwater*; the race was invented in place and time. As such, whiteness is a discourse, subjectivity, and social practice. In US history and as a social construction, whiteness expanded with the whitening of the Irish, Germans, Russian Jews, Slavs, and Italians. By racializing whiteness Du Bois marked what had been left unmarked; he rendered the transparent visible. Not merely an abstraction, Du Bois adds, whiteness bespeaks the power to name and assign value, and it is a possession that pays real dividends; it produces wealth for the self and poverty for self's other. Imperialism, however, is not forever as shown by the dark world rising, and white supremacy is not humanism. Instead "a belief in humanity is a belief in colored men."[21]

As Du Bois points out, people of color understand whites well. We speak their languages and often share their ideologies. Our subjectivities are therewith constituted by their discourses. We have been schooled in the grammar, history, economy, and society of our colonizers. Our subject matter is white studies, and our well-being and life chances depend to a large degree on how well we have mastered the elements of white studies. By contrast, Third World studies is a part of what Du Bois saw as the dark world rising, and our commitments and affiliations must align with a belief in humanity, in colored peoples and their struggles for liberation.

Third World freedom movements in the United States and the world led to responses by the master class evidenced in whiteness discourse and practices. Starting in the 1960s whiteness branched into two streams, an ethnic revival movement and a resurgence of white identity politics, both employing the ideology of self-determination as voiced by Third World peoples. Decrying the essentialism and poverty of whiteness, ethnic revivalists searched for their roots as Americans of Irish, Scottish, German, and Italian descent. They organized social clubs, parades, games, commemorations, and holidays to affirm their newfound ethnic pride.[22] I remember how in 1983 the Marxist and then born-again Christian and eminent US historian Eugene Genovese teased me that he too deserved a seat at the post-1968 ethnic studies table. Gene excelled in unflinching critique, which is what I admired about him. Of course, as we know, Gene was correct, insofar as (Chicago) ethnic studies began as white studies.

The second variety of whiteness decried racialism while organizing on that very basis. The ideologies of nonracialism and color-blindness advanced political and social movements grounded in white identity politics. Partisans applauded the civil rights gains of the 1960s, but, they demurred, those had moved the pendulum too far. Affirmative action gave unfair and undeserving advantages to women and people of color by crippling white men. It was affirmative or reverse discrimination. In addition bilingual education and busing to achieve racial parity, protected by the Supreme Court, and multicultural education have divided what was formerly a united, homogeneous nation, which was founded on the bedrock of European civilization and the English language. Taking back America is the aim and agenda of this brand of white nationalist politics.

Expressions of that "return" include state and national movements for English only and English as the official language, which were recurrent throughout much of US history but underwent revival beginning in the 1980s. Another is the banning of post-1968 ethnic studies, primarily Chicana/o studies, in Arizona's public schools in 2010 because, the law states, ethnic studies promotes "resentment toward a race or class of people" and advocates the overthrow of the US government. Supporters of the law charge post-1968 ethnic studies with teaching (indoctrinating) reverse racism or white hatred and disloyalty to the nation-state.

Both streams of the white backlash and revival flow from the repository and power of whiteness and white studies. Refusing the essentialism of whiteness can liberate and ethnic celebrations can affirm, but taken to their logical extreme, they can devolve to white supremacy. As the Southern Poverty Law Center reported in 2008, white supremacist groups in the United States grew by 54 percent since 2000, increasing from 602 groups in that year to 888 groups in 2007 and 926 groups a year later.

White studies comprises and secures the normative discourse and state of whiteness and white supremacy. Critical white studies, by contrast, strives to dismantle white power, not by erasing whiteness but by making it visible. As Haney-López points out in *White by Law*, whites must come to terms with their white consciousness and subjectivities to deconstruct whiteness and disavow its privileges. Color-blindness works against that project of racializing whiteness, and it sustains white supremacy by denying race and its powers and consequences.

Like critical theory, critical white studies seeks to promote social change and liberation from the forces and devices that enslave humanity, white and nonwhite. Like critical race theory, critical white studies rejects the liberalism of nonracialism and white ethnic revival and its multiculturalist agenda because racism lives and power, not culture, is the agent of oppression. Like racial formation and critical race theory, critical white studies recognizes that racism in the United States is pervasive and structures the dominant order, and those relations of power are based upon white supremacy and privilege and nonwhite subservience and poverty. It is important to note that critical white studies begins at home, with whites and whiteness, and is not a project of white benevolence or uplift of nonwhite peoples.[23]

Summary

The master's tools can dismantle the master's house but, as Lorde points out, only temporarily and partially. The master's tools fail to supply alternative languages and ideologies freed from oppression or the discourses and material manifestations of the ruling class. Racial formation emerges from a historical conjuncture of US sociology's turn away from race toward ethnicity and the detour by Third World liberation movements into cultural nationalism and racial politics. Like a countersentence, racial formation theory intervenes in US sociology's cult of ethnicity, notions of the declining significance of race, and the postracial state, but it is still constrained by the discourses it critiques.

Whiteness is the central feature of US history and society as shown by racial formation and critical race theory. While the prevailing discourse racializes and thereby foregrounds nonwhiteness and naturalizes and thereby renders invisible whiteness, critical white studies features whiteness as a discourse and property of value.[24] Additionally, as feminists of color have pointed out about second-wave feminism, whiteness obscures the distinctions of race, gender, and class. In their critique of patriarchy, second-wave feminists assumed a universal "woman," while their claims were limited to white, middle-class women. Moreover whiteness entails privileges of race (white), gender (man), sexuality (heterosexual), class (owner), and nation (citizen), as explained by the theory of social formation.

EIGHT

SOCIAL FORMATION

Racial formation and critical race theory emerged from US sociology's and legal scholarship's confining cage of ethnicity and slighting of race and hence their liberating timbre.[1] But their insufficiencies were clearly evident to those who experienced multiple, intersecting forms of oppression. A journalist and teacher, Elise Johnson McDougald, described the condition of black women in Alain Locke's *Survey Graphic* in 1925. Although diverse in experiences, McDougald noted, black women as a collective were subjected to the handicaps and indignities of race, gender, and class. "Like women in general, but more particularly like those of other oppressed minorities," she wrote, "the Negro woman has been forced to submit to over-powering conditions. Pressure has been exerted upon her, both from without and within her group. Her emotional and sex life is a reflex of her economic station." But, she observed, "feminist efforts are directed chiefly toward the realization of the equality of the races, the sex struggle assuming a subordinate place."[2]

Third World Women

That inferior position of gender in the struggle for racial equality changed with a new wave of African American feminists like Frances Beale, a former NAACP youth leader and a member of the international affairs commission of the Student Nonviolent Coordinating Committee (SNCC). At a 1968 SNCC meeting in New York City, Beale presented a paper on the impact of racism and

sexism on the lives of African American women and proposed a black wom-
en's caucus to explore those particular concerns. Capitalism, she pointed out,
exploits all workers, but white workers can subscribe to a false consciousness
of racial superiority, and black men a feeling of dominion over black women.
Capitalism relegates women workers "to a state of enslavement" and black
women to the bottom of the ladder of class, race, and gender. Moreover the
state's sterilization campaigns exert control over black and Puerto Rican wom-
en's bodies and sexuality, and the white women's movement, largely a middle-
class project, excludes the masses of black women whose struggles are against
gender but also class, racial, and sexual oppressions.[3]

Beale formed with others the Black Women's Liberation Caucus, which
split from SNCC in 1969 and changed its name to the Black Women's Alliance
(BWA). Widening its purview and circle with the recognition that, in Beale's
words, "the complexities of intersecting oppressions [are] more resilient than
the distinctions of the particular groups," the BWA established solidarity with
other women of color, including American Indians, Asians, and Latinx. That
outreach led to BWA renaming itself the Third World Women's Alliance,
which stated as its goals "to make a meaningful and lasting contribution to
the Third World community by working for the elimination of the oppression
and exploitation from which we suffer" and to create a socialist society free
from "the pressures of racism, economic exploitation, and sexual oppression."[4]

Perceiving a similar marginalization from the civil rights and women's
movements, African American women formed the Combahee River Collective in 1974. Sisters Beverly and Barbara Smith with Demita Frazier crafted
the statement that articulated most persuasively the case for what became theorized as intersectionality. Barbara Smith recalled years later, "We wanted to
integrate a race/class analysis with an antisexist analysis and practice. And we
didn't just want to add on racism and class oppression like white women did."[5]
The statement begins with an explication of the Collective's politics: "We
are actively committed to struggling against racial, sexual, heterosexual, and
class oppression, and see as our particular task the development of integrated
analysis and practice based upon the fact that the major systems of oppression
are interlocking. The synthesis of these oppressions creates the conditions of
our lives."[6]

The ideologies and practices of the Third World Women's Alliance and
Combahee River Collective worked at the intersections of race, gender, sexuality, and class, unlike other African American women's organizations that
might have stressed race and gender but glossed sexuality and class.[7] The interlocking systems of oppression, their synthesis, became a basis for the legal

scholar Kimberlé Crenshaw's foundational 1989 essay, "Demarginalizing the Intersection of Race and Sex," in which she named the "multidimensionality of Black women's experience" *intersectionality*. "Because the intersectional experience is greater than the sum of racism and sexism," Crenshaw explained, "any analysis that does not take intersectionality into account cannot sufficiently address the particular manner in which Black women are subordinated."[8] Other African American scholars expanded upon the intersections of gender, race, and nation, among them the sociologist Patricia Hill Collins, and other women of color deployed the intersections of race, gender, sexuality, class, and nation,[9] but few have theorized fully the articulation.

Perhaps the most thorough exposition is found in the US sociologist Evelyn Nakano Glenn's *Unequal Freedom: How Race and Gender Shaped American Citizenship and Labor* (2002), in which she describes genderings and racializations as "linked identities" that are "relational." Also, she notes, gender and race comprise ideologies that constitute individuals and groups and supply mobilizing tools for political work. Moreover those discourses of race and gender are mapped onto the US economy as a central axis of the labor (class) system and the nation-state, wherein property, whiteness, and manhood constituted freedom and defined the "citizen worker" and his entitlements. Power, Glenn proposes, is *a* factor in those relational identities at both the micro and macro levels.

Instead power is *the* organizing principle within the social formation, and thus its locations and articulations are the objects of analysis. For Third World studies power is expressed along the lines of color and gender, but also and more comprehensively sexuality, class, and nation. Those expressions of power constitute discourses, not mere identities, and they are made real in the material and social relations. We in Third World studies must develop an accurate apprehension of the human condition by building upon racial formation theory and expanding upon intersectionality and its permutations.[10] Social formation theory, although derivative of the discourses of the ruling class, I contend, advances a language and ideology not of that prior order.

Theorizing Social Formation

Like racial formation, social formation is much cited and undertheorized.[11] Marx originated the term to designate both the structure and stage of society, as in social organization and social development (precapitalist, capitalist, socialist). Over time and with its spread into disciplines as disparate as anthropology, cultural studies, history, psychology, and religious studies, the term's usage and meaning acquired less precision. David Krasner, for instance, examines the social formation of cakewalking in his history of African American theater and performance, and Ian Burkitt's social formation describes the development of human personality in society and its networks and relations.[12] The social formation of landscape, according to the art historian Denis Cosgrove, is shaped by Europeans' ways of seeing and representing themselves and their world, and Christopher Elwood conceives of the place of the sacred within society as its social formation.[13] To the African historians Shula Marks and Anthony Atmore, social formation embraces the totality of society and describes "the exact nature of the particular diversity and unity of economic and social relations which characterise a society during a specific epoch."[14]

Zhongqiao Duan traces the roots of Marx's social formation and proposes that Marx saw the term as descriptive of both the form and stage of society. In *German Ideology* (1846), Duan reports, Marx describes the "form of society" as the product of human interactions, and *social formation* first appears in *The Eighteenth Brumaire of Louis Bonaparte* (1851) to indicate a stage of social development.[15] The idea for social formation, Duan speculates, comes from Marx's readings in geology, as seen in his notes in 1851 on J. F. W. Johnston's *Lectures on Agricultural Chemistry and Geology*. Rock strata constituted "formations," the agricultural chemist explained, which possessed unique natures and revealed changes over time. Marx assimilated those scientific ideas into his writings: "Just as one should not think of sudden changes and sharply delineated periods in considering the succession of the different geological formations, so also in the case of the creation of the different economic formations of society."[16] Intent on a science of history and society, Marx summoned geology to perform that work of validation.

By analogy, then, each stage of human history differs from and yet is linked to successive strata; each is thus unique, comprising a social formation, while providing the platform for the next layer, the next stage of development. The span of human history, then, embraces the sum of those evolving progressions from one stage to the next. So while *form of society* represents a static construct, *social formation* connects society's stages over time. Accordingly *social formation* specifies both the social structure and its evolution. Further, as Marks and Atmore proposed, social formations are characterized by their mode of production, which is "the combination of forces and relations of production together with the mechanisms which make possible its continued functioning, and include within its definition economic, juridico-political and ideological structures."[17] Marx classified the modes of production as Asiatic, ancient, feudal, and modern, and described them as the sum total of the relations of production that composes "the economic structure of society, the real foundation, on which rises a legal and political superstructure and to which correspond definite forms of social consciousness."[18]

Althusser references but falls short of defining social formation in his discussion of the materialist dialectic and unevenness exhibited in the relations of colonizer and colonized, development and underdevelopment. Economism, he explains, would favor the means and relations of production as the main cause of that unevenness, but "real history" shows a greater complexity in "the permutations of the principal role between the economy, politics, theory, etc." His translator, with expressions of gratitude from Althusser for clarifying his terminology, defines *social formation* as "society" so-called or "the concrete complex of . . . economic practice, political practice and ideological practice . . . at a certain place and stage of development."[19] Similarly Barry Hindess and Paul Hirst, citing Marx's *Reading Capital*, defines *social formation* as society or the "society effect" produced by the mode of production and economic, political, and ideological structures.[20]

Without delving into the tangle of definitions involving the terms *mode of production*, *base*, and *superstructure*, *social formation theory* subscribes to Marx's formulation of social formation as the structure of society in its totality and its changes, not as stages, over space/time. Because the subjects of Third World studies are the oppressed as produced by nationalism, imperialism, world-system, education, subjectification, and racial formation—all, the consequences of power—social formation specifies the locations and articulations of power around the axes of race, gender, sexuality, class, and nation. Although power is itself suspect as a discrete category, social formation theory deploys the term without explication except to define power as agency or ability. Further, despite its diffuse and immaterial quality, as theorized by Foucault, social formation theory insists on locating power and acknowledging its manifestations to point to, apprehend, and transform its workings. That is, while appreciating the complexities and shifting, ephemeral qualities of power, we in Third World studies must name the oppressors and the oppressed and understand oppression to resist it and create alternative discourses and practices.

Social formation, then, marks the forms of society in their entirety and their passage and changes over space/time. Power and its articulations around the discourses and material manifestations of race, gender, sexuality, class, and nation conceive and cultivate the social structure. Intended to behave as closed systems, the formations of and relations in society are designed by their creators, those who hold and wield power, to function as a whole to actualize control and privileges. But because of human agency and ceaseless contestations, the social formation is not a closed or self-regulating system, neither is its direction predetermined. The social formation accordingly is historical or specific to space/time, though subject to change and transformation.

Social formation attends to the multiplicity of forces at work in the exercise of power. It demands a complexity in our thinking and politics to ascertain how social categories overlap, interact, conflict with, and interrupt each other. Social formation is not solely the intersections or sum of oppressions; it accounts for those meeting points but also their resistances (and accommodations) and the mutually constituting and shifting relations between discourses and the material conditions. Finally social formation theory supplies a rubric for affiliations among discourses of racial formation, feminist, queer, Marxist, and critical theories and for solidarities in political insurgencies emanating from people of color and across imposed divides of race, gender, sexuality, class, and nation.

Power, according to social formation theory, invents and utilizes social categories as discrete entities to divide and thereby rule. When we attend to racial and not to gender and sexual liberation, we succumb to that oppressive regime. Segregation is also the rule within each of those social categories, constituting binary and hence oppositional and hierarchical relations. Race (white and nonwhite), gender (man and woman), sexuality (straight and queer), class (owners and workers), and nation (citizen and alien) differentiate to designate the normative, privileged group. In addition distinguishing the material conditions (society) from discourses (language and ideology) involves a deception that privileges the "real" over the "fictive" when, instead of binary oppositions, they are mutually constituted and constituting.[21]

The real materializes under the sign of biology and nature. Even as raced, gendered, and sexualized bodies indicate natural, normal, and desired anatomies, class and nation and their apparatuses and interpellations conjure a necessary human condition, albeit an evolving one of evolution, growth, and progress. Those appeals to science, the body, and the natural world summon the material; simultaneously they are discourses that actualize those categories and distinctions. They are also apparitions devised by the mind.

To visualize the social formation, imagine separate spheres of race, gender, sexuality, class, and nation that converge to share common ground and diverge to differentiate because they are elastic, expanding and contracting over space/time. Think in terms of singularities and multiplicities, stasis and change. Fundamental to that dynamic is class, by which I mean the economy or the modes, means, and relations of production, involving land, labor, and capital. Upon that foundational base arises the superstructure of society, composed of the nation or polity, including the citizens, laws, police, prisons, schools, and so forth; race, inclusive of kinship, ethnicity, culture, religion, and so forth; and gender and sexuality as discourses and material relations. Social formation theory accepts Marxism's distinction between base (economy) and superstructure (the rest of society) and their mutually constituting relations; that is, the base is foundational for society while affecting and being influenced by the superstructure.

Simply, the economy is the provisioning function that enables human life and undergirds society as a whole. Hunters and gatherers, pastoralists, and agriculturalists organize themselves on the bases of their provisioning choices. They conceive of land variously to suit their economies; hunters and gatherers and pastoralists generally see land and its resources as open, even as they often move within defined territorial limits, while agriculturalists settle the land, even as they might move to seek more fertile soil and water. All three economic systems deploy labor, again, to maximize production and install and affirm social hierarchies. Gender divisions of labor in patriarchal societies relegate women to secondary tasks such as gathering and agriculture, when hunting and pastoralism, reserved for men, supply proteins, carry greater prestige, and produce greater returns insofar as animals are capital for accumulation. Like gender, slavery and migrant labor support the base and superstructure, while the superstructure regulates those labor systems. Hence land, labor, and capital organize society even as society shapes the means and relations of production.

Like the relations between base and superstructure, social formation theory understands the spheres of race, gender, sexuality, class, and nation to form solitary as well as convergent formations, such as gendered and sexualized races, sexualized genders, racialized and gendered labor systems, divinely ordained nations and destinies, and so forth. Moreover, depending upon place and time, each sphere can expand and contract in prominence and importance. The context affects subject positions, which exist in relation to that environment. For instance, a working-class consciousness can diminish the distinctions of race and gender when on strike for higher wages and better working conditions. In a movement against police profiling and violence, as we witnessed in Ferguson, Missouri, and New York City in 2014, thousands marched chanting "Hands up, don't shoot!" and "I can't breathe" across social divides.

To start, to prevent solidarities, the ruling class names, classifies, and divides its subjects; this imposition of order segregates. Policing of those borders punishes, disallows, and diminishes discursive and material transgressions of race, gender, sexuality, class, and nation. Further, the state recognizes no language for multiple, convergent forms of oppression or, in the liberating language of the Combahee River Collective, the interlocking systems of oppression. In her foundational essay naming intersectionality, Crenshaw points out that in *DeGraffenreid v. General Motors* (1976) the court held that black women could charge race or gender discrimination "but not a combination of both." Although other courts have allowed race or gender suits under Title VII of the Civil Rights Act (1964), Crenshaw notes, *DeGraffenreid*'s treatment of black women's claims as aberrant suggests black men as the standard for racial discrimination and white women for claims of gender discrimination.[22] Crucially the law is silent on the daily oppression and exploitation experienced by black women workers who fall between the cracks of race, gender, and class. They, in the discourse of the state, do not exist.

While power and its accomplices, such as Gramscian hegemonic classes,[23] can segregate to rule on the bases of race, gender, sexuality, class, and nation, they can also advance controls through convergences. Hypersexuality, for instance, can simultaneously summon race and gender, namely African men and Asian women and Latinx; likewise in the discourse of nation, the "alien" and "illegal" figures race, Asians and Latinx. Religion, especially Islam since 2001, summons radicalism, terrorism, and threats to universal freedoms, while criminality condemns young black men and Latinx. The intersection of those discourses, their thick saturation can produce a condition that resembles neither its separate parts nor its cumulative effects but "the particular manner" of black women's subjugation, in Crenshaw's analysis, and something entirely different. Those articulations show the complexity and malleability of the social formation, together with the need for an entirely new discourse to recuperate the purposefully unimaginable under the language and ideology of the ruling class.

Social formation theory explicates the interlocking systems of oppression as environments or contexts within which privileges and identifications take place. The categories of white men, straight, owner, and citizen are least susceptible to those oppressive environments of race, gender, sexuality, class, or nation. The categories of nonwhite women, queer, worker, and alien are most vulnerable to oppression in the social formation. In the former the norm is unmarked and invisible; in the latter the norm's opposition is marked as aberrant and visible even as the other enables the self's subjectivity. Consider the contexts of the social formation such as personal interactions, popular culture, the media, churches, schools, and the like. Within the United States the normative of race, gender, sexuality, class, and nation is largely invisible in those environments, while the nonnormative queer requires recurrent and constant justification and explanation. For theory's sake, those remain pure types when, in fact, complexities predominate. For instance, white women might share the race, sexuality, class, and nation of the normative figure but deviate on the basis of gender, which forms their oppressive (and liberating) environment. The examples multiply.

| | |

Power, however, is not total or final. The oppressed have always contested the designs of the ruling class, producing change. Where there is oppression, the US Marxist historian Herbert Aptheker declared, there is resistance. Fixity is a fiction of rule; the social formation is always in motion, in formation because of struggle. It is this contest, produced by human agency, that allows for social transformations and the charting of novel possibilities and futures.

Producing the Social Formation

As critical race theory shows, a key apparatus of the state that produces the social formation is the laws and legal system. In the United States the Page Act (1875) and the Exclusion Act (1882) reveal the convergences of race, gender, and sexuality and of race and class; prostitution or sexual deviance, the Page Act contends, is synonymous with Asian (Chinese and Japanese) women, and the arrival of Chinese workers, in the language of the Exclusion Act, "endangers the good order of certain localities." Asian women because of their race, gender, and sexuality and Chinese workers because of their race and class imperiled the "good order" of the nation-state and were thus prohibited from entering the United States.

Those examples show how migration, including migrant labor, is a matter of nation building and national security. The 1930 US census tracked Mexicans and Mexican Americans while the state forcibly removed them as "excess" labor during the Great Depression. Around the same time the nation-state facilitated the "repatriation" of Filipino migrants. Similarly, under the smoke of an undeclared "war on terror" following September 11, 2001, the federal government moved the oversight of immigration from the Justice Department to the newly created Department of Homeland Security. US immigration laws thus not only define members of the nation and the "illegal"; they interpellate subjects and subjectivities, producing race, gender, sexuality, class, and nation, or the social formation. In 2015, a Republican presidential candidate suggested religion, Islam, as a red flag for exclusion and danger.

Although my rendition of the social formation's production is limited to the United States, readers should remember that social formation theory purports to explain society broadly across space/time. Accordingly the ancient Greeks privileged men over women, citizens over aliens, superiors over inferiors, and the free over the enslaved. They ordered their world by naming and attributing natures to places and peoples and arranged them in hierarchies of beauty, merit, and worth. Those taxonomies and their discourses of geographical and biological determinism were exertions of imperial powers long before the (European) Enlightenment and humanism, the rise of the nation-state, mercantile capitalism, and imperialism and colonialism.

In the United States during the colonial period we find precedents of American Indian land alienation, deployment of Indian, African, and women's labor, controls over African women's sexuality and reproductive capacities, racialized citizenship and its rights, and patriarchy and gender relations. Those discourses and practices of race, gender, sexuality, class, and nation, composing the social formation, produced the postcolonial nation: the United States. Because it is formative in the constitution of the US nation-state the colonial period deserves our examination.

In colonial Virginia the first racialized law was enacted in 1639, some thirty-two years after the colony's founding and twenty years after the first Africans arrived, to produce race, gender, sexuality, and nation by denying African men guns and ammunition. The act called on the colony to provide arms to all persons "except Negroes." Guns in hunting supplied meat or provisions provided by men for their heterosexual families, and the force of arms took land from and defended the colony against Indians, the duties and rights of citizens. "Except Negroes" thereby invented and installed distinctions of race as well as gender, sexuality, and nation.

Four years later, in 1643, colonial Virginia sought to regulate the labor of African women by levying a tithe or tax on African, not European women. That head tax was designed to coax African women's productive labor outside the household to earn their keep. European women, although mostly indentured at the time, were ideally destined as wives of European men and confined to the domestic sphere and were thus shielded from the tax. Although racialized and gendered, the 1643 law sought to control and exploit labor (class), specifically African women's labor, revealing the multiple pivots of that act.[24]

Extending that logic during the 1670s and perhaps indicative of a swelling class of the unemployed, a poll tax was imposed on all men over the age of sixteen—white, black, mulatto—and Indian women. Revealing in the statute's language are the presence of mulattoes in the colony, the result of what later became known as miscegenation, and Indian women. Also the exemption of European women from the tax on African and Indian women shows the hand of patriarchy based upon the ideals of white womanhood and the heterosexual, white family. The white woman remained the protected category.

In 1662 the Virginia Colony mandated that the children of African women inherit the condition of their mother, not their father, as was usual for Europeans. The statute, based upon the property rights of men over women, masters over slaves, reinforced the notion that slavery was inherited and thus a matter of birth, blood, and race. It also encouraged rape by white masters for the reproduction of a next generation of slaves and unfree, unpaid laborers. The 1662 act naturalized a racialized class position, the condition of bondage, and it moved the idea of race toward the one-drop rule for blacks and alleged purity for whites.[25] Produced by the act were race, gender, sexuality, class, and nation and their intersections inscribed on the bodies of African women and their children. Maryland made those demarcations clear with its 1664 law forbidding interracial marriage *and* defining slavery as a lifetime condition.

Free land, paid for by the alienation of Indian lands, and free labor, purchased in African bondage, comprising the means and relations of production, were the gifts of race, gender, sexuality, class, and nation. Those ties of discourse and material conditions were simply reiterated when a 1669 Virginia court found that Anthony Johnson was "a Negroe" and *by consequence* "an alien" or noncitizen. Antonio, an enslaved African, arrived in Virginia Colony in 1621, shortly after the first Africans landed. There he worked for a master on a tobacco plantation along the James River, and about a year later he was among the five survivors of the fifty-seven on the Bennett plantation after a Powhatan Indian attack. Over the next twenty years Antonio became Anthony; he married an enslaved African woman, Mary; and together they had four children. Anthony and Mary Johnson gained their freedom during the 1640s and farmed some 250 acres on the colony's eastern shore. They kept cattle and had two African servants. In 1669 a settler jury of white men ruled that Anthony Johnson was black and thus an alien and as a result could not deed land to his son. Instead the jury awarded the property to a white settler.[26] Herein race and citizenship and with it property rights intersect such that white and citizen and black and alien formed exclusive and polar pairs, albeit linked in that privilege accrued from poverty.

Amid discontent in Virginia Colony over declining tobacco prices, a perceived need for more land, anxieties over white manhood and property rights, and additional restrictions on slaves and servants, Nathaniel Bacon mobilized those grievances into a movement and then rebellion, as we saw. For several months in 1675 and 1676 Bacon fashioned a coalition united in a hatred of Indians, a desire for more land, and a restoration of patriarchal honor and rights. With a force of four hundred armed men, English and African, landowners and servants and slaves, they pressed Virginia's governor from Jamestown to the sea, from whence he sailed for England and returned with reinforcements.

The revolt ended after Bacon died from dysentery in October 1676 and by the force of English troops, but the movement achieved its goals of property and rights. Land, the colony's rulers declared, was a right of white men or citizens, and not of Africans or Indians who were aliens. White women, as the dependents of white men, belonged to their husbands and fathers. As a consequence the rebellion in which claims over land found expression in disregard of racial or class lines was used by Virginia Colony to buttress the divide between whites and blacks, men and women. The colony's laws and practices gave coherence to what was at first an amorphous set of beliefs around race, gender, sexuality, class, and citizenship. The institutionalization of those social categories throughout the seventeenth century, social formation theory points out, accompanied the growing need for plantation land and labor.[27]

In 1705 Virginia's colonizers deployed racialized religion to determine that Indians and Africans, not being Christians, were "incapable in law" and were thus excluded from the courts to testify for or against Europeans or citizens. The use of the word *Christians* was racialized as white because Africans and Indians could convert to Christianity, as they did, but were still incapable in law. Racialized religion resonates throughout US and world history down to our present moment. In the late nineteenth century, as we learned, Christianity was synonymous with civilization in Kaiser Wilhelm II's call to defend Europe's "holiest possession," and that juxtaposition of Christian/European civilization against anti-Christian/Asian civilization reappears in the twentieth and twenty-first centuries. The 1705 Virginia statute rendered Africans and Indians incapable in law and placed them beyond the reach of membership and rights.

In 1854 Asians and Pacific Islanders, as nonwhites, joined Indians and Africans in that disqualification. California's chief judge Hugh Murray ruled in the case of *The People v. George W. Hall* (1854), in which Hall, "a free white citizen of this State," was convicted of murder on the testimony of Chinese witnesses. California's law specifies, the chief judge recalled, "no Indian or Negro shall be allowed to testify as a witness in any action in which a White person is a party." The intent of the law was to shield the "European white man" from the testimony of "the degraded and demoralized caste," such as "the Negro, fresh from the coast of Africa, or the Indian of Patagonia, the Kanaka, South Sea Islander, or New Hollander." The citizen or white person was entitled to the "protection for life and property," in a reference to the Constitution, whereas those "not of white blood" or "black, yellow, and all other colors" were excluded from that guarantee and protection.[28]

A mere three years later that racialized citizenship was clearly articulated by Chief Justice Roger Taney, who delivered the majority opinion in the *Dred Scott v. John F. A. Sandford* (1857) decision. As the chief justice put it, the question before the Court was simply this: "Can a negro, whose ancestors were imported into this country, and sold as slaves, become a member of the political community formed . . . by the Constitution . . . and as such become entitled to the rights, and privileges, and immunities, guaranteed by that instrument to the citizen?" American Indians, he reasoned, were a free and independent people but "under subjection to the white race," and Africans were "regarded as beings of an inferior order, and altogether unfit to associate with the white race, either in social or political relations; and so far inferior, that they had no rights which the white man was bound to respect." Moreover, Taney contended, the 1790 Naturalization Act affirmed Congress's intention to limit citizenship to free white persons and not extend it to American Indians, who were members of alien nations, or Africans, who were slaves and thus property. The distance and distinction, he concluded, was clear between "the citizen race," or whites, and "persons of color" or those "not included in the word citizens" and who were of "another and different class of persons."

Asians were the last among that class "not included in the word citizens" to gain admittance into the "citizen race," and among Asians, Japanese were the last admitted, in 1952. Rendered "aliens ineligible to citizenship" since 1790, as we know, Asians were denied real property and relegated to the laboring class in most western states; their testimonies were excluded from cases involving whites; and although subject to US laws, they could not participate in the public sphere, like women and dependents. Women citizens who married alien men after 1907 and Asian men or "aliens ineligible to citizenship" after 1922 lost their US citizenship.[29] Those laws, though repealed in 1931, regulated Asians on the basis of race, gender, sexuality, and nation. The alienation of Asians from US society was justified on the basis of their biology and the discourses of race, gender, and sexuality, which disqualified them from full membership in the nation-state.

The foundational Naturalization Act of 1790, cited by Chief Justice Taney in *Dred Scott*, defines the citizen as a free white person and therewith produces race, gender, sexuality, class, and nation. The modern nation-state, as we know, was founded upon the principle of sovereignty, which involves the definition of the nation's territory and subjects or peoples called races. The word *nation*, meaning "birth," indicates blood relation, which in turn is an attribute of race; common descent, then, whether real of fictive, determines a nation's people or race.[30] As described by John Jay, a founding father and the first chief justice of the Supreme Court, Americans were "one united people—a people descended from the same ancestors, speaking the same language, professing the same religion, attached to the same principles of government, very similar in their manners and customs."[31]

With the rise of republicanism, subjects became citizens who participated in the political process because of their qualities, sometimes called natures (virtues). Those ideas derived from ancient Greece, in which inhabitants of city-states, the polis, were men who occupied the public sphere because they possessed civic virtues, unlike women and aliens. The public sphere was a place where rulers and citizens met to debate and discuss matters of rule. The attributes of gender, then, formed a dividing line for citizenship. In the United States since the nation's founding, white women were citizens, but, as dependents of white men, they were without the full rights of citizenship. Women's voting rights came over a hundred years later, in 1920.

A quality of citizenship and under capitalism, property is the cornerstone of the economy and state. Possessions, both real (land) and material, including objects and people such as wives, children, and slaves, conferred virtues, citizenship, rights, civic participation, and full manhood. Property qualifications for voting or engagement in the public sphere were repealed in the mid-nineteenth century, but their existence throughout the colonial and postcolonial periods attests to their significance in the formation of the US nation-state. Property conveyed freedom insofar as ownership was the basis for individualism and (economic) self-determination.[32] *Propriety* in our time still conveys virtuous conduct.

Propertied white men conjured throughout much of US history the virtues of race, gender, sexuality, class, and nation. Conversely nonwhites were denied real property and, in fact, constituted property. As we have seen, American Indians in *Johnson v. M'Intosh* (1823) could not possess land, and African Americans in *Dred Scott* (1857) were deemed to be property. Alien land laws denied Asian Americans landownership as "aliens ineligible to citizenship." Those binary oppositions in the social formation manufactured property and rights through dispossession and a denial of rights. Insofar as whiteness confers rights and privileges, which are values and assets that their owners could use and enjoy, whiteness is property.[33] In sum and as intersecting relations, whiteness was purchased by nonwhiteness, manhood by dependency, heterosexuality by deviancy, property by property disqualification, and citizenship by alienation.

| | |

While far from exhaustive, the foregoing history of laws and the creation of the US social formation illustrates the interlocking systems of oppression inclusive of race, gender, sexuality, class, and nation. Rarely solitary, those constructed spheres implicate one another and expand and contract depending upon their environments and times. Resistances by the oppressed against those articulations of power are, like power itself, diffuse, influential, multivocal, and persistent. In countless acts both individual and collective, the oppressed contested their states of oppression in the courts, through social movements and political campaigns, as workers in fields and factories, in schools, and in everyday life around language and ideologies. The dialectic of oppression and resistance stimulates change and movement in the social formation, exposing the locations and articulations of power and revealing the insufficiency of totalizing systems and the possibility of agency.

Summary

Although race makes the headlines, Third World feminism and its capacious, prescient articulation of intersecting oppressions hold greater explanatory value for Third World studies. The Third World feminist insight that the major systems of oppression are interlocking, we must remember, emerges from integrated analysis and the conditions of lived lives. Social formation theory arises from that union of theory and experience, engages oppression within the confines of its discourses, but only as a strategic necessity, and aspires to replace those tools with entirely new languages, ideologies, and practices not of the ruling class to map and clear out a common ground for solidarities across the taxonomies and environments that divide and rule.

NINE

SYNTHESES

Third World studies is the discourse and practice of liberation. Its subjects are the oppressed, the world's masses, especially of the Third World, and not we, the people of the US Constitution. That instrument in fact limited citizenship and rights to "free white persons." Instead of pursuing civil rights for inclusion within that white settler nation-state, students of the Third World Liberation Front aligned themselves with the people of the Third World, colonial and postcolonial subjects yearning, striving for freedom. Third World liberation descends from that "problem of the twentieth century," the stirring of colonized peoples against their colonial masters and former masters. The anticolonial movement, articulated as antiracism and self-determination or discursive and material freedoms, pushed back against some four hundred years of world history, during which European empires had spread over the planet. Third World studies comprises an aspect of that global revolution and involves the creation of, through struggle, "a new language, a new ideology, a new world consciousness."

That achievement, as we have seen, requires a mastery of the discourses of the ruling class, a strategic necessity, to engage and end oppression. But it also demands discourses and relations not of the master's design. The former, deploying the master's tools to dismantle his house, is the first step and occupies most of my discussion of Third World studies. The latter, the articulation of new languages, ideologies, and practices, was begun by Third World feminists, is the intention of social formation theory, and is the future of Third World studies. That comprehensive work of deconstruction and reconstruction has just begun. But we are not without shoulders upon which to stand; post-1968 ethnic studies and its related fields, feminist and queer studies in particular, have extended the Third World studies horizon in their efforts to locate and understand the workings of power. That apprehension, in turn, can point the way to liberation.

If divide and rule is a principal strategy of power, then syntheses can work against those expressions of power. In this final chapter I provide two syntheses that illustrate the bordered and borderless worlds of race, gender, sexuality, class, and nation. The first synthesis surveys ideas from and practices in feminist and queer theories and post-1968 ethnic studies that elucidate the subjects of Third World studies. The second supplies an intellectual history to situate Third World studies and restate the connections between theory and practice, discourse and practice in the formations of nation and race, imperialism and colonialism, and modernity and postmodernity.

Synthesis One

This first synthesis connects Third World studies with feminist and queer theory and follows the threads that link the four, now divided fragments of post-1968 ethnic studies: African American, Asian American, Latinx, and Native American studies. We are a kindred people united by oppression and exploitation, although rendered separate by the distinctions of race, gender, sexuality, class, and nation. Our alienations and incapacities, discursive and material, locate power and its articulations and are a measure of our subjugation.

GENDER AND SEXUALITY

Feminist and queer theories appear throughout this text, especially in our consideration of intersectionality, subjectivity, and experience and on giving voice. An important additional concept is the idea of *performance* as advanced by the US continental philosopher and critical theorist Judith Butler. In *Gender Trouble* (1999), Butler considers Julia Kristeva's critique of Lacan's phallocentrism and observes that Kristeva falls short because she accepts Lacan's biological explanation for language. Instead, Butler argues, Foucault's insight that sexuality is not anatomy or nature but is historically constituted in place and time and by culture supplies a more fundamental deconstruction of Lacan. Following Foucault, man and woman, heterosexual and homosexual are not differentiated by biology but by discourse; gender and sexuality accordingly implicate power and power relations and are made and performed. As

Simone de Beauvoir noted in *Second Sex* (1949), Butler reminds us, women are not born, they are made; women are a "cultural accomplishment."[1] The French writer, lesbian, and feminist theorist Monique Wittig adds that "man" is the unmarked self and only "woman" is sexed.

Although we might disagree with some of the implications embraced by those ideas, that discussion of discourse and subjectivities surely deserves our full consideration. For example, Wittig extends her point of normative man and deviant, sexualized woman to the lesbian, who, as a "third sex," is neither man nor woman. While biology might manufacture a unitary, discursive field of gender and sexuality, she argues, language is the site of the creation of those physical bodies made real and normal through enactments and performances.[2] Those ideas about discourse and subjectivities suggest that race, like gender and sexuality, is a discourse and performance.

Many of the understandings of self and society form parallels in feminist and Third World studies, for instance, the biological versus the social contrasts of the real and conjured, like materiality and discourse, sex and gender, sex and sexuality, race and racial formation, and identity and subjectivity. Substance and positivism inhabit the former of those binaries; the latter, language, ideology, and poststructuralism. Feminism and Third World studies have gravitated toward the explanations of discourse and poststructuralism while arguing that the distinctions are false choices and are, in fact, seamlessly connected in that practices materialize discourses. Race, gender, and sex are made, and bi- and multiracials, bi- and transgenders, and bi- and transsexuals embody the verity of continuities.[3] Invented oppositions and border-crossing prohibitions implicate power, and binaries and their regulations constitute oppression.[4]

Additionally feminist and Third World studies share a move from liberalism to radicalism and from a single to a multiple frame of analysis. First-wave feminists were mainly suffragists like Elizabeth Cady Stanton and Susan B. Anthony. Their cause was the vote for white women, which they achieved in 1920 with passage of the Nineteenth Amendment. Like the Seneca Falls Convention (1848) and National Woman Suffrage Association (1869) that advocated white women's equality with white men, the Niagara Movement (1905) and National Association for the Advancement of Colored People (1910) sought to end racial segregation and to promote equality among the races. Those liberal ideas of gender and racial equality reemerged in the 1960s with the women's and civil rights movements.

Second-wave feminism saw "woman" as its subject matter, while civil rights discourse embraced race as its object of analysis. Betty Friedan's *Feminist Mys-*

tique (1963) and the National Organization of Women (1966) were inspired by "the problem with no name," the persistent problem of discrimination against white women. Martin Luther King Jr. and his Southern Christian Leadership Conference scored racial discrimination and segregation and advocated civil rights, equality under the law, and citizenship within the nation-state. Both movements succeeded in having laws passed to render illegal gender and racial discrimination, resulting in the so-called postfeminist and post–civil rights eras, when, presumably, gender- and color-blindness prevails. Differences have led to inequality, some propose, and sameness will result in equality.

In the 1970s critical thinkers focused on power and expanded the purview of feminist theory through class and Marxist analyses, and Third World women denied the essentialism of the universal woman by pointing to intersectionality and the particularities of race, cultures, imperialism, and colonization.[5] Sexuality is a key for many of those intellectuals, both third-wave feminists and Third World women, because their subject positions were multiply expressed. Adrienne Rich, the US poet and feminist, wrote from her experience as a lesbian, characterizing "compulsory heterosexuality" as a violent political institution created by men to establish and claim their sexual and property rights over and access to women. Lesbianism in that environment is an act of resistance against the norms and privileges of gender, sexuality, and class.[6]

Power, not difference, is the principal analytical category for radical feminists of the third wave and Third World theorists. Marxism, revolution, and anti-imperialism worldwide were the driving forces behind that realization and surge. For those intellectuals and activists, race, gender, sexuality, class, and nation are socially produced, historical, contingent, contextual, relational, and contested.

POST-1968 ETHNIC STUDIES

Post-1968 ethnic studies, while a companion, also departs from critical feminist and queer theories. As ethnic studies, the field's distinction was its focus on race and the US racial formation. Further, as we know, post-1968 ethnic studies separated into subfields of African American, Asian American, Latina/o, and Native American studies largely on the basis of self-determination. That is, each group reserved the right to speak for and to itself. For many of the field's founders, the black/white racial binary was the dominant relation of race, while the others, nonblacks and nonwhites, composed ethnic or cultural groups worthy of heritage celebrations but of little consequence to the principal order of race. As we saw, San Francisco State College administrators and faculty named and considered ethnic studies in that way, a field for blacks and nonblack, ethnic others. Some scholars understand the histories of those nonblack, ethnic others as derivative of the African American experience; the full weight of oppression fell on black bodies, they hold, and lesser measures spilled over to those on the sidelines.

All binaries, social formation theory informs us, are creations of power to divide and therewith rule. Rulers have used the black/white binary at least since Bacon's Rebellion (1675–76), a class uprising of whites and blacks for patriarchal and citizenship rights over lands and goods held by American Indians. Clearly the black/white binary fails to explain those origins and the consequences of the rebellion that institutionalized white freedom over black and American Indian alienation and bondage, involving race but also gender, class, and nation. When power foregrounds the black/white binary, as seen in the 1968 formation of ethnic studies and in contemporary US social relations, whites and blacks become visible, while nonblack, nonwhite others—Asians, Latinx, and Native Americans—disappear or are assimilated and essentialized into whiteness or blackness. Binaries are creations of the self in relation to its other and thus are acts of power to reserve privilege for the self through dominion over the other.

Third World studies accordingly departs from post-1968 ethnic studies and its focus on race and, for some, its embrace of the primacy of the black/white binary.[7] The locations and articulations of power in society broadly are the subject of Third World studies. Moreover the US nation-state is not the originating site of Third World studies; the world is. Even as Third World studies benefits from the insights of feminist and queer theories, the emerging field subscribes to many of the ideas of post-1968 ethnic studies, including racial formation theory. While hardly exhaustive, I highlight a few of the theoretical advances made by African American, Asian American, Latina/o, and Native American studies that remain vital concepts for Third World studies.

| | |

As we understand it, Third World studies begins with European imperialism and conquest of the world. That spread was both discursive and material, involving taxonomies that named, described, and ranked lands and waters, peoples, and all life forms on the planet. That mastery was also materially achieved through conquest, colonization, and the expropriation of resources, labor, and culture. The United States started as a periphery and settler colony of England and, as such, was designed to extract wealth for the benefit of capital in Europe. The base of that settler colony was American Indian land worked by American Indian, European, and African labor. Tilled land produced wealth, mainly tobacco, for export to companies in England, and that pattern, repeated throughout the Third World, eventuated into capitalism's world-system. Capital, labor, and culture coursed through the system to enrich the core at the expense of the peripheries. Relatedly, development of the core and underdevelopment of the periphery were designed and structured, constituting the spaces and workings of Third World studies.

In the United States, including island possessions in the Caribbean and Pacific, the settler colonists claimed native lands on the bases of conquest and instruments of dispossession. Land thereby became possessions and, as such, held value under capitalism. Laws protected those properties held by the citizen race and white men. Those same property rights extended over women and enslaved Africans, who, after the decline of European indentures, provided the main source of labor for the plantations of the New World. After the end of the African slave trade and slavery, Latinx and indentured Asians supplied the labor for America's plantations and mines. In sum, in the United States, which is simply one locus of Third World studies, Native Americans supplied the land, and Asians and Latinx joined African Americans in the fields and factories of the social formation, constituting the means and relations of production.

Despite being of the same class, Third World peoples in the United States were segregated by race, gender, and nation. Again divide and rule was the design of oppression. After the late nineteenth century, African Americans joined the ranks of free, citizen labor even as they held diminished rights as citizens and workers. Asians and Latinx were classed as bound, alien labor and were deployed to retard African American mobility and threaten white workers. Additionally white and nonwhite labor was divided by gender, whereby men held better positions and received higher wages than women and children, who were dependents of men. Considering those impediments to working-class solidarity, the instances of solidarity among that oppressed class are remarkable.

| | |

A spatial consciousness of community is one of the more important ideas of African American studies for Third World studies. Consider the immense distances embraced by the African continent and its islands, together with

Africa's richly diverse languages and cultures; Africa and the African are European essentialisms and dispersals. So *pan-Africanism* is a brilliant, liberating concept and subjectivity that turns European hegemony against itself. At the same time we understand pan-Africanism as another essentialism that removes specificities and retards national liberation, as Fanon points out. Still, to mobilize a resistance movement in the oppressor's language and name is a remarkable and liberating idea, albeit a strategic essentialism but a necessary first step toward greater freedoms.

Studies of pan-Africanism depict it as a movement of ideas and emotions, and they trace a topography of the insurgency that erupts in the diaspora, not in Africa, and circulates, like the Atlantic triangle, among Europe, America, and Africa. As we saw, pan-Africanism's intellectual foundation rests upon the idea and consciousness called *négritude* by the Martinican poet Aimé Césaire.[8] The Senegalese poet Léopold Senghor described négritude as "the sum of the cultural values of the black world" and "rooting oneself in oneself, and self-confirmation: confirmation of one's being."[9] The context of that rooting was the uprooting of African history, bodies, and subjectivities by European colonizers. Africa had no history, Europeans charged, and Africans had no culture; before Europeans, Africa was mired in stasis and barbarism. Europe stirred Africa, giving it movement, and Christianized and civilized the Dark Continent's peoples. Educated in Paris, Césaire, Senghor, and other black intellectuals voiced a countersentence in the colonizers' tongue. Négritude, they proclaimed, distills the qualities indigenous to Africa before the destruction brought by Europeans, and blackness is an affirmative subjectivity that unites Africans worldwide, disavows assimilation, and opposes colonialism and inhumanity.

Pan-Africanism, it is important to remember, arose in the African diaspora among Western-educated intellectuals in conversation with the discourses of imperialism. Displacement and exile, the sense of a lost past and subjectivity robbed, and ambivalence toward the West fired a pride of color and black solidarity and a determination to reclaim the African past. African liberation movements called for national independence and Africa for Africans, and the First Pan-African Congress in London (1900) called for solidarity along the color line and self-determination and antiracism. As the Jamaican Marcus Garvey, founder of the Universal Negro Improvement Association in Harlem, made plain, the movement for dignity was a contest over power. Pan-Africanism as a discourse and political movement aimed to advance the people's agency and dignity as a global community.

Those pan-Africanist discourses and practices engaged Africans in America, Europe, and Africa, and although articulated by black intellectuals in the core, they were intended to mobilize the nonwhite masses of Africa and the Third World. Like Africans, a race invented by Europeans, Asians and Americans (Indians) are European essentialisms that homogenize nations, histories, and cultures often at odds with each other. Using the master's tools to dismantle his house, Third World peoples have deployed the taxonomies of oppression to resist colonization and dependency in pan-African, pan-Asian, pan-American, and pan-Indian movements in the United States and the world.

Asian American history intersects with the African American past in the world-system of labor, as we have seen, in the transition from African slaves to Asian coolies. Theorizing *migrant labor* is probably the most important project of Asian American studies for Third World studies.[10] The US sociologists Lucie Cheng and Edna Bonacich lay the foundations for that understanding. Migrant labor, they explain, is an element and product of the world-system. Migrant labor is not immigration. As a study of migrant workers in Western Europe indicates, immigration falls under race relations, while migrant labor arises from a critique of international capitalism. Race relations studies assimilation, or how immigrants become citizens within the nation-state, whereas migrant labor circulates within the capitalist world-system. The former follows the consensus model in that immigrants melt into a new whole, while the latter follows the conflict model, wherein race, class, gender, and nation divide and collide.[11]

In the United States Asian migrant laborers illustrate the utility of the theory. Starting in the 1840s Chinese worked the mines, railroads, and farms in the West and, mirroring the requirements of those industries, were overwhelmingly men. Women were less than ideal because, while reproduction enabled the next generation of laborers, children born in the United States were, unlike their parents, citizens under the Fourteenth Amendment. A workforce of mainly men therefore, coupled with miscegenation laws, controlled Asians' birthrates, thereby limiting their presence and curtailing their political influence in the United States. In 1875 under the Page Act, we know, Asian women migrants were barred from entering the United States, reducing further the numbers of children and citizens.

Migrant labor worked best when migrants moved, following the seasons, and when they were no longer useful returned to Asia. Asians, since 1790 classified as "aliens ineligible to citizenship," were easily denied rights and were thus eminently exploitable. In 1882 the United States excluded Chinese (men) workers, we recall, signaling the end of their utility to their employers. Prior to the 1875 and 1882 exclusions, there were no national immigration laws;

there were no illegal immigrants before the late nineteenth century, when northern European immigration prevailed. When the "wretched refuse" of Emma Lazarus's poem on the Statue of Liberty turned a darker hue, the state, guided by the science of eugenics, imposed "national quotas" to limit their numbers. The Immigration and Nationality Act (1924) favored Anglo-Saxons with annual quotas of 65,721 (Britain) and 25,957 (Germany) while discriminating against southern Europeans (5,802 from Italy; 307 from Greece). Least favored were Africans, Asians, and Pacific Islanders, with annual quotas of about 100. In addition, to monitor the flow of southern and eastern Europeans, Asians, and Mexicans, the state established the Bureau of Immigration (1891) and Border Patrol (1925), and, as we saw, the US census began to count Asians (1870) and Mexicans (1930).

US immigration laws regulated Asian and Mexican migrant labor. In the 1880s, after the exclusion of Chinese laborers, Japanese migrants replaced them in Hawai'i and along the West Coast. The Gentlemen's Agreement (1908) restricted Japanese workers, and, following a period of South Asian migration, the "Barred Zone" Act (1917) limited their entry. The Literacy Act (1917) reduced Mexican migrants by requiring a literacy test and an eight-dollar head tax. Beginning in the early 1900s Filipino migrants were recruited to supplant the Japanese, but in 1934 they too faced exclusion. Mexican migrants worked with Japanese and Filipinos in the West's fields, and during the Great Depression Filipinos and Mexicans were "repatriated." Excess or idle labor was not part of the design for migrant labor.

| | |

Mexican American or Chicana/o studies, like Asian American studies, centers on that idea of migrant labor. Fences at national borders, whether along the Atlantic and Pacific Oceans or along continental expanses, produce the migrant and the illegal and withhold and confer national membership and rights. Largely because of the prominence of the border in Chicana/o studies, the field is notable for theorizing those borderlands that constitute the subject. As Gloria Anzaldúa, the originator of *borderlands theory*, put it, the US border with Mexico is an "unnatural" boundary and a "third country," holding stabilizing as well as destabilizing potential.[12] That topography of displacement and loss is also a mapping of affirmation, locating not merely separations but connections as well. Borderlands are alive with crossings that produce hybrid peoples, languages, and subjectivities that repudiate polarities, the insular nation-state, and the distinctions between the periphery and core. Like postcolonial theory, binaries do not inhabit those borderlands, and movement, not stasis, animates and actualizes new, myriad bodies and formations.

Enlightening is Anzaldúa's account of the origins of borderlands theory.[13] The place was Vermont in the dead of winter. Displaced was the author, Anzaldúa, at Norwich University in an alien environment among an alien people. She is the center—working-class, lesbian, racial-minority woman—and her home is the borderlands; she is the familiar while Vermont's America is the strange, her alien other. She writes to return home, seeking solace in words. Her explication of borderlands, Anzaldúa declares, is to produce knowledge (when European high theory silences intellectuals of color as incapable) and to spread an understanding of Chicanas/os in her way, in her language, which is "mestiza style," or code-switching in a mobile tongue of English, Spanish, Spanglish, *pocho, chola/o*, and back again. Such writing, she concedes, requires faith and stubbornness because of constant disparagement and rejection from Anglo and Chicano "malestream." Her intention nonetheless is to push against all boundaries, which divide and oppress.

Space, the land is at the heart of borderlands theory. As Anzaldúa reminds us in poetic, not narrative form (the former eliciting freedom; the latter structure):

> The land
> was Mexican once
> was Indian always
> and is.
> And will be again.[14]

Native American studies, foremost, compels us to consider the geographies of power. Indigeneity and sovereignty bespeak those spatial domains. Unlike the world-system of possession and dispossession, indigenous peoples populate not the Third but the Fourth World.[15] The Fourth World is without national borders; it is unbounded.[16] Native peoples share that Fourth World; land and, for island natives, the seas are inalienable and managed for the common good. Indigeneity references those differences in epistemologies and worldviews; the land/seas and people are undivided, they are related discursively and materially. People emerge from the land/seas that sustain them and interpellate their subjectivities. Ways of knowing are spiritual, mysteries of the eternal (time) and unbounded (space). Discursive self-determination, then, involves a decolonization of the mind to cleanse it from the polluting languages and ideologies of the colonizers.[17]

Some in Native American studies have cited indigeneity and sovereignty

The Fourth World. When seen from space, our planet has no borders. Photo from NASA.

as the features that separate their field from post-1968 ethnic studies. Third World studies, however, considers all Third World peoples as inhabitants of the Fourth World, a borderless world, and all were subjected to the discourses and material conditions created and imposed by European imperialism. Indigeneity's sacred affiliation with the land/seas and its spatial consciousness of the Fourth World appear to contradict the claims to sovereignty. As we learned, sovereignty is a European concept that, in the name of self-determination, delineates nation-states with borders, rulers, and peoples and races. Sovereignty distinguishes spaces and confers power, underwriting the imperialism that conquered, exploited, and oppressed indigenous peoples of the Third World.

In the United States sovereignty justified the nation-state and its extensions across the continent and overseas, eventuating in Native American dispossession. At first the state considered American Indians as constituting sovereign nations with treaty rights (Treaty of Greenville, 1795) and Hawaiians as members of the Hawaiian Kingdom. Imperialism and the absorption of land and peoples, we learned, reduced American Indians to "domestic dependent nations" that required federal wardship and plenary rule, and, with US aid, whites overthrew the Hawaiian queen (1893) and the United States annexed the islands (1898). "Termination" sought the end of American Indian sovereignty, and for some Indians extinction demanded the restoration of sovereignty as the means of survival and self-determination. Many Hawaiians similarly subscribe to that strategy.

At the same time Native Americans have shown us some of the pitfalls of the national turn in post-1968 ethnic studies and Third World liberation movements. Sovereignty is an imperial, not an indigenous or Third World discourse and practice. Membership in the nation-state can but will not ultimately lead to liberation, and human, not civil rights pursued before international and not national bodies pave alternative paths toward self-determination. Survival is a human, not a civil right. Moreover indigenous and Third World discourses can articulate languages and ideologies not of the ruling world order. Instead of the conquest and appropriation of the environment, they teach us the verity of our kinship with the land, water, and all animate and inanimate forms. They soar on the wings of the imagination and have us view from space our true home—the Fourth World—absent boundaries or distinctions between waters, lands, and nations. Our earth and its peoples are indeed one.

Synthesis Two

In this intellectual history of Third World studies I point to the relations between discourse and material conditions and the fictions of equivalences such as multiculturalism and Third World studies and postcolonialism and post-1968 ethnic studies. As we understand it in Third World studies, the material base of the world-system is capitalism that began as mercantile capitalism such as pursued by Italian city-states of the eleventh and twelfth centuries. Mercantile capitalism advanced to industrial and monopoly capitalism in the eighteenth and nineteenth centuries, to finance and international capitalism in the twentieth century, and to transnational capitalism in the twenty-first century.

Political expressions of those material bases include the city-state (Italy) and sovereign nation-state (Europe), arising from mercantile capitalism. Imperialism and extensions of sovereignty to extraterritorial colonies emerged from industrial and monopoly capitalism. International bodies such as the League of Nations and United Nations, founded on the principle of the sovereign nation-state, accompanied finance and international capitalism, and, some believe, a new world order and empire based on juridical authority is emerging from transnational capitalism. Enabling and driving those regimes of material relations are discourses.

Sovereignty and the nation or race are foundational discourses of the nation-state. Imperialism reduced nation or race to empire or race in the encounter with non-European others in the Third World. As Kaiser Wilhelm II proposed in his fear of the "yellow peril," the nations of Europe were united on the bases of civilization and Christianity against the immanent, threatening forces of savagery and barbarism. Enlightenment ideas of humanism and positivism, both deemed universal, upheld the primacy of the (European) individual and the triumph of (European) science over nature. As imperial sciences, taxonomy disciplined an unruly world, imposing order; structuralism explained society; and modernity justified colonization and the world-system.

Contrarily anticolonialism and the twentieth century's color line deployed (European) humanism and its values of self-determination and racial equality to counter colonial discourses and material relations. Following independence, Third World liberation devolved into nationalisms and nation-states as ends in themselves, thereby aligning with the ruling internationalism, multilateralism of nation-states. The states of disorder exemplified by the internecine wars between white brothers, the First and Second World Wars, prompted the internationalism that followed in their wake and was designed to restore order and avoid the spectacle of whites and nonwhites killing whites. Disillusionment with positivism, structuralism, and modernism prompted another discursive turn that recognized fragmentation, multiplicity, fluidity, contingency, and indeterminacy in those states of disunity. Critical theory, deconstruction, poststructuralism, and postmodernism reflect and explain those conditions and environments.

MULTICULTURALISM

Two dominant ideas, multiculturalism and postcolonialism, require our consideration because of their associations with Third World studies. The former is an imposter and the latter a pretender that blunts the transformative edge of Third World studies. Recall the cultural turn to (post-1968) ethnic studies at the formation of Third World studies in 1968. (Chicago) ethnic studies led the move from race to culture (ethnicity) and cultural pluralism. Multiculturalism, though, is as old as the US republic itself, embraced by the eighteenth-century myth of the "American," this new man who eschews old, European traditions and embraces unique American traits of rugged individualism, democracy, and meritocracy. The late nineteenth century's unprecedented immigration altered that myth to become the "melting pot," wherein a mind-boggling diversity of cultures melded with the "native" majority to produce the "new American." In the aftermath of the Nazi white supremacist experiment and in the midst of internationalism, decolonization, and talk of universal brotherhood, ethnicity supplanted race as the principal divide of the postwar twentieth century. Pluralism and an appreciation of cultural diversity promised relief from race riots in the United States and demands of Africa for Africans and Asia for Asians in the Third World. Whites too have ethnicities, and on that basis all are equal. "Many cultures, one US nation-state" is still the motto.

Multiculturalism is not Third World studies. It descends from race relations and the turn from race to ethnicity. Race relations studied colonial subjects and problem minorities to forestall their self-determination and keep them in their place of subservience to preserve social order. Chicago sociology's move from race relations to ethnic studies spawned at least three variants on the theme of ethnicity. *Multiculturalism*, or the celebration of cultural diversity and intercultural competence, is the most prominent of those offspring. The second variety affirms the *declining significance of race* and emphasizes class over culture.[18] Class divisions and the growing underclass explain, better than race or ethnicity, social hierarchies. The third sees a *postethnic America* in which hybridity is the norm and solution to conflicts arising from racial and ethnic differences.[19] The new face of America is a woman with the physical features of all races and cosmopolitan tastes.[20]

Those moves from race to ethnicity, class, and postethnicity are what racial formation theory critiques. In that critical sense racial formation theory converses with race relations, (Chicago) ethnic studies, multiculturalism, and the notions of the declining significance of race and postethnic America. Racial formation theory accordingly is a member of those discursive formations, albeit in opposition to them.

POSTCOLONIALISM

Like *poststructural* and *postmodern*, the "post" in *postcolonial* is a temporal marker that denotes "past" or "beyond," as in past structuralism, beyond modernity, and beyond colonialism.[21] As such "post" describes a condition or state derivative of the past and in anticipation of an indeterminate future. Displacing or succeeding past discourses, "post" theories reveal the limitations of the original and provide more robust explanations of social relations. Allied in their endorsement of multiplicity, fluidity, contingency, and indeterminacy, those critical theories direct their aim at discourses of structuralism, modernity, and colonialism and, as we observed, essentialisms and binaries and their spatial and temporal hierarchies.[22] As a conversation on colonialism, postcolonialism patterns its critique on colonial discourse. Herein colonialism is the organizing principle.

To wit, colonialism deploys race to divide and rule; postcolonialism rejects race and celebrates hybridity. Colonialism's positivism gives way to indeterminacy, structuralism to ambiguities and contradictions, modernity to disorder, and the global to the local.[23] Resistance at the local level erodes totalizing discourses and colonial hegemony, and continuities and multiplicities reveal the falsity of binaries. In that engagement we see the power of the sentence, which sets the parameters of the conversation, in the light of postcolonialism's countersentence. Postcolonialism responds in the negative to colonialism's affirmative claims and is thereby held in check by the prior discourse.

Moreover while postcolonialism vacates the nation-state as a bankrupt, European notion responsible for dictatorial, corrupt, and oppressive Third World nation-states, it fails to mobilize resistance to neocolonialism and dependency. Transnationalism or flight across borders, which is postcolonialism's answer to the nation-state, is also a feature of capitalism and culture and not an easy option for the oppressed masses, and postcolonialism's facile transits from core to periphery, colonizer to colonized diminish our ability to name and resist power, oppression, and the oppressor.

Postcolonialism's assertion that it supplanted Third World studies rests largely on its critique of the global color line and Third World struggles for self-determination and antiracism. What it neglects in its race to primacy is the efficacy of that history and the continuing explanatory power of structuralism's world-system, dependency, and neo- and internal colonial theories. A possible reason for its aversion to the collapsed Third World while purporting to speak for it is postcolonialism's deep and entangling roots in the language and ideologies of the West. Postcolonialism's major figures cut their intellectual teeth on European literatures and continental philosophy; they engage in conversation with those discourses; they inhabit and receive acclaim in academic sanctuaries of privilege in Europe and the United States; and they write for their peers and not the masses of the Third World. In the dense discourse of postcolonial theory, the subaltern cannot speak.

The postcolonial "condition" does not suggest struggle or engagements with power. Postcolonialism's celebration of hybridity, diversity, difference and alterity, and multiculturalism hints at its intellectual genealogy, and, like global capitalism, it thrives in environments of transnationalism, global localism, and multiplicities. A politics of location such as the discourse of difference can mask the vertical relations of power that locate privilege and poverty, ruler and the oppressed. Disillusionment over the Third World's embrace of the colonizers' patriarchal nation-state is merited on the basis of self-determination and choice, but it also testifies to colonized minds and neocolonialism and dependency. Despite their best intentions, Bandung and other Third World alliances succumbed to Bretton Woods (1944), the World Bank (1944), the International Monetary Fund (1945), the General Agreement on Tariffs and Trade (1947–48), and the World Trade Organization (1995). Through those means multinational and transnational corporations came to dominate the nation-state and world.[24]

Third World victims of capitalism's new world order are not the enemy or the problem, and exploitation and oppression still prey upon the teeming masses. Even as the Third World created material Europe during the four-hundred-year-old imperial reign of the colonial project, the Third World inspired not postcolonialism, which arose in the West, but the generation of anticolonial discourses. Colonialism in the Third World, the problem of the twentieth century, is the breeding ground for the discourse and practice of liberation, not Europe, Marxism, or poststructuralism. While Marxism dismissed the Third World as a place and people without history (agency), poststructuralism engaged French Marxism and post-Marxist theory.

Third World studies emerges from an intellectual genealogy at odds with race relations, ethnic studies, multiculturalism, and postcolonialism. Third World studies, as we know, originates within the Third World. Algeria and the French war against Algerian self-determination (1954–62) influenced many of the major figures cited in this introduction to Third World studies, including Althusser, Derrida, Fanon, and Sartre, together with Jean-François Lyotard and Hélène Cixous. Born in colonial Algeria, Cixous witnessed firsthand oppression, alterity, and exploitation, and her criticism of Freud's phallocentrism resonated with his declaration that the feminine was a dark, unexplored continent (Africa).[25] Racism and sexism populate Marx, Freud, and the imperial vision.

Instead of a temporal and spatial marker, the "post" in poststructuralism, postmodernity, and postcolonialism should speak against those discourses of rule. Likewise Third World studies should critique and oppose, discursively and materially, structuralism, modernity, and colonialism (a negative good) and advance alternative languages and ideologies to the master's tools (a positive good). In those ways Third World studies identifies oppression and exploitation while pointing the way toward self-determination and liberation.

Summary

The Third World, voiced exquisitely in the "final communiqué" radiating from Bandung, devolved into abject nationalisms of warring states, cultures, and discourses following the exemplar of nation-states and imperial dictates. In the United States national culture, perhaps best expressed as black (and brown, red, and yellow) power, mobilized even as it dispersed; divide and rule is a prominent arsenal of the ruling class in the social formation. Third World studies, while descending from that lineage of nationalism and sovereign nation-states, pursues a different path, thanks to the Third World women who insisted on the synthesis of multiple forms of oppression. Not singly or one above the other, they insightfully testified from their experiences, race, gender, sexuality, class, and nation compose the totality of their daily lives. That complex reality had no name prior to that articulation, and because of its utility for rule there was no language to express the particular nature of Third World women's oppression. In this text I name and theorize it as social formation.

As we began, Third World studies is not multiculturalism or (Chicago and post-1968) ethnic studies, identity politics or intellectual affirmative discrimination. The task of Third World studies is not the disuniting of America. Heritage months and cultural celebrations trivialize the work of Third World studies. In the twenty-first century the field in the United States faces challenges from those who would return to the founding proposition of one united people devoid of diversity, sharing a common language and culture. That nostalgia has roots in white supremacy. Others, starting with some of the founders of (post-1968) ethnic studies, see the field's value as a celebration of marginalized cultures to promote national inclusion and belonging. That liberal ideal of assimilation leaves intact US history and society, which were conceived in power and dedicated to the proposition of inequality; they require not reform but revolution and fundamental transformation.

Syntheses suggest a coming together as opposed to separations into discrete and often sovereign parts. Divide and rule, segregation is not an option here. Third World studies, I suggest, is a synthesis of related but disparate genesis, speaking European tongues to engage European ideologies in creolized languages. The empire strikes back with colonial mimicry and hybridity that can destabilize and undermine the univocal original;[26] crossings can, at the same time, signify hegemony and submission to the ruling class. The Third World also appropriated First World discourses of sovereignty, equality, and self-determination. As we saw, those syntheses liberated even as they circumscribed. Third-wave feminist theory intersects with Third World studies in locating power and its articulations, and queer theory teaches Third World studies to abandon the norm for the deviant.[27]

In that regard the so-labeled retarded, disabled, and freak, like inferior peoples, the bisexual, pervert, poor, and alien (race, gender, sexuality, class, and nation), were once regarded as degenerations and transgressions of nature, god, and civilization.[28] Third World people, as dependents like women and children, signified deprivation or lack in their incapacity to think, participate in law, own and transfer property, and become full-fledged citizens. As "curiosities" and like "freaks," Third World peoples and their bodily parts, especially genitals, were pornographically exhibited and inspected in salons, museums, world's fairs, and carnivals. In the seeing came the knowing, and in the knowing came possession. That link between deficient bodies, whether of race, gender, or class, and perverse sexualities applied to mental capacities wherein feeble-mindedness and sexual promiscuity demanded the sterilization of those "high-grade defectives,"[29] as in the US Supreme Court's ruling in *Buck v. Bell* (1927). Interestingly some of my best students in Third World studies have urged me to include ability as a category in social formation theory. I see their point.[30]

New syntheses, not the discourses of the master class, are the future of Third World studies, which must nonetheless arise from the foundations of the old. Liberation of and self-determination for the masses, not national sovereignty, should remain the discourse and practice of that new dispensation for Third World studies, while antiracism, the other solution to the problem of the twentieth century, should give way to ending all forms of oppression as produced in the social formation. Further, self-determination is not of the solitary self, as European humanism holds, but of the self in dialogue with society; the indigenous worldview of collective selves in kinship with all animate and inanimate forms expresses best, I believe, that new language and understanding of liberation. That borderless, shared Fourth World inhabited by custodians, not owners, testifies to the imagination and power of Third World studies.

NOTES

Introduction

1. I use the designation (post-1968) ethnic studies to distinguish this variety of ethnic studies from the earlier ethnic studies of the Chicago school of sociology, as I explain later in this introduction.
2. I subscribe to this nongendered form of Latina/o that implicates race, gender, sexuality, class, and nation and their intersections.

One. Subjects

1. "A Non-White Struggle toward New Humanism, Consciousness."
2. "An Interview with Pat Sumi," 259.
3. Hare, "The Battle for Black Studies," 33, 47.
4. Ferreira, "From College Readiness to Ready for Revolution!"
5. *Peninsula Observer*, January 20–27, 1969, cited in Ferreira, "From College Readiness to Ready for Revolution!," 123.
6. Hare, "The Battle for Black Studies," 33–34.
7. Mandela, *No Easy Walk to Freedom*, 163, 189.
8. Fanon, *The Wretched of the Earth*, 35–36, 311, 315.
9. Fanon, *The Wretched of the Earth*, 314.
10. Quoted in Kahin, *The Asian-African Conference.*
11. While revolutionary in the sense described, decolonization failed to end neocolonialism and European and US hegemony, as I explain in chapter 2.
12. The language of this statement draws heavily from the Black Students Union's principles written in late 1966 or early 1967. See Orrick, *Shut It Down!*, 108–9. The most comprehensive published account of the San Francisco State strike is Orrick, *Shut It Down!* See also eyewitness accounts by two San Francisco State students, Bill Barlow and Peter Shapiro, a San Francisco State faculty member, Robert Chrisman, and two University of California, Davis sociologists, James McEvoy and Abraham Miller, in McEvoy and Miller, *Black Power and Student Rebellion*, 12–31, 222–32, 277–97.

13. Memmi, *The Colonizer and the Colonized*, 147, 153; Fanon, *The Wretched of the Earth*, 246.

14. *Daily Gater*, May 22, 1969. For the location of the Third World Liberation Front within this context of Third World struggles and not the US civil rights movement, see Ferreira, "All Power to the People"; Maeda, *Chains of Babylon*.

15. Bloom and Martin, *Black against Empire*, 275.

16. On the complexities of the conference and the political stakes for Vietnamese and Third World women in the United States, see Wu, *Radicals on the Road*, 219–65.

17. *Asian Women*, 79, 80.

18. As first published in Du Bois, "The Freedmen's Bureau," 354. See Du Bois, "To the Nations of the World." See also Du Bois, *The Souls of Black Folk*, 10; Du Bois, "The Color Line Belts the World." Racists used similar language on the problem of the twentieth century. See, e.g., Stoddard, *The French Revolution in San Domingo*, vii; Stoddard, *The Rising Tide of Color against White World-Supremacy*, v–vii. Portions of this section appear in Okihiro, "Japan, World War II, and Third World Liberation."

19. Du Bois, "The African Roots of War." For a more contemporary analysis of colonialism and racism, see Miles, *Racism and Migrant Labour*; Miles, *Racism*.

20. Harrison, *When Africa Awakes*, 5, 6, 96–97.

21. Stoddard, *The Rising Tide of Color against White World-Supremacy*.

22. For an account of this conflict and the rise and fall of white men, see Lake and Reynolds, *Drawing the Global Colour Line*.

23. As represented in a commissioned painting. See *Review of Reviews* (London), December 1895, 474–75.

24. Zimmern, *The Third British Empire*, 82.

25. Du Bois, "The Color Line Belts the World," 30.

26. Thorne, "Racial Aspects of the Far Eastern War of 1941–1945," 336. See also Füredi, *The Silent War*, 29–30; Horne, *Race War!*, 251–53.

27. Sun Yat-sen as described in Duara, "Introduction," 2–3.

28. Tinker, *Race, Conflict and the International Order*, 12–14; Füredi, *The Silent War*, 2, 27–28, 34.

29. Gordon, *Assimilation in American Life*, 60–83.

30. Füredi, *The Silent War*, 34, 50, 86–87.

31. Park, *Race and Culture*, 82. For a "state of the field" affirmation of Park's views specific to the US South, see Thompson, *Race Relations and the Race Problem*.

32. See, e.g., Banton, *Race Relations*; Miles, *Racism after "Race Relations."*

33. Park and Burgess, *Introduction to the Science of Sociology*, 578.

34. Thompson, *Race Relations and the Race Problem*, vii; Tinker, *Race, Conflict and the International Order*, 12–14, 42–48; Füredi, *The Silent War*, 2, 7.

35. See Morris, *The Scholar Denied* for an important corrective to the claim that Chicago sociology marked the start of modern sociology in the United States.

36. Matthews, *Quest for an American Sociology*, 90–91.

37. Quoted in Raushenbush, *Robert E. Park*, 50. For a review of the Chicago school of sociology, see Abbott, *Department and Discipline*.

38. See, e.g., Thomas and Znaniecki, *The Polish Peasant in Europe and America*; Yu, *Thinking Orientals*.

39. Boas, introduction to *Handbook of American Indian Languages*; Stocking, *Delimiting Anthropology*.

40. Persons, *Ethnic Studies at Chicago*, 34–35. Another midwestern idea was the hypothesis that proposed the American frontier as the leveler of ethnic and class distinctions. See Turner, *The Frontier in American History*.

41. Likewise in the 1960s race riots prompted a study of their causes and remedy. See *Report of the National Advisory Commission on Civil Disorders*.

42. Chicago Commission on Race Relations, *The Negro in Chicago*.

43. Bogardus, "A Race-Relations Cycle"; Ross and Bogardus, "The Second-Generation Race Relations Cycle." See also E. Franklin Frazier's version of Robert Park's cycle in "Theoretical Structure of Sociology and Sociological Research." Park coined the term *marginal man* in "Human Migration and the Marginal Man."

44. Park, introduction to *The Japanese Invasion*, xvi.

45. See, e.g., Park, "The Nature of Race Relations," 81–116; Park, "Racial Assimilation in Secondary Groups with Particular Reference to the Negro," 610–11. See also Lyman, "Race Relations as Social Process," 370–401.

46. Compare the resuscitation of ethnicity and assimilation in Alba and Nee, "Rethinking Assimilation Theory for a New Era of Immigration."

47. Park, introduction to *The Japanese Invasion*, xiii, xiv.

48. Park, introduction to *The Japanese Invasion*, xv.

49. Sartre, preface to Fanon, *The Wretched of the Earth*, 7, 9.

50. Woodson, *The Mis-education of the Negro*, 192.

51. Orrick, *Shut It Down!*, 102.

52. See Yu, *Thinking Orientals*, for a description of this evolution.

53. For a useful survey of this "model minority" literature, see Osajima, "Asian Americans as the Model Minority," 165–74. For a critique of that turn from race to ethnicity, see Yoo, *Growing Up Nisei*, 9–11, 149–71.

54. Orrick, *Shut It Down!*, 101.

55. *Daily Gater*, April 16, 1968.

56. *Daily Gater*, April 26, May 1, May 16, May 21, May 22, 1968.

57. For accounts of the strike, see Orrick, *Shut It Down!*, 37–70; Smith et al., *By Any Means Necessary*; Bloom and Martin, *Black against Empire*, 269–87.

58. Quoted in Bloom and Martin, *Black against Empire*, 270.

59. President S. I. Hayakawa, press release. The president who settled the strike, Hayakawa distinguished between African and Asian Americans; the latter, he believed, possessed intact cultures and were like Europeans assimilating into the mainstream. Maeda, *Chains of Babylon*, 56–58.

60. San Francisco State Strike Bulletin. See also San Francisco State Strike Committee, "On Strike, Shut It Down."

61. "Demands and Explanations."

62. Joint Agreement.

63. McDermid, "Strike Settlement," 229. Of course teaching and writing under the sign of "ethnic studies" can arise from a Third World consciousness.

64. At the University of California, Berkeley, the Third World Liberation Front demanded a "Third World College," while referring to "Asian Studies, Black Studies, Chicano Studies, Native American Studies" as "ethnic studies programs." Third World Liberation Front, University of California, Berkeley, "Strike Demands."

65. Hare, "A Conceptual Proposal for a Department of Black Studies," 159.

66. Hare, "A Conceptual Proposal for a Department of Black Studies," 163.

67. See Bloom and Martin, *Black against Empire*, 271, which describes Hare's "Conceptual Proposal" as having "an anti-imperialist framework."

68. Hare, "A Conceptual Proposal for a Department of Black Studies," 166.

69. See Robinson, *Black Nationalism in American Politics and Thought*, 104–17, which contends that black nationalism of the 1960s and 1970s adopted the "ethnic paradigm" of the Chicago school of sociology. Compare Hare, "The Battle for Black Studies," for his articulation of black education as a means for liberation through the transformation of the black community and the academy.

70. Orrick, *Shut It Down!*, 116.

71. Smith et al., *By Any Means Necessary*, 140.

72. Malcolm X, "The Ballot or the Bullet," 13–21.

73. Quoted in Bloom and Martin, *Black against Empire*, 32.

74. See Williams, *Negroes with Guns*.

75. Mao, "Statement Supporting the American Negroes in Their Just Struggle Against Racial Discrimination by US Imperialism," 69–71.

76. Speech by Robert Williams at the Peking Rally on August 8, 1966, from the *Peking Review*, August 12, 1966, reprinted in Wu, *As Peking Sees Us*, 86, 87. William L. Van Deburg writes that the term *black power* entered the US political lexicon on June 16, 1966, when Stokely Carmichael declared in a speech in Greenwood, Mississippi, "We been saying freedom for six years and we ain't got nothin'. What we gonna start saying now is Black Power!" To which his audience shouted back, "Black Power!" (*New Day in Babylon*, 31–32).

77. Murch, *Living for the City*, 108–11.

78. Quoted in Murch, *Living for the City*, 116.

79. Franklin, *From the Movement*, 100–102.

80. Bloom and Martin, *Black against Empire*, 67.

81. Bloom and Martin, *Black against Empire*, 269, 270, 271.

82. Quoted in Wu, *As Peking Sees Us*, 29. Ernesto "Che" Guevara was an Argentine Marxist and revolutionary in Cuba and Latin America. Patrice Lumumba was a Congolese freedom fighter and the first democratically elected prime minister of the Republic of the Congo. Ho Chi Minh was the Vietnamese communist leader of the independence movement and was the first president of the Democratic Republic of Vietnam.

83. Cruse, "Negro Nationalism's New Wave" and "Revolutionary Nationalism and the Afro-American." Both essays are included in Cruse, *Rebellion or Revolution?*, 68–96.

84. Carmichael, "Toward Black Liberation," 639.

Two. Nationalism

1. See Robinson, *Black Nationalism in American Politics and Thought*, for precision in conceptualizing black nationalism, for a critique of black nationalism as a timeless, generalized notion of peoplehood and self-determination, and for a narration of black nationalism as a specific formation, historically situated and relationally and mutually constituted with the dominant order.

2. Williams, *Crusader* 8.3 (1967): 11.

3. Ture, "Afterword, 1992," 188.

4. The remarkable Williams, like Du Bois and others before him, remained staunchly internationalist while pursuing black nationalism because, he explained, it is anti-imperialist. *Crusader* 8.3 (1967): 11.

5. Conversely, among the US ruling class, that consciousness raised concern of a black insurrection. See, e.g., Füredi, *The Silent War*, 161; Horne, *Race War!*, 115–24.

6. *Chicago Defender*, March 3, 1945, quoted in Von Eschen, *Race against Empire*, 7–8.

7. Prashad, *The Darker Nations*, 6–11.

8. Mathurin, *Henry Sylvester Williams and the Origins of the Pan-African Movement*, 60–65.

9. Du Bois, "To the Nations of the World"; and Lewis, *W. E. B. Du Bois*.

10. Du Bois, "The Freedmen's Bureau," 354. This same wording appears in his classic, *Souls of Black Folk*, 10.

11. Du Bois, "The Color Line Belts the World," 30.

12. The language "having no rights a white man is bound to respect" comes from Chief Justice Roger Taney's ruling in *Dred Scott v. Sandford* (1857).

13. Du Bois, *Color and Democracy*, 241, 246, 248–49, 252, 280. See also Weale, *The Conflict of Colour*.

14. Pearson, *National Life and Character*, 84, 85. On Pearson and his book's reception, see Lake and Reynolds, *Drawing the Global Colour Line*, 75–94.

15. Pearson, *National Life and Character*, 85.

16. Stoddard, *The Rising Tide of Color against White World-Supremacy*, 4, 5, 7. See also Weale, *The Conflict of Colour*, 98–99, on the colored "invasion" of the white world for work.

17. Stoddard, *The Rising Tide of Color against White World-Supremacy*, 16.

18. Stoddard, *The French Revolution in San Domingo*, vii.

19. Prashad, *The Darker Nations*.

20. Quoted in Prashad, *The Darker Nations*, 30.

21. Legum, *Pan-Africanism*, 29, 155.

22. Thorne, "Racial Aspects of the Far Eastern War," 341, 342. See also Thorne, *The Issue of War*, 119–20, 125–31, 135–36; Dower, *War without Mercy*; Füredi, *The Silent War*, 18; Koshiro, *Trans-Pacific Racisms and the U.S. Occupation of Japan*; Horne, *Race War!*

23. Horne, *Race War!*, xiv. Black intellectuals like Du Bois and Aimé Césaire had pointed out that the parentage of Nazi white supremacy was European humanism and colonial discourse. Du Bois, *The World and Africa*, 23; Césaire, *Discourse on Colonialism*, 36–37. See also Tinker, *Race, Conflict and the International Order*, 42–48.

24. Thorne, "Racial Aspects of the Far Eastern War," 377.

25. Quoted in Füredi, *The Silent War*, 42–43, 44.

26. Füredi, *The Silent War*, 40.

27. Nehru, *The Discovery of India*, 443, 448. See also Mates, *Nonalignment*, 46–48, 57–62.

28. Nehru, *The Discovery of India*, 488–89, 492, 495–96, 498–502, 584.

29. Mohamad, *A New Deal for Asia*, 15–17, 68.

30. Horne, *Race War!*, 189, 196. See also Thorne, *The Issue of War*, 155, 156; Mishra, *From the Ruins of Empire*, 245–53.

31. Churchill, *The Second World War*, 206.

32. Quoted in Von Eschen, *Race against Empire*, 26.

33. Quoted in Horne, *Race War!*, 77, 78. For another overdrawn assessment of a British defeat at the hands of the Japanese, see Leasor, *Singapore*.

34. Iriye, *Power and Culture*, 4–10, 34–35, 49–50, 64–65; LaFeber, *The Clash*, 192, 214–15, 217; Thorne, *The Issue of War*, 154.

35. Thorne, *The Issue of War*, 144, 145–46, 148.

36. Iriye, *Power and Culture*, 97–98, 118–19; Thorne, *The Issue of War*, 113, 115.

37. Thorne, *The Issue of War*, 153. See also Horne, *Race War!*, 198, 219, 279, 288–89.

38. As cited in Horne, *Race War!*, 312.

39. Duara, "Introduction," 1.

40. Füredi, *Colonial Wars and the Politics of Third World Nationalism*, 272.

41. Leasor, *Singapore*, 5, 306. See also Thorne, *The Issue of War*, 47, 201–3.

42. Füredi, *The Silent War*, 1.

43. A classic text on neocolonialism is Nkrumah, *Neo-Colonialism*.

44. Quoted in Kahin, *The Asian-African Conference*.

45. Wright, *The Color Curtain*, 133–34. On African Americans and Bandung, see Von Eschen, *Race against Empire*, 167–73.

46. See Prashad, *The Darker Nations*.

47. Mates, *Nonalignment*, 48.

48. Kahin, *The Asian-African Conference*, 11, 43.

49. Wright, *The Color Curtain*, 208.

50. "Final Communique of the Asian-African Conference," Bandung, April 24, 1955, in Kahin, *The Asian-African Conference*, 76–85.

51. Balibar, "The Nation Form," 86, 90–93.

52. See Kelley and Kaplan, *Represented Communities*, 14.

53. Balibar, "The Nation Form," 96–103. In this connection see Patricia Hill Collins's important essay "It's All in the Family."

54. For instance, African freedom from France in the 1960s required membership in the Communauté Financière Africaine (African Financial Community), which obliged fourteen African nations, former French colonies, to deposit most of their foreign currency reserves into the French Treasury and give France and French companies the first right to buy their natural resources.

55. Kelley and Kaplan, *Represented Communities*, 9.

56. Kelley and Kaplan, *Represented Communities*, 15–17.

57. Compare Hardt and Negri, *Empire*, which depicts the UN as a juridical formation of

empire and world order following the transition from nation-state to postmodern, global apparatuses of imperial right.

58. Fanon, *The Wretched of the Earth*, 209.

59. Fanon, *The Wretched of the Earth*, 233, 247. At the same time, in "The Pitfalls of National Consciousness," Fanon warns that nationalism and the nation-state must yield to "political and social consciousness" (203).

60. Ture and Hamilton, *Black Power*, 55.

61. For insightful studies of nationalism in postcolonial states, see Duara, *Decolonization*.

62. See Bruyneel, *The Third Space of Sovereignty* for a discursive articulation of a "third space of sovereignty" that teeters on the nation's boundaries and troubles the "false choice" of inside/outside the US nation-state. By contrast, while I agree with Bruyneel's analysis of sovereignty as discourse, I herein trace the idea of sovereignty as a material condition while recognizing the union of discourse and material condition, which I discuss in chapter 3.

63. This discussion of international law draws from Anaya, *Indigenous Peoples in International Law*, 9–38. See also Howard, *Indigenous Peoples and the State*, which follows Anaya but adds a discussion of Pacific Islanders, specifically the Maori peoples.

64. For a discussion of this concept, see Pateman, "The Settler Contract," 35–78.

65. Quoted in Anaya, *Indigenous Peoples in International Law*, 24.

66. Deloria and Lytle, *The Nations Within*, 1–3.

67. Anaya, *Indigenous Peoples in International Law*, 41.

68. Anaya, *Indigenous Peoples in International Law*, 48.

69. Coulter, "The Law of Self-Determination and the United Nations Declaration on the Rights of Indigenous Peoples," 6.

70. Césaire, *Discourse on Colonialism*, 43.

Three. Imperialism

1. Space/time because they are intersecting, relational constructs.

2. See, e.g., Bunbury, *A History of Ancient Geography*, 148–49; Gillis, *Islands of the Mind*, 5–10.

3. *Hippocrates*, 105, 107, 109, 113, 115.

4. *Hippocrates*, 133–35, 137.

5. Bunbury, *A History of Ancient Geography*, 395–97; Tozer, *A History of Ancient Geography*, 179.

6. Aristotle, *The Politics*, 74, 165.

7. Stoneman, introduction to *The Greek Alexander Romance*, 3.

8. Thomson, *History of Ancient Geography*, 134–35.

9. Bodin, *Method for the Easy Comprehension of History*, ix, xi–xiii.

10. For a discussion of Plato's views on "race," see Hannaford, *Race*, 30–43.

11. Travelers, including Marco Polo, traders, and missionaries in the thirteenth and fourteenth centuries had dispelled the idea of an uninhabitable tropical zone. Lach, *Asia in the Making of Europe*, 32, 35–36, 43, 47–48.

12. Isaac, *The Invention of Racism in Classical Antiquity*, 74–75, 124.

13. Bodin, *Method for the Easy Comprehension of History*, 86, 87, 92–96, 97, 101, 102, 103, 116–19.
14. Hannaford, *Race*, 156.
15. Blumenbach, *On the Natural Varieties of Mankind*, 71–81, 98, 99.
16. Blumenbach, *On the Natural Varieties of Mankind*, 100, 101, 102, 104, 110, 111, 113.
17. Blumenbach, *On the Natural Varieties of Mankind*, 188, 192, 193, 196–203, 207, 209, 210, 211–12, 215; Bodin, *Method for the Easy Comprehension of History*, 102, 107.
18. Blumenbach, *On the Natural Varieties of Mankind*, 223–57.
19. Blumenbach, *On the Natural Varieties of Mankind*, 269; Hannaford, *Race*, 207, 208.
20. Bodin, *Method for the Easy Comprehension of History*, 143.
21. Blumenbach, *On the Natural Varieties of Mankind*, 224.
22. Blumenbach, *On the Natural Varieties of Mankind*, 275, 276; Hannaford, *Race*, 211, 212.
23. Hegel, *Lectures on the Philosophy of History*, 83, 84.
24. Kant, *Physical Geography*, 63, 64. See also Eze, "The Color of Reason."
25. Gobineau, *The Inequality of Human Races*, 24, 25, 27, 28, 31.
26. At the same time the Princeton geographer Arnold Guyot remained convinced of climate's sway over human energies and capacities. Guyot, *The Earth and Man*. See also Nott and Gliddon, *Indigenous Races of the Earth*. On the prevalence of that view among nineteenth-century scientists, see Livingstone, "The Moral Discourse of Climate."
27. Gobineau, *The Inequality of Human Races*, 36–62.
28. Gobineau, *The Inequality of Human Races*, 116, 146, 150–51, 154–67, 179.
29. Quoted in Gould, *The Mismeasure of Man*, 115.
30. See, e.g., the controversy stirred by Bernal's *Black Athena*.
31. Hobson, *Imperialism*, introduction.
32. Lenin, *Imperialism*.
33. As Paul Gilroy reminds us in *The Black Atlantic*.
34. Quoted in Murphey, *A History of Asia*, 222.

Four. World-System

1. Wallerstein, *World-Systems Analysis*.
2. On 1968, see, e.g., Ali and Watkins, *1968*.
3. Hobson, *Imperialism*, part 1, chapters 4, 6–7.
4. Frank, *Capitalism and Underdevelopment in Latin America*.
5. Hobson, *Imperialism*, part 2, chapter 4.
6. Similarly see Rodney's *How Europe Underdeveloped Africa*.
7. See, e.g., Cardoso and Enzo, *Dependency and Development in Latin America*.
8. As Richard White points out, conquest is not synonymous with dependency, and dependency is not solely economic but is also simultaneously political, cultural, and environmental. White, *The Roots of Dependency*.
9. Herein I reference Gramsci, *Selections from the Prison Notebooks*.
10. As seen in his Gramsci, *Selections from the Prison Notebooks, Notebook 1*. Gramsci first describes hegemony in "Notes on the Southern Question" (1926).

11. Gramsci, *Selections from the Prison Notebooks, Notebook 4*, 377. On war of position and war of maneuver, see *Notebook 6*, 109; *Notebook 7*, 168.

12. Althusser, *Essays on Ideology*.

13. Memmi, *Colonizer and Colonized*.

14. Memmi, *The Liberation of the Jew*, 182–83.

15. E.g., see Fusco, *English Is Broken Here*.

16. See, e.g., Rosa, *Local Story*.

17. On the complexity of Hawaiian pidgin, see Bickerton, *Roots of Language*; Bickerton, "Pidgins and Language Mixture," 31–43; and Roberts, "The TMA System of Hawaiian Creole and Diffusion," 45–70.

18. See, e.g., Sakoda and Siegel, *Pidgin Grammar*. At the same time, the ruling class and their instruments, notably the schools, stigmatized and sought to extinguish pidgin as the inarticulate expressions of inferior, uncivilized peoples.

19. Ngũgĩ, *Decolonising the Mind*, 4.

20. Quoted in *Observer* (London), July 6, 1952.

21. Tobias, "Amos Tutuola and the Colonial Carnival"; Low, "The Natural Artist."

22. Zabus, *The African Palimpsest*. Compare Tabron, *Postcolonial Literature from Three Continents*.

23. See Frank, *Capitalism and Underdevelopment in Latin America*, xvii–xviii.

24. Smith, *Conquest*. While the Spanish conquistadors commonly saw American Indians as subhuman and as sites of pollution, as Smith maintains, the Catholic Church debated whether Indians had souls, and Bartolomé de las Casas (ca. 1484–1566), the bishop of Chiapas, New Spain, chronicled Spanish atrocities committed against Indians and advocated Indian equality and the abolition of slavery.

25. Smith, *Conquest*, 15. For a more nuanced interpretation of conquest and American Indian women, see Chávez-García, *Negotiating Conquest*.

26. Trexler, *Sex and Conquest*.

27. For a history of the colony's labor systems, see Morgan, *American Slavery, American Freedom*.

28. Quoted in Nash et al., *The American People*, 38–39.

Five. Education

1. Fanon, *The Wretched of the Earth*, 233, 247.

2. The philosopher John Dewey wrote earlier of schooling for social change and teachers as facilitators and partners in the learning process. See, e.g., *The School and Society*; *Democracy and Education*; *My Pedagogic Creed*.

3. Freire, *Pedagogy of the Oppressed*, 19–20, 23–24, 58–59, 67–68, 71–73.

4. The old humanism, as we will see, advanced positivism, colonialism, and racism.

5. Quoted in Okihiro, *Island World*, 82–83.

6. Quoted in Okihiro, *Island World*, 83.

7. Quoted in Okihiro, *Island World*, 84–85.

8. Quoted in Okihiro, *Island World*, 98.

9. A history of education in Hawai'i calls Richard Armstrong "the father of American

education" because, although he was the second holder of the position, he intro-
duced an educational system and curriculum where none existed before (Wist, *A Century of Public Education in Hawaii*, 59).

10. Quoted in Okihiro, *Island World*, 117, 118.
11. Quoted in Okihiro, *Island World*, 122, 123.
12. Quoted in Okihiro, *Island World*, 129.
13. "Canon" because in the academy the struggle was centrally over "great books" and the literary canon, and "culture" because at least since the 1920s the term referred broadly to the contest between traditional/conservative and unconventional/liberal values.
14. Bloom, *Closing*, 25–43.
15. Levine, *The Opening of the American Mind*.
16. Levine, *Opening*, 3–33.
17. D'Souza, *Illiberal*, 1–23. On the radical professoriate, see Kimball, *Tenured Radicals*.
18. Malcolm X, *Malcolm X on Afro-American History*, 17, 22.
19. Cleaver, "Education and Revolution," 46, 51.

Six. Subjectification

1. Mills, *The Sociological Imagination*, 3–5, 196–97, 205, 211, 223, 226.
2. For definitions of modernism and postmodernism, see Williams, *Politics of Modernism*; Jameson, *Postmodernism*.
3. Poststructuralist feminist theorists like Julia Kristeva, Hélène Cixous, and Luce Irigaray reject Lacan's phallocentrism and instead offer that language is androgynous and pre-Oedipal.
4. From Matsuda, *Words That Wound*.
5. I expand on these ideas in chapter 9.
6. Marx, *Eighteenth Brumaire*, 71.
7. Williams, *Keywords*, 126–29.
8. Scott, "Difference," 25. Readers must keep in mind that Third World studies is an examination not of difference but of power.
9. Scott, "Experience," 34
10. Neihardt, *Black Elk Speaks*, 1.
11. On the layered, complicated text that accents Black Elk's speech, see Neihardt, *The Sixth Grandfather*. For a biography of Black Elk, see Steltenkamp, *Nicholas Black Elk*.
12. For critical readings of the text, see Holler, *The Black Elk Reader*.
13. Menchú told her story in 1982 to the anthropologist Elisabeth Burgos-Debray in Paris; Burgos-Debray published her representation of that account in Spanish the following year, and Ann Wright's English translation appeared as *I, Rigoberta Menchú: An Indian Woman in Guatemala*. On the controversy generated by the book, see Stoll, *Rigoberta Menchú and the Story of All Poor Guatemalans*; Arias, *The Rigoberta Menchú Controversy*; Grandin, *Who Is Rigoberta Menchú?*.
14. In "The Margin at the Center" Beverley contends that testimonios are testimony in the juridical sense and not oral histories, which are "documents." I disagree with that distinction.

15. Gugelberger and Kearney, "Voices for the Voiceless," 4, 9.
16. Marín, "Speaking Out Together."
17. Domitila and Viezzer, *Let Me Speak!*, 15.
18. Venuti, *The Translation Studies Reader*, 13.
19. Schleiermacher's 1813 lecture, "On the Different Methods of Translating," as translated by Susan Bernofsky, appears in Venuti, *The Translation Studies Reader*, 43–63.
20. Benjamin, "The Task of the Translator," 69–82.
21. Gayatri Chakravorty Spivak, "The Politics of Translation," in Venuti, *The Translation Studies Reader*, 369.
22. Venuti, *The Translation Studies Reader*, 20.

Seven. Racial Formation

1. See Omi and Winant, *Racial Formation in the United States*, 38–51, for a critique of nation-based theory.
2. For a useful review of these origins, see Lyman, "Race Relations as Social Process."
3. Lyman, "Race Relations as Social Process." For a history of the term *miscegenation*, see Pascoe, *What Comes Naturally*, 28.
4. See, e.g., Park, "The Nature of Race Relations" and "Racial Assimilation in Secondary Groups," 610–11.
5. Omi and Winant, *Racial Formation*, 61.
6. Omi and Winant, *Racial Formation*, 62.
7. Mills, *The Racial Contract*, 70, 73, 127.
8. See Roediger, *The Wages of Whiteness*.
9. Horkheimer, "Traditional and Critical Theory."
10. Derrida, *Of Grammatology*.
11. For some of critical race theory's key ideas, see Delgado and Stefancic, *Critical Race Theory*. For some of its influential writings, see Crenshaw et al., *Critical Race Theory*.
12. A founding text for critical race theory is Bell, *Race, Racism, and American Law*.
13. Haney-López, *White by Law*.
14. See, e.g., Ignatiev, *How the Irish Became White*; Brodkin, *How Jews Became White Folks*.
15. The literary critic Brent Hayes Edwards calls African diasporic practices a "mood," not a census, map, or museum (*The Practice of Diaspora*, 318).
16. Anderson, *Imagined Communities*. The study I cited in chapter 2 by Kelley and Kaplan, *Represented Communities*, is an important critique of Anderson's *Imagined Communities*.
17. For helpful analyses of the US census, visit the Bureau of the Census website, www.census.gov.
18. For a recent historical study of whiteness, see Painter, *The History of White People*.
19. Du Bois, "Souls of White Folk," 29.
20. See, e.g., Allen, *The Invention of the White Race*, based upon his *Class Struggle and the Origin of Racial Slavery*, a pamphlet published in 1975.
21. Du Bois, "Souls of White Folk," 49.
22. See, e.g., Jacobson, *Roots Too*.

23. Consult two key texts: Frankenberg, *White Women, Race Matters*; Lipsitz, *The Possessive Investment in Whiteness*.

24. See, e.g., Roediger's *Wages of Whiteness*; Harris, "Whiteness as Property"; Lipsitz's *The Possessive Investment in Whiteness*.

Eight. Social Formation

1. Omi and Winant, *Racial Formation in the United States*, 2–3, 14–24. Besides ethnicity, Omi and Winant critique class-based and, as I noted earlier, nation-based theories.

2. McDougald, "The Struggle of Negro Women for Sex and Race Emancipation," 81, 82.

3. Beale, "Double Jeopardy." Beale's Third World consciousness embraced black and Puerto Rican women in the United States and in "non-white countries," especially India, where, she charged, the United States was sponsoring sterilization clinics for men and women.

4. Springer, *Living for the Revolution*, 45–49, 185.

5. From an interview in Springer, *Living for Revolution*, 60. Barbara Smith, on the suggestion of her friend Audre Lorde, went on to found the influential Kitchen Table Women of Color Press in 1980.

6. "The Combahee River Collective Statement," 26.

7. See, e.g., Anderson-Bricker, "'Triple Jeopardy.'"

8. Crenshaw, "Demarginalizing the Intersection of Race and Sex," 139, 140.

9. Collins, "It's All in the Family" and "Gender, Black Feminism, and Black Political Economy"; Davis, *Women, Race, and Class*; Mullings, *On Our Own Terms*; Moraga, *Loving in the War Years*; Glenn, "Racial Ethnic Women's Labor."

10. For an articulation of race and gender building upon Third World women's intersectionality and the search for a new language, see Mills, "Intersecting Contracts."

11. The introductory paragraphs in this section come from Okihiro and Tsou, "On Social Formation," 74–76.

12. Krasner, *Resistance, Parody and Double Consciousness in African American Theatre*; Burkitt, *Social Selves*.

13. Cosgrove, *Social Formation and Symbolic Landscape*; Elwood, *The Body Broken*.

14. Marks and Atmore, *Economy and Society in Pre-Industrial South Africa*, 38n9.

15. Duan, *Marx's Theory of the Social Formation*, 9–10, 11.

16. Quoted in Duan, *Marx's Theory of the Social Formation*, 12.

17. Marks and Atmore, *Economy and Society in Pre-Industrial South Africa*, 38n9.

18. Quoted in Duan, *Marx's Theory of the Social Formation*, 15.

19. Althusser, *For Marx*, 212–13, 233.

20. Hindess and Hirst, *Mode of Production and Social Formation*, 46–48.

21. Binaries form the principal architecture of these discourses, but they can also triangulate, as proposed by Claire Jean Kim in *Bitter Fruit* and "The Racial Triangulation of Asian Americans."

22. Crenshaw, "Demarginalizing the Intersection of Race and Sex," 141–43.

23. On hegemony and ideology, see Gramsci, *Selections from the Prison Notebooks*; Mouffe, "Hegemony and Ideology in Gramsci."

24. Brown, *Good Wives, Nasty Wenches, and Anxious Patriarchs*, 108. An earlier statute, enacted in 1639, called on the governor and council to provide arms and ammunition to "all persons except Negroes," but it did not forbid Africans from owning guns, nor was the act directed at Africans (Higginbotham, *In the Matter of Color*, 32).

25. Brown, *Good Wives, Nasty Wenches, and Anxious Patriarchs*, 132.

26. Nash, *The American People*, 70–71; Brown, *Good Wives, Nasty Wenches, and Anxious Patriarchs*, 107–8.

27. On Bacon's rebellion, see Brown, *Good Wives, Nasty Wenches, and Anxious Patriarchs*, chapter 5.

28. Reproduced in Odo, *The Columbia Documentary History of the Asian American Experience*, 19–21.

29. Haney-López, *White by Law*, 46–47.

30. See, e.g., Balibar, "The Nation Form," 96–103.

31. Jay, "Concerning the Dangers from Foreign Force and Influence."

32. Reich, "The New Property."

33. Harris, "Whiteness as Property."

Nine. Syntheses

1. Butler, *Gender Trouble*, 142.

2. See, e.g., Lacquer, *Making Sex*.

3. For a groundbreaking work on the transsexual, revealing the distinction between body and gender, see Harry, *The Transsexual Phenomenon*.

4. Garber, *Vested Interests* and *Vice Versa*.

5. See, e.g., Firestone, *The Dialectic of Sex*; Millett, *Sexual Politics*; Mohanty, "Under Western Eyes."

6. Rich, "Compulsory Heterosexuality and Lesbian Existence."

7. I am not suggesting, nonetheless, abandoning the black/white binary entirely as an object of study and as a basis for political action. What I am cautioning against is the binary and its primacy that can exclude as well as include.

8. See his classic, *Discourse on Colonialism*.

9. Senghor, "Negritude," 179. The West Indian writer and educator Edward Blyden called that inheritance the "African personality."

10. That work began with Cheng and Bonacich, *Labor Immigration under Capitalism*.

11. Castles and Kosack, *Immigrant Workers and Class Structure in Western Europe*.

12. Anzaldúa, *Borderlands/La Frontera*.

13. Anzaldúa, "On the Process of Writing *Borderlands/La Frontera*."

14. Anzaldúa, *Borderlands/La Frontera*, 113.

15. Manuel, *The Fourth World*.

16. Compare Castells, *End of Millennium*, which uses *fourth world* to designate peoples bypassed by technology.

17. See Smith, *Decolonizing Methodologies*.

18. See, e.g., Wilson, *The Declining Significance of Race*.

19. See, e.g., Hollinger, *Postethnic America*.

20. "The New Face of America," *Time*, November 18, 1993, front cover.

21. For a confused intellectual genealogy of postcolonial theory and post-1968 ethnic studies, see Singh and Schmidt, *Postcolonial Theory and the United States*.

22. Often cited as postcolonialism's founding texts are Edward W. Said's *Orientalism* and *Culture and Imperialism*.

23. See Walter D. Mignolo's important critique of modernity, or "the colonial matrix of power," which, he argues, consists of four heads (knowledge and subjectivity; racism, gender, and sexuality; authority; and economy) and two legs (theology or secular philosophy and patriarchy). In this, Mignolo contends, colonialism or modernity is the primary power driving the social formation, and the "decolonial" response is the precolonial, noncapitalist, communal world. See his trilogy: *Local Histories/Global Designs*; *The Darker Side of the Renaissance*; and *The Darker Side of Western Modernity*.

24. For critiques of postcolonialism, see the essays by Arif Dirlik and Ella Shohat in McClintock et al., *Dangerous Liaisons*.

25. Much of this analysis comes from Young, *White Mythologies*.

26. Bhabha, *The Location of Culture*.

27. For a synthesis of feminist, queer, and disability theories through Butler's performance theory, see Samuels, "Critical Divides."

28. See, e.g., Black, *War against the Weak*; Garland-Thomson, *Extraordinary Bodies*; Fiedler, *Freaks*.

29. From H. H. Goddard, director of a school for the feebleminded in Vineland, New Jersey.

30. At the same time I am unconvinced that the European, post-Enlightenment notion of "defective" bodies transfers as easily across (Third and Fourth World) cultures as race, gender, sexuality, class, and nation. That is, as theory, disability works best in European, not Third World discourses.

BIBLIOGRAPHY

Archival Sources

"Demands and Explanations." N.d. San Francisco State Strike Collection, Box "Third World Liberation Front," Folder 164, San Francisco State University Library Archives.

Joint Agreement. March 18, 1969. San Francisco State Strike Collection, Box "Third World Liberation Front," Folder 164, San Francisco State University Library Archives.

President S. I. Hayakawa, press release, December 6, 1968. Box "College of Ethnic Studies: Origins—Asian American Studies," Folder "College of Ethnic Studies: Origins," San Francisco State University Library Archives.

San Francisco State Strike Bulletin. N.d. San Francisco State Strike Collection, Box "Third World Liberation Front," Folder 164, San Francisco State University Library Archives.

San Francisco State Strike Committee. "On Strike, Shut It Down." Pamphlet. N.d. Box "Ephemera Files LARC, San Francisco State University—Strike, 1968–1969," Folder "San Francisco State University—Strike, 1968," San Francisco State University, Labor Archives and Research Center.

Third World Liberation Front, University of California, Berkeley. "Strike Demands." January 1969. San Francisco State Strike Collection, Box "Third World Liberation Front," Folder 164, San Francisco State University Library Archives.

Secondary Sources

Abbott, Andrew. *Department and Discipline: Chicago Sociology at One Hundred.* Chicago: University of Chicago Press, 1999.

Alba, Richard, and Victor Nee. "Rethinking Assimilation Theory for a New Era of Immigration." *International Migration Review* 31.4 (1997): 826–74.

Alcoff, Linda Martín. "The Problem of Speaking for Others." In *Who Can Speak? Au-*

thority and Critical Identity, ed. Judith Butler and Robyn Wiegman. Urbana: University of Illinois Press, 1995.

Ali, Tariq, and Susan Watkins. *1968: Marching in the Streets*. New York: Free Press, 1998.

Allen, Theodore W. *Class Struggle and the Origin of Racial Slavery: The Invention of the White Race*. Hoboken, NJ: Hoboken Education Project, 1975.

———. *The Invention of the White Race*. Vol. 1. London: Verso, 1994.

———. *The Invention of the White Race*. Vol. 2. London: Verso, 1997.

Althusser, Louis. *Essays on Ideology*. London: Verso, 1984.

———. *For Marx*. Trans. Ben Brewster. London: Verso, 1969.

Anaya, S. James. *Indigenous Peoples in International Law*. New York: Oxford University Press, 2000.

Anderson, Benedict R. *Imagined Communities: Reflections on the Origin and Spread of Nationalism*. London: Verso, 1983.

Anderson-Bricker, Kristen. "'Triple Jeopardy': Black Women and the Growth of Feminist Consciousness in SNCC, 1964–1975." In *Still Lifting, Still Climbing: Contemporary African American Women's Activism*, ed. Kimberly Springer. New York: New York University Press, 1999.

Anzaldúa, Gloria. *Borderlands/La Frontera: The New Mestiza*. San Francisco: Spinsters/Aunt Lute Books, 1987.

———. "On the Process of Writing *Borderlands/La Frontera*." In *The Gloria Anzaldúa Reader*, ed. AnaLouise Keating. Durham, NC: Duke University Press, 2009.

Arias, Arturo, ed. *The Rigoberta Menchú Controversy*. Minneapolis: University of Minnesota Press, 2001.

Aristotle. *The Politics*. Trans. Benjamin Jowett. Cambridge: Cambridge University Press, 1988.

Asian Women. Berkeley: N.p., 1971.

Balibar, Étienne. "The Nation Form: History and Ideology." In *Race, Nation, Class: Ambiguous Identities*, by Étienne Balibar and Immanuel Wallerstein. London: Verso, 1991.

Banton, Michael. *Race Relations*. New York: Basic Books, 1967.

Beale, Frances. "Double Jeopardy: To Be Black and Female." In *Words of Fire: An Anthology of African-American Feminist Thought*, ed. Beverly Guy-Sheftall. New York: New Press, 1995.

Bell, Derrick A. *Race, Racism, and American Law*. Boston: Little, Brown, 1973.

Benjamin, Walter. "The Task of the Translator." 1955. In *Illuminations*. Trans. Harry Zohn. Ed. Hannah Arendt. New York: Schocken Books, 1969.

Bernal, Martin. *Black Athena: The Afroasiatic Roots of Classical Civilization*. Vol. 1. New Brunswick, NJ: Rutgers University Press, 1987.

———. *Black Athena: The Afroasiatic Roots of Classical Civilization*. Vol. 2. New Brunswick, NJ: Rutgers University Press, 1991.

———. *Black Athena: The Afroasiatic Roots of Classical Civilization*. Vol. 3. New Brunswick, NJ: Rutgers University Press, 2006.

Beverley, John. "The Margin at the Center: On *Testimonio* (Testimonial Narrative)." In *De/Colonizing the Subject: The Politics of Gender in Women's Autobiography*, ed. Sidonie Smith and Julia Watson. Minneapolis: University of Minnesota Press, 1992.

Bhabha, Homi K. *The Location of Culture*. London: Routledge, 1994.

Bickerton, Derek. "Pidgins and Language Mixture." In *Creole Genesis, Attitudes and Discourse: Studies Celebrating Charlene J. Sato*, ed. John R. Rickford and Suzanne Romaine. Amsterdam: John Benjamins, 1999.

———. *Roots of Language*. Ann Arbor, MI: Karoma, 1981.

Black, Edwin. *War against the Weak: Eugenics and America's Campaign to Create a Master Race*. New York: Four Walls Eight Windows, 2003.

Bloom, Allan. *Closing of the American Mind*. New York: Simon and Schuster, 1987.

Bloom, Joshua, and Waldo E. Martin Jr. *Black against Empire: The History and Politics of the Black Panther Party*. Berkeley: University of California Press, 2013.

Blumenbach, Johann Friedrich. *On the Natural Varieties of Mankind*. Ed. Thomas Bendyshe. New York: Bergman, 1969.

Boas, Franz. Introduction to *Handbook of American Indian Languages*. Bulletin 40. Bureau of Ethnology, Smithsonian Institution. Washington, DC: Government Printing Office, 1911.

Bodin, John. *Method for the Easy Comprehension of History*. Trans. Beatrice Reynolds. New York: Columbia University Press, 1945.

Bogardus, Emory S. "A Race-Relations Cycle." *American Journal of Sociology* 35.4 (1930): 612–17.

Brodkin, Karen. *How Jews Became White Folks and What That Says about Race in America*. New Brunswick, NJ: Rutgers University Press, 1998.

Brown, Kathleen M. *Good Wives, Nasty Wenches, and Anxious Patriarchs: Gender, Race, and Power in Colonial Virginia*. Chapel Hill: University of North Carolina Press, 1996.

Bruyneel, Kevin. *The Third Space of Sovereignty: The Postcolonial Politics of US-Indigenous Relations*. Minneapolis: University of Minnesota Press, 2007.

Bunbury, E. H. *A History of Ancient Geography*. Vol. 1. London: John Murray, 1883.

Burkitt, Ian. *Social Selves: Theories of the Social Formation of Personality*. London: Sage, 1991.

Cardoso, Fernando Henrique, and Faletto Enzo. *Dependency and Development in Latin America*. Berkeley: University of California Press, 1979.

Carmichael, Stokely. "Toward Black Liberation." *Massachusetts Review* 7 (Autumn 1966): 639–51.

Castells, Manuel. *End of Millennium*. Malden, MA: Blackwell, 1998.

Castles, Stephen, and Godula Kosack. *Immigrant Workers and Class Structure in Western Europe*. London: Oxford University Press, 1973.

Césaire, Aimé. *Discourse on Colonialism*. 1955. Trans. Joan Pinkham. New York: Monthly Review Press, 2000.

Chávez-García, Miroslava. *Negotiating Conquest: Gender and Power in California, 1770s to 1880s*. Tucson: University of Arizona Press, 2004.

Cheng, Lucie, and Edna Bonacich, eds. *Labor Immigration under Capitalism: Asian Workers in the United States before World War II*. Berkeley: University of California Press, 1984.

Chicago Commission on Race Relations. *The Negro in Chicago: A Study of Race Relations and a Race Riot*. Chicago: University of Chicago Press, 1922.

Churchill, Winston S. *The Second World War*. Vol. 4: *The Hinge of Fate*. Boston: Houghton Mifflin, 1950.

Cleaver, Eldridge. "Education and Revolution." *Black Scholar* 1.1 (1969): 44–52.

Collins, Patricia Hill. "Gender, Black Feminism, and Black Political Economy." *Annals of the American Academy of Political and Social Science* 568 (2000): 41–53.

———. "It's All in the Family: Intersections of Gender, Race, and Nation." *Hypatia* 13.3 (1998): 62–82.

"The Combahee River Collective Statement." In *Home Girls: A Black Feminist Anthology*, ed. Barbara Smith. Latham, NY: Kitchen Table Women of Color Press, 1983.

Cosgrove, Denis. *Social Formation and Symbolic Landscape*. Madison: University of Wisconsin Press, 1998.

Coulter, Robert T. "The Law of Self-Determination and the United Nations Declaration on the Rights of Indigenous Peoples." *UCLA Journal of International Law and Foreign Affairs* 15 (Spring 2010): 1–28.

Crenshaw, Kimberlé. "Demarginalizing the Intersection of Race and Sex: A Black Feminist Critique of Antidiscrimination Doctrine, Feminist Theory and Antiracist Politics." *University of Chicago Legal Forum* (1989): 139–67.

Crenshaw, Kimberlé, Neil Gotanda, Gary Peller, and Kendall Thomas, eds. *Critical Race Theory: The Key Writings That Formed the Movement*. New York: New Press, 1995.

Cruse, Harold. "Negro Nationalism's New Wave." *New Leader* (1962): 16–18.

———. *Rebellion or Revolution?* New York: William Morrow, 1968.

———. "Revolutionary Nationalism and the Afro-American." *Studies on the Left* 2.3 (1962): 12–25.

Davis, Angela Y. *Women, Race, and Class*. New York: Random House, 1981.

Delgado, Richard, and Jean Stefancic. *Critical Race Theory: An Introduction*. New York: New York University Press, 2001.

Deloria, Vine, Jr., and Clifford M. Lytle. *The Nations Within: The Past and Future of American Indian Sovereignty*. New York: Pantheon, 1984.

Derrida, Jacques. *Of Grammatology*. Trans. Gayatri Chakravorty Spivak. Baltimore: Johns Hopkins University Press, 1997.

Dewey, John. *Democracy and Education: An Introduction to the Philosophy of Education*. New York: Macmillan, 1916.

———. *My Pedagogic Creed*. Washington, DC: Progressive Education Association, 1929.

———. *The School and Society*. Chicago: University of Chicago Press, 1915.

Domitila Barrios de Chungara with Moema Viezzer. *Let Me Speak! Testimony of Domitila, a Woman of the Bolivian Mines*. Trans. Victoria Ortiz. New York: Monthly Review Press, 1978.

Dower, John W. *War without Mercy: Race and Power in the Pacific War*. New York: Pantheon, 1986.

D'Souza, Dinesh. *Illiberal Education*. New York: Free Press, 1991.

Duan, Zhongqia. *Marx's Theory of the Social Formation*. Aldershot, UK: Avebury, 1995.

Duara, Prasenjit. "Introduction: The Decolonization of Asia and Africa in the Twentieth Century." In *Decolonization: Perspectives from Now and Then*, ed. Prasenjit Duara. London: Routledge, 2004.

Du Bois, W. E. Burkhardt. "The African Roots of War." *Atlantic Monthly* 115 (May 1915): 707–14.

———. *Color and Democracy: Colonies and Peace.* 1945. New York: Oxford University Press, 2007.

———. "The Color Line Belts the World." *Collier's Weekly,* October 20, 1906, 30.

———. "The Freedmen's Bureau." *Atlantic Monthly* 87.521 (1901): 354–65.

———. "To the Nations of the World." In *Report of the Pan-African Conference, Held on the 23rd, 24th, and 25th July, 1900, at Westminster Town Hall, Westminster, S.W.* London, 1900. Reprinted in *W. E. B. Du Bois: A Reader*, ed. David Levering Lewis. New York: Henry Holt, 1995.

———. *The Souls of Black Folk.* Chicago: A. C. McClurg, 1903.

———. *The World and Africa.* New York: International, 1946.

Edwards, Brent Hayes. *The Practice of Diaspora: Literature, Translation and the Rise of Internationalism.* Cambridge, MA: Harvard University Press, 2003.

Elwood, Christopher. *The Body Broken: The Calvinist Doctrine of the Eucharist and the Symbolization of Power in 16th Century France.* New York: Oxford University Press, 1999.

Eze, Emmanuel Chukwudi. "The Color of Reason: The Idea of 'Race' in Kant's Anthropology." *Bucknell Review* 38.2 (1995): 200–241.

Fanon, Frantz. *The Wretched of the Earth.* Trans. Constance Farrington. New York: Grove Press, 1968.

Ferreira, Jason Michael. "All Power to the People: A Comparative History of Third World Radicalism in San Francisco, 1968–1974." PhD diss., University of California, Berkeley, 2003.

———. "From College Readiness to Ready for Revolution! Third World Student Activism at a Northern California Community College, 1965–1969." *Kalfou: A Journal of Comparative and Relational Ethnic Studies* 1.1 (2014): 117–44.

Fiedler, Leslie A. *Freaks: Myths and Images of the Secret Self.* New York: Simon and Schuster, 1978.

Firestone, Shulamith. *The Dialectic of Sex: The Case for Feminist Revolution.* New York: Morrow, 1970.

Firmin, Joseph-Anténor. *The Equality of the Human Races (Positivist Anthropology).* Trans. Asselin Charles. New York: Garland, 2000.

Foucault, Michel. *Power/Knowledge: Selected Interviews and Other Writings, 1972–1977.* Ed. and trans. Colin Gordon. Brighton, UK: Harvester, 1980.

Frank, Andre Gunder. *Capitalism and Underdevelopment in Latin America: Historical Studies of Chile and Brazil.* New York: Monthly Review Press, 1969.

Frankenberg, Ruth. *White Women, Race Matters: The Social Construction of Whiteness.* Minneapolis: University of Minnesota Press, 1993.

Frazier, E. Franklin. "Theoretical Structure of Sociology and Sociological Research." *British Journal of Sociology* 4.4 (1953): 293–311.

Freire, Paulo. *Pedagogy of the Oppressed*. Trans. Myra Bergman Ramos. New York: Herder and Herder, 1972.

Füredi, Frank. *Colonial Wars and the Politics of Third World Nationalism*. London: I. B. Tauris, 1994.

———. *The Silent War: Imperialism and the Changing Perception of Race*. London: Pluto Press, 1998.

Fusco, Coco. *English Is Broken Here: Notes on Cultural Fusion in the Americas*. New York: New Press, 1995.

Garber, Marjorie B. *Vested Interests: Cross-Dressing and Cultural Anxiety*. New York: Routledge, 1992.

———. *Vice Versa: Bisexuality and the Eroticism of Everyday Life*. New York: Simon and Schuster, 1995.

Garland-Thomson, Rosemarie. *Extraordinary Bodies: Figuring Physical Disability in American Culture and Literature*. New York: Columbia University Press, 1997.

Gillis, John. *Islands of the Mind: How the Human Imagination Created the Atlantic World*. New York: Palgrave Macmillan, 2004.

Gilroy, Paul. *The Black Atlantic: Modernity and Double-Consciousness*. Cambridge, MA: Harvard University Press, 1993.

Glenn, Evelyn Nakano. "Racial Ethnic Women's Labor: The Intersection of Race, Gender and Class Oppression." *Review of Radical Political Economics* 17.3 (1985): 86–108.

———. *Unequal Freedom: How Race and Gender Shaped American Citizenship and Labor*. Cambridge, MA: Harvard University Press, 2002.

Gobineau, Arthur de. *The Inequality of Human Races*. Trans. Adrian Collins. New York: Howard Fertig, 1967.

Gordon, Milton M. *Assimilation in American Life: The Role of Race, Religion, and National Origins*. New York: Oxford University Press, 1964.

Gould, Stephen Jay. *The Mismeasure of Man*. New York: Norton, 1996.

Gramsci, Antonio. *Selections from the Prison Notebooks*. Ed. and trans. Quintin Hoare and Geoffrey Nowell-Smith. London: Lawrence and Wishart, 1971.

Grandin, Greg. *Who Is Rigoberta Menchú?* London: Verso, 2011.

Gugelberger, Georg, and Michael Kearney. "Voices for the Voiceless: Testimonial Literature in Latin America." *Latin American Perspectives* 18.3 (1991): 3–14.

Guyot, Arnold Henry. *The Earth and Man: Lectures on Comparative Physical Geography in Its Relation to the History of Mankind*. New York: Sheldon, Blakeman, 1849.

Haney-López, Ian. *White by Law: The Legal Constructions of Race*. New York: New York University Press, 1996.

Hannaford, Ivan. *Race: The History of an Idea in the West*. Washington, DC: Woodrow Wilson Center Press, 1996.

Hardt, Michael, and Antonio Negri. *Empire*. Cambridge, MA: Harvard University Press, 2000.

Hare, Nathan. "The Battle for Black Studies." *Black Scholar* 3.9 (1972): 32–47.

———. "A Conceptual Proposal for a Department of Black Studies." In William H. Orrick Jr., *Shut It Down! A College in Crisis: San Francisco State College, October*

1968–April 1969. A Staff Report to the National Commission on the Causes and Prevention of Violence. Washington, DC: Government Printing Office, 1969.

Harris, Cheryl I. "Whiteness as Property." *Harvard Law Review* 106.8 (1993): 1707–91.

Harrison, Hubert H. *When Africa Awakes: The "Inside Story" of the Stirrings and Strivings of the New Negro in the Western World*. New York: Porro Press, 1920.

Harry, Benjamin. *The Transsexual Phenomenon*. New York: Julian, 1966.

Hegel, G. W. F. *Lectures on the Philosophy of History*. Trans. J. Sibree. London: George Bell and Sons, 1881.

Higginbotham, A. Leon, Jr. *In the Matter of Color: Race and the American Legal Process. The Colonial Period*. Oxford: Oxford University Press, 1978.

Hindess, Barry, and Paul Hirst. *Mode of Production and Social Formation: An Auto-Critique of Pre-Capitalist Modes of Production*. London: Macmillan, 1977.

Hippocrates. Vol. 1. Trans. W. H. S. Jones. Cambridge, MA: Harvard University Press, 1923.

Hobson, J. A. *Imperialism: A Study*. London: James Nisbet, 1902.

Holler, Clyde, ed. *The Black Elk Reader*. Syracuse, NY: Syracuse University Press, 2000.

Hollinger, David A. *Postethnic America: Beyond Multiculturalism*. New York: Basic Books, 1995.

Horkheimer, Max. "Traditional and Critical Theory." In *Critical Theory: Selected Essays*. Trans. Matthew J. O'Connell et al. New York: Seabury Press, 1972.

Horne, Gerald. *Race War! White Supremacy and the Japanese Attack on the British Empire*. New York: New York University Press, 2004.

Howard, Bradley Reed. *Indigenous Peoples and the State: The Struggle for Native Rights*. DeKalb: Northern Illinois University Press, 2003.

Ignatiev, Noel. *How the Irish Became White*. New York: Routledge, 1995.

"An Interview with Pat Sumi." In *Roots: An Asian American Reader*, ed. Amy Tachiki et al. Los Angeles: UCLA Asian American Studies Center, 1971.

Iriye, Akira. *Power and Culture: The Japanese-American War, 1941–1945*. Cambridge, MA: Harvard University Press, 1981.

Isaac, Benjamin. *The Invention of Racism in Classical Antiquity*. Princeton, NJ: Princeton University Press, 2004.

Jacobson, Matthew Frye. *Roots Too: White Ethnic Revival in Post–Civil Rights America*. Cambridge, MA: Harvard University Press, 2006.

Jameson, Fredric. *Postmodernism, or, the Cultural Logic of Late Capitalism*. Durham, NC: Duke University Press, 1992.

Jay, John. "Concerning the Dangers from Foreign Force and Influence." Federalist No. 2. In *The Federalist Papers: Alexander Hamilton, James Madison, John Jay*. Ed. Ian Shapiro. New Haven, CT: Yale University Press, 2009.

Kahin, George McTurnan. *The Asian-African Conference, Bandung, Indonesia, April 1955*. Ithaca, NY: Cornell University Press, 1956.

Kant, Immanuel. *Physical Geography*. In *Race and the Enlightenment: A Reader*. Ed. Emmanuel Chukwudi Eze. Cambridge, MA: Blackwell, 1997.

Kelley, John D., and Martha Kaplan. *Represented Communities: Fiji and World Decolonization*. Chicago: University of Chicago Press, 2001.

Kim, Claire Jean. *Bitter Fruit: The Politics of Black-Korean Conflict in New York City.* New Haven, CT: Yale University Press, 2000.

———. "The Racial Triangulation of Asian Americans." *Politics and Society* 27.1 (1999): 105–38.

Kimball, Roger. *Tenured Radicals: How Politics Has Corrupted Our Higher Education.* New York: Harper and Row, 1990.

Koshiro, Yukiko. *Trans-Pacific Racisms and the U.S. Occupation of Japan.* New York: Columbia University Press, 1999.

Krasner, David. *Resistance, Parody and Double Consciousness in African American Theatre, 1895–1910.* New York: St. Martin's Press, 1997.

Lach, Donald F. *Asia in the Making of Europe.* Vol. 1: *The Century of Discovery.* Chicago: University of Chicago Press, 1965.

Lacquer, Thomas. *Making Sex: Body and Gender from the Greeks to Freud.* Cambridge, MA: Harvard University Press, 1990.

LaFeber, Walter. *The Clash: A History of U.S.-Japan Relations.* New York: Norton, 1997.

Lake, Marilyn, and Henry Reynolds. *Drawing the Global Colour Line: White Men's Countries and the International Challenge of Racial Equality.* Cambridge: Cambridge University Press, 2008.

Leasor, James. *Singapore: The Battle That Changed the World.* Garden City, NY: Doubleday, 1968.

Legum, Colin. *Pan-Africanism: A Short Political Guide.* New York: Frederick A. Praeger, 1965.

Lenin, Vladimir. *Imperialism: The Highest Stage of Capitalism.* New York: International, 1937.

Levine, Lawrence W. *The Opening of the American Mind: Canons, Culture, and History.* Boston: Beacon Press, 1996.

Lipsitz, George. *The Possessive Investment in Whiteness: How White People Profit from Identity Politics.* Philadelphia: Temple University Press, 2006.

Livingstone, David N. "The Moral Discourse of Climate: Historical Considerations of Race, Place and Virtue." *Journal of Historical Geography* 17.4 (1991): 413–34.

Lorde, Audre. "The Master's Tools Will Never Dismantle the Master's House." In *Sister Outsider.* Freedom, CA: Crossing Press, 1984.

Low, Gail. "The Natural Artist: Publishing Amos Tutuola's *The Palm-Wine Drinkard* in Postwar Britain." *Research in African Literature* 37.4 (2006): 15–33.

Lyman, Stanford M. "Race Relations as Social Process: Sociology's Resistance to a Civil Rights Orientation." In *Race in America: The Struggle for Equality,* ed. Herbert Hill and James E. Jones Jr. Madison: University of Wisconsin Press, 1993.

McClintock, Anne, Aamir Mufti, and Ella Shohat, eds. *Dangerous Liaisons: Gender, Nations, and Postcolonial Perspectives.* Minneapolis: University of Minnesota Press, 1997.

McDermid, Nancy. "Strike Settlement." In *Academics on the Line,* ed. Arlene Kaplan Daniels et al. San Francisco: Jossey-Bass, 1970.

McDougald, Elise Johnson. "The Struggle of Negro Women for Sex and Race Emancipation." In *Words of Fire: An Anthology of African-American Feminist Thought,* ed. Beverly Guy-Sheftall. New York: New Press, 1995.

McEvoy, James, and Abraham Miller, eds. *Black Power and Student Rebellion*. Belmont, CA: Wadsworth, 1969.

Maeda, Daryl J. *Chains of Babylon: The Rise of Asian America*. Minneapolis: University of Minnesota Press, 2009.

Malcolm X. "The Ballot or the Bullet." 1964. In *From the Movement toward Revolution*, ed. Bruce Franklin. New York: Van Nostrand Reinhold, 1971.

———. *Malcolm X on Afro-American History*. New York: Pathfinder Press, 1967.

Mandela, Nelson. *No Easy Walk to Freedom*. Ed. Ruth First. London: Heinemann, 1965.

Manuel, George. *The Fourth World: An Indian Reality*. New York: Free Press, 1974.

Mao Tse-tung. "Statement Supporting the American Negroes in Their Just Struggle against Racial Discrimination by U.S. Imperialism." 1966. In *As Peking Sees Us: "People's War" in the United States and Communist China's America Policy*, by Yuan-li Wu. Stanford, CA: Hoover Institution Press, 1969.

Marín, Lynda. "Speaking Out Together: Testimonials of Latin American Women." *Latin American Perspectives* 18.3 (1991): 51–68.

Marks, Shula, and Anthony Atmore, eds. *Economy and Society in Pre-Industrial South Africa*. London: Longman, 1980.

Marx, Karl. *Eighteenth Brumaire of Louis Bonaparte*. Trans. Daniel DeLeon. Chicago: C. H. Kerr, 1907.

Mates, Leo. *Nonalignment: Theory and Current Policy*. Belgrade: Institute of International Politics and Economics, 1972.

Mathurin, Owen. *Henry Sylvester Williams and the Origins of the Pan-African Movement, 1869–1911*. Westport, Conn.: Greenwood, 1976.

Matsuda, Mari J. *Words That Wound: Critical Race Theory, Assaultive Speech, and the First Amendment*. Boulder, Colo.: Westview Press, 1993.

Matthews, Fred H. *Quest for an American Sociology: Robert E. Park and the Chicago School*. Montreal: McGill-Queen's University Press, 1977.

Memmi, Albert. *The Colonizer and the Colonized*. Boston: Beacon Press, 1967.

———. *The Liberation of the Jew*. Trans. Judy Hyun. New York: Orion Books, 1966.

Menchú, Rigoberta. *I, Rigoberta Menchú: An Indian Woman in Guatemala*. Ed. Elisabeth Burgos-Debray. Trans. Ann Wright. London: Verso, 1984.

Mignolo, Walter D. *The Darker Side of the Renaissance: Literacy, Territoriality, and Colonization*. Ann Arbor: University of Michigan Press, 2003.

———. *The Darker Side of Western Modernity: Global Futures, Decolonial Options*. Durham, NC: Duke University Press, 2011.

———. *Local Histories/Global Designs: Coloniality, Subaltern Knowledges, and Border Thinking*. Princeton, NJ: Princeton University Press, 2000.

Miles, Robert. *Racism*. London: Routledge, 1989.

———. *Racism after "Race Relations."* London: Routledge, 1993.

———. *Racism and Migrant Labour: A Critical Text*. London: Routledge and Kegan Paul, 1982.

Millett, Kate. *Sexual Politics*. New York: Doubleday, 1970.

Mills, Charles W. "Intersecting Contracts." In *Contract and Domination*, by Carole Pateman and Charles Mills. Cambridge, UK: Polity Press, 2007.

———. *The Racial Contract*. Ithaca, NY: Cornell University Press, 1997.

Mills, C. Wright. *The Sociological Imagination*. New York: Oxford University Press, 1959.

Mishra, Pankaj. *From the Ruins of Empire: The Intellectuals Who Remade Asia*. New York: Farrar, Straus and Giroux, 2012.

Mohamad, Mahatir. *A New Deal for Asia*. Tokyo: Tachibana, 1999.

Mohanty, Chandra. "Under Western Eyes: Feminist Scholarship and Colonial Discourses." In *Feminism without Borders: Decolonizing Theory, Practicing Solidarity*. Durham, NC: Duke University Press, 2003.

Moraga, Cherríe. *Loving in the War Years*. Cambridge, MA: South End Press, 1983.

Morgan, Edmund S. *American Slavery, American Freedom: The Ordeal of Colonial Virginia*. New York: Norton, 1975.

Morris, Aldon D. *The Scholar Denied: W. E. B. Du Bois and the Birth of Modern Sociology*. Berkeley: University of California Press, 2015.

Mouffe, Chantal. "Hegemony and Ideology in Gramsci." In *Gramsci and Marxist Theory*, ed. Chantal Mouffe. London: Routledge and Kegan Paul, 1979.

Mullings, Leith. *On Our Own Terms: Race, Class, and Gender in the Lives of African American Women*. New York: Routledge, 1997.

Murch, Donna Jean. *Living for the City: Migration, Education, and the Rise of the Black Panther Party in Oakland, California*. Chapel Hill: University of North Carolina Press, 2010.

Murphey, Rhoads. *A History of Asia*. 2nd edition. New York: HarperCollins, 1996.

Nash, Gary B., et al. *The American People: Creating a Nation and Society*. 4th edition. New York: Longman, 1998.

Nehru, Jawaharlal. *The Discovery of India*. London: Meridian Books, 1956.

Neihardt, John G. *Black Elk Speaks: Being the Life Story of a Holy Man of the Oglala Sioux*. New York: William Morrow, 1932.

———. *The Sixth Grandfather: Black Elk's Teachings as Given to John G. Neihardt*. Ed. Raymond J. DeMallie. Lincoln: University of Nebraska Press, 1984.

"The New Face of America." *Time*, November 18, 1993, front cover.

Ngũgĩ wa Thiong'o. *Decolonising the Mind: The Politics of Language in African Literature*. Oxford: James Currey, 1986.

Nkrumah, Kwame. *Neo-Colonialism: The Last Stage of Imperialism*. London: Nelson, 1965.

"A Non-White Struggle toward New Humanism, Consciousness." *Daily Gater* [San Francisco State College], May 22, 1969.

Nott, Josiah Clark, and George R. Gliddon. *Indigenous Races of the Earth; Or, New Chapters of Ethnological Inquiry*. Philadelphia, PA: J. B. Lippincott, 1857.

Odo, Franklin, ed. *The Columbia Documentary History of the Asian American Experience*. New York: Columbia University Press, 2002.

Okihiro, Gary Y. *Island World: A History of Hawai'i and the United States*. Berkeley: University of California Press, 2008.

———. "Japan, World War II, and Third World Liberation." *Rikkyo American Studies* 31 (March 2009): 77–100.

Okihiro, Gary Y., and Elda Tsou. "On Social Formation." *Works and Days* 24.1–2 (2006): 69–88.

Omi, Michael, and Howard Winant. *Racial Formation in the United States: From the 1960s to the 1980s*. New York: Routledge, 1994.

Orrick, William H., Jr. *Shut It Down! A College in Crisis: San Francisco State College, October 1968–April 1969*. A Staff Report to the National Commission on the Causes and Prevention of Violence. Washington, DC: Government Printing Office, 1969.

Osajima, Keith. "Asian Americans as the Model Minority: An Analysis of the Popular Press Image in the 1960s and 1980s." In *Reflections on Shattered Windows: Promises and Prospects for Asian American Studies*, ed. Gary Y. Okihiro et al. Pullman: Washington State University Press, 1988.

Painter, Nell. *The History of White People*. New York: Norton, 2010.

Park, Robert Ezra. "Human Migration and the Marginal Man." *American Journal of Sociology* 33.6 (1928): 881–93.

———. Introduction to *The Japanese Invasion: A Study in the Psychology of Inter-Racial Contacts*, by Jesse Frederick Steiner. Chicago: A. C. McClurg, 1917.

———. "The Nature of Race Relations." In *Race and Culture*. Glencoe, IL: Free Press, 1950.

———. *Race and Culture*. Glencoe, IL: Free Press, 1950.

———. "Racial Assimilation in Secondary Groups with Particular Reference to the Negro." *American Journal of Sociology* 19.5 (1914): 606–23.

Park, Robert E., and Ernest W. Burgess. *Introduction to the Science of Sociology*. Chicago: University of Chicago Press, 1926.

Pascoe, Peggy. *What Comes Naturally: Miscegenation Law and the Making of Race in America*. New York: Oxford University Press, 2009.

Pateman, Carole. "The Settler Contract." In *Contract and Domination*, by Carole Pateman and Charles Mills. Cambridge, UK: Polity Press, 2007.

Pearson, Charles H. *National Life and Character: A Forecast*. London: Macmillan, 1893.

Persons, Stow. *Ethnic Studies at Chicago, 1905–45*. Urbana: University of Illinois Press, 1987.

Prashad, Vijay. *The Darker Nations: A People's History of the Third World*. New York: New Press, 2007.

Raushenbush, Winifred. *Robert E. Park: Biography of a Sociologist*. Durham, NC: Duke University Press, 1979.

Reich, Charles A. "The New Property." *Yale Law Journal* 73.5 (1964): 733–87.

Report of the National Advisory Commission on Civil Disorders. New York: Bantam Books, 1968.

Rich, Adrienne. "Compulsory Heterosexuality and Lesbian Existence." In *Blood, Bread, and Poetry: Selected Prose, 1979–1985*. New York: Norton, 1986.

Roberts, Sarah Julianne. "The TMA System of Hawaiian Creole and Diffusion." In *Creole Genesis, Attitudes and Discourse: Studies Celebrating Charlene J. Sato*, ed. John R. Rickford and Suzanne Romaine. Amsterdam: John Benjamins, 1999.

Robinson, Dean E. *Black Nationalism in American Politics and Thought*. Cambridge: Cambridge University Press, 2001.

Rodney, Walter. *How Europe Underdeveloped Africa*. Washington, DC: Howard University Press, 1974.

Roediger, David R. *The Wages of Whiteness: Race and the Making of the American Working Class*. New York: Verso, 1991.

Rosa, John. *Local Story: The Massie-Kahahawai Case and the Culture of History*. Honolulu: University of Hawai'i Press, 2014.

Ross, Robert H., and Emory S. Bogardus. "The Second-Generation Race Relations Cycle: A Study in *Issei-Nisei* Relationships." *Sociology and Social Research* 24.4 (1940): 357–63.

Said, Edward W. *Culture and Imperialism*. New York: Vintage Books, 1994.

———. *Orientalism*. New York: Vintage Books, 1979.

Sakoda, Kent, and Jeff Siegel. *Pidgin Grammar: An Introduction to the Creole Language of Hawai'i*. Honolulu, HI: Bess Press, 2003.

Samuels, Ellen Jean. "Critical Divides: Judith Butler's Body Theory and the Question of Disability." *NWSA Journal* 14.3 (2002): 58–76.

Sartre, Jean-Paul. Preface to *The Wretched of the Earth*, by Frantz Fanon. Trans. Constance Farrington. New York: Grove Press, 1968.

Scott, Joan W. "Experience." In *Feminists Theorize the Political*, ed. Judith Butler and Joan W. Scott. New York: Routledge, 1992.

Senghor, Léopold Sédar. "Negritude: A Humanism of the Twentieth Century." In *The Africa Reader*, ed. Wilfred Cartey and Martin Kilson. New York: Random House, 1970.

Singh, Amritjit, and Peter Schmidt, eds. *Postcolonial Theory and the United States: Race, Ethnicity, and Literature*. Jackson: University Press of Mississippi, 2000.

Smith, Andrea. *Conquest: Sexual Violence and American Indian Genocide*. Cambridge, MA: South End Press, 2005.

Smith, Linda Tuhiwai. *Decolonizing Methodologies: Research and Indigenous Peoples*. London: Zed Books, 1999.

Smith, Robert, Richard Axen, and DeVere Pentony. *By Any Means Necessary: The Revolutionary Struggle at San Francisco State*. San Francisco: Jossey-Bass, 1970.

Spivak, Gayatri Chakravorty. "Can the Subaltern Speak?" In *Marxism and the Interpretation of Culture*, ed. Cary Nelson and Lawrence Grossberg. London: Macmillan, 1988.

———. "The Politics of Translation." In *Outside in the Teaching Machine*. New York: Routledge, 1993.

Springer, Kimberly. *Living for the Revolution: Black Feminist Organizations, 1968–1980*. Durham, NC: Duke University Press, 2005.

Steltenkamp, Michael F. *Nicholas Black Elk: Medicine Man, Missionary, Mystic*. Norman: University of Oklahoma Press, 2009.

Stocking, George W., Jr. *Delimiting Anthropology: Occasional Inquiries and Reflections*. Madison: University of Wisconsin Press, 2001.

Stoddard, T. Lothrop. *The French Revolution in San Domingo*. Boston: Houghton Mifflin, 1914.

———. *The Rising Tide of Color against White World-Supremacy*. New York: Charles Scribner's Sons, 1920.

Stoll, David. *Rigoberta Menchú and the Story of All Poor Guatemalans*. Boulder, Colo.: Westview Press, 1999.

Stoneman, Richard. Introduction to *The Greek Alexander Romance*. Trans. Richard Stoneman. London: Penguin Books, 1991.

Tabron, Judith. *Postcolonial Literature from Three Continents: Tutuola, H.D., Ellison, and White*. New York: Peter Lang, 2003.

Thomas, William I., and Florian Znaniecki. *The Polish Peasant in Europe and America: Monograph of an Immigrant Group*. 5 vols. Chicago: University of Chicago Press, 1918–20.

Thompson, Edgar T., ed. *Race Relations and the Race Problem: A Definition and Analysis*. Durham, NC: Duke University Press, 1939.

Thomson, J. Oliver. *History of Ancient Geography*. Cambridge: Cambridge University Press, 1948.

Thorne, Christopher. *The Issue of War: States, Societies, and the Far Eastern Conflict of 1941–1945*. New York: Oxford University Press, 1985.

———. "Racial Aspects of the Far Eastern War of 1941–1945." *Proceedings of the British Academy* 66 (1980): 329–77.

Tinker, Hugh. *Race, Conflict and the International Order: From Empire to United Nations*. New York: St. Martin's Press, 1977.

Tobias, Steven M. "Amos Tutuola and the Colonial Carnival." *Research in African Literature* 30.2 (1999): 66–74.

Tozer, H. F. *A History of Ancient Geography*. 2nd edition. London: Cambridge University Press, 1935.

Trexler, Richard. *Sex and Conquest: Gendered Violence, Political Order, and the European Conquest of the Americas*. Ithaca, NY: Cornell University Press, 1995.

Ture, Kwame. "Afterword, 1992." In *Black Power: The Politics of Liberation*, by Kwame Ture and Charles V. Hamilton. New York: Vintage Books, 1992.

Ture, Kwame, and Charles V. Hamilton. *Black Power: The Politics of Liberation*. New York: Vintage Books, 1992.

Turner, Frederick Jackson. *The Frontier in American History*. New York: Henry Holt, 1920.

Van Deburg, William L. *New Day in Babylon: The Black Power Movement and American Culture, 1965–1975*. Chicago: University of Chicago Press, 1992.

Venuti, Lawrence, ed. *The Translation Studies Reader*. 2nd edition. New York: Routledge, 2004.

Von Eschen, Penny M. *Race against Empire: Black Americans and Anticolonialism, 1937–1957*. Ithaca, NY: Cornell University Press, 1997.

Wallerstein, Immanuel. *World-Systems Analysis: An Introduction*. Durham, NC: Duke University Press, 2004.

Weale, B. L. Putnam [pseudo. B. Lenox Simpson]. *The Conflict of Colour: The Threatened Upheaval throughout the World*. New York: Macmillan, 1910.

White, Richard. *The Roots of Dependency: Subsistence, Environment, and Social Change among the Choctaws, Pawnees and Navajos*. Lincoln: University of Nebraska Press, 1988.

Williams, Raymond. *Keywords: A Vocabulary of Culture and Society*. New York: Oxford University Press, 1983.

———. *Politics of Modernism: Against the New Conformists*. London: Verso, 1989.

Williams, Robert F. *Negroes with Guns*. New York: Marzani and Munsell, 1962.

Wilson, William J. *The Declining Significance of Race: Blacks and Changing American Institutions*. Chicago: University of Chicago Press, 1978.

Wist, Benjamin O. *A Century of Public Education in Hawaii, 1840–1940*. Honolulu, HI: Hawaii Education Review, 1940.

Woodson, Carter G. *The Mis-education of the Negro*. Washington, DC: Associated Publishers, 1933.

Wright, Richard. *The Color Curtain: A Report on the Bandung Conference*. New York: World, 1956.

Wu, Judy Tzu-Chun. *Radicals on the Road: Internationalism, Orientalism, and Feminism During the Vietnam Era*. Ithaca, NY: Cornell University Press, 2013.

Yoo, David K. *Growing Up Nisei: Race, Generation, and Culture among Japanese Americans of California, 1924–49*. Urbana: University of Illinois Press, 2000.

Young, Robert. *White Mythologies: Writing History and the West*. London: Routledge, 1990.

Yu, Henry. *Thinking Orientals: Migration, Contact, and Exoticism in Modern America*. New York: Oxford University Press, 2001.

Zabus, Chantal. *The African Palimpsest: Indigenization of Language in the West African Europhone Novel*. Amsterdam: Rodopi, 1991.

Zimmern, Alfred. *The Third British Empire*. London: Humphrey Milford, 1926.

INDEX

NOTE: Page numbers followed by *f* indicate a figure.

ability/disability, 172, 185n23
affirmative action programs, 104, 135
African American feminism, 139–41
African American studies, 12, 16–17, 114; at Merritt College, 34; at San Francisco State College, 27–31; Third World studies and, 156–66
Afro-American Association (AAA), 33–34
"Afterword, 1992" (Carmichael), 37
In re Ah Yup decision, 128
Albuquerque, Alfonso de, 72
Alcoff, Linda Martín, 115–16
Alexander the Great, 60–61, 63, 67
Alexander VI, Pope, 73
Algeria's revolution, 5, 38–39, 170
Allen, Ernest, 34–35
Allende, Salvatore, 83–84
Althusser, Louis, 81, 92, 122, 170; on ideological hegemony of the state, 109; on liberation of consciousness, 93–94; on social formation and economism, 143
Alvarado, Roger, 27
American Board of Commissioners for Foreign Missions, 96–97
American Indians. *See* Native Americans
American Missionary Association, 97
ancient Egypt, 66–67

Anderson, Benedict, 130
Annales d'histoire économique et sociale, 79
Anthony, Susan B., 157
anticolonial movements, 155, 167; Bandung Conference of 1955 and, 6, 17–18, 36, 47–48, 170–71; black power analogies of, 35–37; cultivation of national culture in, 9, 50–51, 93, 106, 179n59; education and, 93–106; end to white supremacy in, 41–47; European historiography of, 46–47; Fanon's focus on, 17–19, 93; First World responses to, 40–41, 44; indigenous peoples' rights and, 51–56; internationalism in, 41–47, 167; nationalist turn of, 6–7, 9, 12–14, 31, 48–51, 55–56, 167, 178n54; neocolonialist responses to, 28, 31, 49, 56, 169–70, 178n54; pan-Africanism and, 6, 12, 39, 42, 48, 50–51, 67, 160–62; World War I and, 41; World War II and, 42–47
antistructuralism, 109–10
Anzaldúa, Gloria, 163–64
Aptheker, Herbert, 147
Aristotle, 60, 63
Arizona SB 2281 (2010), 2, 135
Armstrong, Clarissa Chapman, 96–97
Armstrong, Richard, 96–97, 181n9
Armstrong, Samuel Chapman, 6, 9, 23, 97–99

Asian Americans, 160; invention of "non-white" categories and, 129; legal challenges to naturalization of, 128, 162–63; migrant labor of, 89–92, 162–63; as model minority, 26, 129; social formations of, 147, 150–51; US census classifications of, 131–32, 163

Asian American studies, 12; Chicago ethnic studies and, 26–27, 175n59; Third World studies and, 156–66

Asians and Pacific Islanders (US census definition), 133

Asian Women, 19

assimilation, 111–12; of American Indians, 95–99, 105; of immigrants, 6, 23–25, 112, 122; of problem races, 111–12, 122, 162

Assimilation in American Life (Gordon), 111–12

Atlanta Compromise, 6

Atlantic Charter, 44–46

Atlantic trade triangle, 69–75, 161

Atmore, Anthony, 142

Bacon, Nathaniel, 87, 150

Bacon's Rebellion, 87, 150, 159

Balibar, Étienne, 48–49

Bandung Conference of 1955, 6, 17–18, 36, 47–48, 170–71

Barred Zone Act of 1917, 133, 163

Barrios de Chungara, Domitila, 118

Beale, Frances, 11–12, 139–40, 184n3

Beauvoir, Simone de, 157

Bell, Derrick A., 183n12

Benjamin, Walter, 118–19

Berlin Conference of 1884–85, 20

Beverley, John, 182n14

Big Foot, 117f

bilingual education, 135

binary oppositions, 3, 129, 158–59, 184n21, 185n7

biological determinism, 61–64, 148

black (blood quantum definition), 131

Black Atlantic, 69

Black Elk Speaks (Niehardt), 116–17

blackness, 129

Black Panther journal, 35

Black Panther Party, 18; on African American liberation, 35; at San Francisco State College, 28–29; slogan of, 15; Ten Point Program of, 34–35

black power (as term), 176n76

Black Power (Carmichael and Hamilton), 36, 51

black power movement: cultivation of cultural identity in, 51; nationalist discourse of, 37–38, 177n1; organic intellectuals of, 32–36, 38, 57; Reagan-era response to, 103–5; revolutionary discourses of, 35–36; third world internationalism and, 31, 38–39, 176n69, 177n4; US fears of, 177n5

Black Student Union (BSU), 34–35, 51, 173n12

black studies. *See* African American studies

black women: marginalization by feminist studies of, 121–22, 139–40, 153; multiple intersecting oppressions of, 139–41

Black Women's Alliance (BWA), 140

Black Women's Liberation Caucus, 11, 140

Bloch, Marc, 79

blood quantum definitions of race, 131

Bloom, Allan, 103–4, 110

Blumenbach, Johann Friedrich, 62–64, 128

Boas, Franz, 23

Bodin, Jean, 61–65

Bogardus, Emory, 24

Bonacich, Edna, 162

borderlands theory, 163–64

Botswana, 4–5

Braudel, Fernand, 79

Bretton Woods, 170

Broca, Paul, 66

Brown, William O., 32

Brown v. Board of Education decision, 100–102

Bruyneel, Kevin, 179n62

Buck v. Bell decision, 172

Burgos-Debray, Elisabeth, 182n13

Burkitt, Ian, 142

Butler, Judith, 156–57

Cape Colony, 86

capitalism, 7, 166–67; Chicago laissez-faire theory of, 83; critical race theory on,

11; imperialist basis of, 7–8, 59–76, 79; Marxist theory on, 125; multiple oppressions of black women by, 140; neocolonial dependency and, 170; search for cheap labor in, 87–92; structured dependency in, 78–84, 92; transnationalist features of, 169–70; US as global hegemon of, 50; world-systems theory of, 77–92

Cardoso, Fernando Henrique, 79

Carlisle Indian Industrial School, 9, 99

Carmichael, Stokely (Kwame Ture), 36, 37, 176n76

Carnegie, Andrew, 100

Cartesian humanism, 108–9. *See also* new humanism

Caucasian (as term), 64

census classifications, 130–33, 147, 163

Center for the Study of Ethnicity and Race, 3

Césaire, Aimé, 51, 56, 161, 177n23

Cheng, Lucie, 162

Cherokee Nation v. Georgia decision, 53

Chicago economic theory, 83

Chicago ethnic studies, 6, 10, 25–31, 36, 111, 173n1; on assimilation of immigrant minorities, 6, 23–25, 112, 122, 167–68; critical responses to, 14; study of Asian Americans in, 26–27

Chicago riot of 1919, 23–24

Chicago sociology, 14, 19, 22–23, 174n35; black sociologists of, 32; endorsement of evolutionary science by, 25; ethnic cycle followed by, 32; focus on race relations in, 6, 10, 13–14, 17, 19, 22–25, 27, 86; transition to ethnic studies of, 25–27, 122, 168; urban focus of, 23–24, 122

Chicana/o studies, 12, 163–64

Chinese Exclusion Act of 1882, 133, 147, 162–63

Christian (as racialized category), 150

Churchill, Winston S., 44

Cicero, 118

Civil Rights Act of 1964, 102, 146

civil rights movement, 12–13, 31, 36, 51, 126–27

Cixous, Hélène, 170

Clark, Kenneth, 35–36

class divisions, 168

Closing of the American Mind (Bloom), 103

code-switching, 164

Cold War, 19, 68; Bandung Conference of 1955 and, 6, 17–18, 36, 47–48, 170–71; funding for area studies during, 29; non-aligned movement of, 38–39, 48; primacy of nation-states in, 49–50

College of San Mateo's College Readiness Program, 16–17

Collins, Patricia Hill, 141

Collins, Terry, 31

colonialism, 84–87; black subjects of, 57, 67; definition of, 68, 84; extractive colonies of, 85–86; indigenous subjects of, 51–56; migrant labor and, 87–92, 162; race relations in, 86–87; religious rationale for, 181n24; rights to land and labor in, 86; settler colonies of, 85–87, 124, 159–60. *See also* imperialism

color-blind policies, 126, 136

colored (US census definition), 133

Columbia University: Boas' anthropology at, 23; comparative ethnic studies at, 3–4, 13; early ethnic studies at, 3; student strikes of 1968 at, 78

Columbus, Christopher, 72–73

Combahee River Collective, 140–41, 146

Communauté Financière Africaine, 178n54

comparative ethnic studies, 3–4, 12

Conference on Discrimination against Indigenous Populations, 54

conquest, 84–87, 180n8; of indigenous peoples, 51–56; migrant labor and, 87–92; race relations in, 86–87; rape and sexual violence in, 84–85, 181n24; religious rationale for, 88, 181n24; rights to land and labor in, 86

consciousness, 93–94; language and voicing of, 109, 113–19; Marx on false forms of, 109; in new humanism, 107–11; role of experience in, 113–14; translation and, 118–19

coolies, 91–92

Cosgrove, Denis, 142

Crenshaw, Kimberlé, 127, 141, 146
creolized language, 82–83, 181n18
critical ethnic studies, 14
critical legal studies, 11, 124, 126
critical race theory, 139; on capitalism, 11; on the legal apparatus of social formation, 147; on whiteness, 124–27, 129, 136, 183n12
critical theory, 124–27, 136
critical white studies, 11, 124, 134–37
Crusader, The, newsletter, 33
Cruse, Harold, 35
cultural nationalism, 3, 6, 13–14, 31, 36. *See also* nationalism
cultural relativism. *See* multiculturalism
Culture and Imperialism (Said), 185n22
culture wars of the 1980s–90s, 8–9, 102–5
curriculum of Third World studies, 15–36; black organic intellectual mobilization of, 32–36; Chicago sociology and, 17, 19, 22–25, 27; foundational texts in, 19, 185n22; internationalism of, 31, 176n69; post-1968 ethnic studies and, 25–31; on self-determination, 17–19, 31–36; Third World Liberation Front's demands for, 1, 5, 13–14, 18–19, 27–31, 36, 93, 102, 105–6, 173n12. *See also* education

da Gama, Vasco, 71–72
Dark Ghetto (Clark), 35–36
Darkwater (Du Bois), 134
Dawes (General Allotment) Act of 1887, 53–54, 131
Declaration on the Rights of Indigenous Peoples of 2007, 55
decolonization movements. *See* anticolonial movements
deconstruction, 125–26
Defence of India Act, 43–44
DeGraffenreid v. General Motors decision, 146
de las Casas, Bartolomé, 181n24
De l'égalité des races humaines (Firmin), 66–67
Deloria, Vine, Jr., 53, 55
"Demarginalizing the Intersection of Race and Sex" (Crenshaw), 141, 146

De Orbe Novo (Pietro Martir de Anghiera), 73
dependency theory, 78–84; on asymmetrical spatial dimensions of imperialism, 78–80, 92; hegemonic production of subjectivities in, 80–83, 107, 109
Derrida, Jacques, 125–26, 170
Descartes, René, 108
Dewey, John, 181n2
Dias, Bartolomeu, 71
Diop, Alioune, 51
Diop, Cheik Anta, 51
discovery doctrine, 52
Doak, William, 131
Doyle, Bertram, 32
Dred Scott v. Sandford decision, 151–52, 177n12
D'Souza, Dinesh, 104, 110
Duan, Zhongqiao, 142
Duara, Prasenjit, 46
Du Bois, W. E. B., 32; on the global color line, 5–6, 19–21, 39–40, 57, 174n18, 177n12; on interracial contracts, 42; on Nazism, 177n23; on the US's Negro problem, 39; on whiteness, 134–35
Dutch East India Company (VOC), 75, 86

education, 8–9, 93–106; Civil Rights Act of 1964 and, 102; of colonial subjects, 99; Immigration Act of 1965 and, 102; liberation of national consciousness through, 93–94, 181n2; Mann's reforms of, 99–100; Puritan ideals of, 95–97, 103, 105; racial and gender hierarchies and segregation in, 94–102, 105–6; Reagan-era multiculturalism in, 102–5, 110, 135, 136, 182n13; US court decisions on, 100–102. *See also* curriculum of Third World studies
Edwards, Brent Hayes, 193n15
Eighteenth Brumaire of Louis Bonaparte, The (Marx), 113, 142
Elwood, Christopher, 142
encomienda system, 86
English East India Company, 75
English language, 135
Enlightenment thought, 61–64, 148

Equality of Human Races, The (Firmin),
66–67
Eratosthenes, 60–61
Erikson, Erik, 111–12
ethnic revivalism, 135–36
ethnic studies. *See* Chicago ethnic studies;
post-1968 ethnic studies
ex-natives, 25–26, 82–83
extractive colonies, 85

Fabie, Ramon, 75
false consciousness, 109
Fanon, Frantz, 3, 25–26, 170; black power
movement and, 32, 35; on essentialist
movements, 161; on national culture, 9,
50–51, 93, 106, 179n59; on négritude,
67; on new humanism, 5, 9–10, 18, 94,
108–9, 111, 121; on Third World liberation, 17–19, 93
Febvre, Lucien, 79
feminism: first wave of, 157; second wave
of, 157–58; third-wave of, 171
Feminist Mystique, The (Friedan), 157–58
feminist studies: marginalization of Third
World women in, 121–22, 139–40, 153,
171; movement for self-determination
in, 12; theory and methodology of, 2,
158; Third World studies and, 156–66.
See also women's studies
Ferdinand II, King of Aragón, 71
Filipino Repatriation Act of 1935, 133, 147
finance capitalism, 78–79
Firetail, Louis, 98*f*
Firmin, Anténor, 65–67
first-wave feminism, 157
First World (as term), 39, 50
Fitzhugh, George, 122
Foreign Mission School, 95–97
formation (as term), 122–23
Foucault, Michel: on power, 108; on pro-
duction of the subject, 110; on sexuality,
156; on social formation, 143; on sub-
altern discourse, 115–16
Four Freedoms, 45–46
Fourteenth Amendment of the Constitu-
tion, 100, 128, 162
Fourth World, 164–66, 172

Frank, Andre Gunder, 79, 83–84
Frankfurt School, 125–26
Frazier, Demita, 140
Frazier, E. Franklin, 32
free colored (US census definition), 133
Freire, Paulo, 3, 9, 93–94, 107, 113, 116
Freud, Sigmund, 110; on the dark feminine
world, 170; on psychosocial stages, 111;
on the unconscious, 109
Friedan, Betty, 157–58
Füredi, Frank, 47

Garrett, James, 35
Garvey, Marcus, 161
Gay Wan Guay, 44
gendered violence, 84–85, 181n24
Gender Trouble (Butler), 156–57
General Agreement on Tariffs and Trade,
50, 170
General Allotment (Dawes) Act of 1887,
53–54, 131
Genovese, Eugene, 135
Gentlemen's Agreement of 1902, 133, 163
geographical determinism, 58–61, 63, 67,
148
German Ideology (Marx), 142
Glenn, Evelyn Nakano, 141
global color line, 5–6, 19–21, 39–41, 57,
167, 169, 174n18; contrast with nation-
alist movements to, 37–38, 177n12;
geographical determinism and, 58–61;
migrations to First World imperial cen-
ters and, 6
Gobineau, Arthur de, 64–65
Godelier, Maurice, 122
Gong Lum v. Rice decision, 100–101
Gordon, Milton, 111–12
Gramsci, Antonio, 14, 32, 83, 92, 115; on
hegemony, 80–81, 109, 146; on liberation of consciousness, 93–94; on pater-
nalism, 98
Great East Asia Conference of 1943, 45
Greater East Asia Co-Prosperity Sphere,
45
Great Society, 102
Greek philosophy, 58–61
Grotius, Hugo, 52

Guevara, Che, 32, 35, 176n82
Guyot, Arnold, 180n26

Hall, George W., 149–50
Hamilton, Charles V., 36, 51
Hampton Normal and Agricultural Institute, 6, 9, 23, 97–99
Haney-López, Ian, 127–29, 136
Hare, Nathan, 16–17, 27–31
Harrison, Hubert H., 20, 32, 37
Hawai'i, 4–5; creolized (pidgin) language of, 82–83, 181n18; indentured labor from, 89–90; mission education in, 8–9, 96–97, 99, 181n9; US census classifications in, 133; US conquest and annexation of, 165–66
Hayakawa, S. I., 175n59
Hegel, G. W. F., 64, 108–9, 113
hegemony, 80–83
Henry the Navigator, Prince of Portugal, 71
Hindess, Barry, 143
Hippocrates, 58–61, 63
Hirst, Paul, 143
Hispanic (US census definition), 131
Hobbes, Thomas, 52
Hobson, J. A., 68, 78–79
Ho Chi Minh, 35, 176n82
homosexual violence, 84–85, 181n24
Hoover, Herbert, 45
Hoover, Robert, 16–17
Horne, Gerald, 43
Hughes, Henry, 122
humanism, 10, 108–9, 113, 121, 148. *See also* new humanism

I, Rigoberta Menchú: An Indian Woman in Guatemala (Menchú), 117–18, 182n13
identity politics, 2–3, 119; performance of identity and, 112–13, 156–57; in post-1968 ethnic studies, 110–13; of whiteness, 135–36
Illiberal Education (D'Souza), 104
immigrant assimilation, 6, 23–25, 111–12, 122, 162, 167–68
Immigration Act of 1965, 102, 104–5, 133
Immigration and Nationality Act of 1924, 163

imperialism, 57–76, 155, 166–67; African Americans as subjects of, 35–36; Asia as original focus of, 68–73, 179n11; Atlantic trade triangle of, 69, 161; capitalist basis of, 7–8, 59–76; the colonized-object of, 107; conquest and colonialism in, 51–56, 84–87, 180n8; creation of a native elite in, 25–26, 82–83; definition of, 68; dependency theory on, 78–84, 92; global color line of, 5–6, 19–21, 37–41, 57, 174n18, 177n12; ideological discourses of space/time in, 57–67, 180n26; internationalist responses to, 38; language and education as weapons of, 8–9, 12, 81–83, 109–10, 122, 181n18; material discourses of, 57–58, 67–75; neocolonial forms of, 28, 31, 49, 56, 169–70, 178n54; in the New World, 72–76; Portuguese navigation and, 69–72; racial dimensions of, 10–11, 15–17, 79–80; Third World Liberation Front's focus on, 7–8, 13; Third World studies' response to, 9–10, 13, 17–19, 31–36, 55–56, 121–22, 159–60, 173n11; of US multilateralism, 50; wars of the twentieth century and, 7, 20–21, 37, 40–47, 49, 68, 167; in world-systems theory, 77–92. *See also* anticolonial movements
indentured labor, 78, 86–92, 130
independence movements. *See* anticolonial movements
Indian Citizenship Act of 1924, 53–54
Indian National Congress, 44
Indian Reorganization Act of 1934, 53–54
Indians. *See* Native Americans
indigenous peoples, 51–56; dependency theory and, 78–84; human rights agenda of, 57; in North America, 52–56, 73–75; rape and sexual violence against, 84–87, 181n24. *See also* Native Americans
Indochinese Women's Conference of 1971, 19
Inequality of Human Races, The (Gobineau), 64–66

Institute for Research in African American Studies, 3
Institute for Social Research (Frankfurt School), 125–26
Institute of Pacific Relations, 21
Institute of Race Relations, 21
Institute of Social and Religious Research, 24
Inter-American Conference of 1899, 48
International Court of Justice (World Court), 54
internationalism, 38–41; in anticolonial movements, 41–47, 167; Bandung Conference of 1955 and, 6, 17–18, 36, 47–48, 170–71; in the black power movement, 31, 38–39, 176n69, 177n4; human rights agenda of, 51, 57; Pan-Africa Conferences and, 6, 12, 39, 42, 48; in post-1968 ethnic studies, 19, 31; in Third World studies, 31, 176n69; during World War II, 38–47
International Labor Organization (ILO), 54–55
International Monetary Fund (IMF), 7, 50, 170
International Trade Organization (ITO), 50
International Treaty Council (ITC), 54
International Year of the World's Indigenous Peoples, 55
interracial mixing, 111–12, 122, 130–31, 162
intersectionality, 11–12, 127, 139–53, 155–56. See also social formation
Ionian philosophy, 58
Isabella, Queen of Spain and Castile, 71

Jackman, Marvin, 34
Jamestown colony, 86
Japan: Meiji Restoration of, 45; pan-Asian vision of, 45–46; Russo-Japanese War victory of, 20–21, 40, 46; threat to white supremacy by, 42–46
Japanese American Citizens League (JACL), 101–2
Jay, John, 152
Jim Crow segregation, 25, 33, 64–66, 89. See also racism

Johnson, Anthony, 149
Johnson, Charles S., 23–24, 32
Johnson, Lyndon B., 102
Johnson v. M'Intosh decision, 52, 152–53
Johnston, J. F. W., 142
jus sanguinis, 49

Kant, Immanuel, 64, 108–9
Kaplan, Martha, 49–50
Kelley, John D., 49–50
King, Martin Luther, Jr., 126, 158
Kitchen Table Women of Color Press, 153
Krasner, David, 142
Kristeva, Julia, 156
Ku Klux Klan, 33

Labriola, Antonio, 80
Lacan, Jacques, 109–10, 121–22, 156, 182n3
laissez-faire capitalism, 83
Lange, Dorothea, 132f
Latin American Students Organization, 26
Latina/o (US census definition), 131, 133
Latinx, 3, 160, 173n2; as cultural/ethnic group, 129; forced expulsions of, 131, 132f, 147, 163; US Census classifications of, 130–31, 133, 147, 163
Latinx studies, 79, 156–66
Law of Nations, or The Principles of Natural Law (Vattel), 52–53
Lazarus, Emma, 163
League against Imperialism and Colonialism, 42
League of Nations, 7, 43, 166
Lectures on Agricultural Chemistry and Geology (Johnston), 142
Lee Kuan Yew, 44
Lenin, Vladimir, 68
Let Me Speak! (Barrios de Chungara), 118
Levine, Lawrence W., 103–4
linguistic structuralism, 109
Linnaeus, Carl, 62–63
Literacy Act of 1917, 163
Locke, Alain, 139
Locke, John, 52, 84
Lorde, Audre, 121
Lum, Martha, 100–101
Lumumba, Patrice, 35, 176n82

Lyotard, Jean-François, 170
Lytle, Clifford M., 53, 55

Mackey, Miles, 96
Macmillan, Harold, 43
Mahatir Mohamad, 44
Malcolm X, 32–36, 51, 105–6
Mandela, Nelson, 17
Mann, Horace, 99–100
Mao Zedong, 3, 32–33, 35
Marable, Manning, 3
Marco Polo, 179n11
Marcus, David C., 101
"The Margin at the Center" (Beverley),
    182n14
Marks, Shula, 142
Marshall, John, 52–53
Marshall, Thurgood, 101
Marx, Karl, 3, 110; on base and superstruc-
    ture, 145; on modes of production,
    142–43; on the silenced masses, 113, 115;
    on social constitutions of the self, 109;
    on social formation, 141–43
Marxism, 11, 27; critical theory and,
    125–27; on false consciousness, 80; in
    feminist theory, 158; on the masses, 16;
    on means and relations of production,
    81; on the nation, 48–49; on oppression
    and resistance, 147, 153; on race, 123; on
    social formation, 122–23; on the Third
    World, 170
materialism, 125
Matsuoka, Yosuke, 45
McAllister, Don, 28f
McCormick, Paul J., 101
McDougald, Elise Johnson, 139
Memmi, Albert, 18, 26, 81–83, 121–22
Menchú, Rigobarta, 117–18, 182n13
Méndez, Sylvia, Gonzalo, and Merome,
    101–2
Méndez v. Westminster, 101–2
mercantile capitalism, 68–69, 79
Merritt College, 34
"Meteorologica" (Aristotle), 60
Method for Easy Comprehension of History
    (Bodin), 61–65
Mexican Americans: citizenship status and
    rights of, 101–2; forced expulsions of,
    131, 132f, 147, 163; US census classifica-
    tions of, 130–31, 133, 147, 163
Mexican American studies, 27
Mignolo, Walter D., 185n23
migrant labor, 87–92, 162–64
Mills, Charles W., 10–11, 123–24
Mills, C. Wright, 107–8, 113–14
Minority Identity Development model, 112
miscegenation. See interracial mixing
Mis-education of the Negro, The (Wood-
    son), 26
Missionary Spelling Book, and Reader, The,
    96
Morris, Aldon, 174n35
mulatto (blood quantum definition), 131
multiculturalism, 103–5, 110, 135–36,
    166–68
multilateralism, 50
Murray, George, 18, 28–29, 35
Murray, Hugh, 149–50

National Association for the Advancement
    of Colored People (NAACP), 101, 157
national consciousness, 93–94
nationalism, 37–56, 166; black power
    discourses of, 37–38, 177n1; indigenous
    peoples' rights and, 51–56; kinship and
    language in, 49; national culture and, 9,
    50–51, 93, 179n59; origin of sovereign
    nation-states and, 48–52, 178n54; racial
    motivations of, 41–48; in Third World
    anticolonial movements, 6–7, 9, 12–14,
    25, 31, 55–56, 167; Third World interna-
    tionalist consciousness and, 38–41; of
    World War I, 41
National Life and Character: A Forecast
    (Pearson), 40–41
National Organization of Women (NOW),
    158
National Women's Suffrage Association,
    157
nation-states. See sovereign nation-states
Native Americans: cultural revival of
    the 1880s of, 116–17; education and
    assimilation of, 95–99, 105; enslaved
    labor of, 88, 90, 181n24; eroded rights

of self-determination of, 53–55; European conquest of Americas and, 73–75, 160; Fourth World of, 164–66; human rights agenda of, 57; Marshall trilogy of decisions on, 52–53; as racial category, 129; rape and sexual violence against, 84–85, 181n24; self-determination goals of, 165–66; social formation of, 148–51; spiritual identity of, 55; in US census data, 130, 131

Native American studies, 12, 27, 156, 164–66

Native Hawaiian and Other Pacific Islander (US census definition), 133

Naturalization Act of 1790, 128, 151–52

natural law, 52–53

négritude, 50–51, 67, 161

Negro (US census definition), 131, 133

The Negro in Chicago, 24

Nehru, Jawaharlal, 43–44, 48

Neihardt, John G., 116–17

neocolonialism and dependency, 28, 31, 49, 56, 83, 169–70, 178n54

"The New Colossus" (Lazarus), 163

New Deal, 102

new humanism, 5, 9–10, 13, 17–19, 94, 108–11, 121–22. *See also* self-determination

New Spain, 84–86, 181n24

Newton, Huey P., 34–35

New World Consciousness. *See* new humanism

Ngũgĩ wa Thiong'o, 82–83

Niagara Movement, 157

Nineteenth Amendment of the Constitution, 157

non-aligned movement, 38–39, 48

nonpersons, 130

North American Indian Brotherhood, 54

Nuremberg War Crimes Trial, 46

objectification, 107

octaroon (blood quantum definition), 131

Omi, Michael, 10, 122–24

On Airs, Waters, and Sites (Hippocrates), 58–59

one-drop rule, 131

"On the Heavens" (Aristotle), 60

On the Natural Varieties of Mankind (Blumenbach), 62–64

Opium War, 90

oral histories, 114, 116–17

Organization of Solidarity with the People of Asia, Africa and Latin American conference, 35

Orientalism (Said), 185n22

Ozawa, Takao, 128–29

Pacific Coast Survey of Race Relations, 24, 26–27

Page Act of 1875, 147, 162

Palm-Wine Drinkard, The (Tutuola), 83

Pan-African Conference of 1900, 6, 39, 48, 50

Pan-African Conference of 1933, 42

Pan-African Conference of 1945, 42

pan-Africanism, 12, 160–62; cultivation of négritude in, 50–51, 67, 161; mobilization goals of, 161–62

pan-Asianism, 45–46

Paris Anthropological Society, 66

Park, Robert E., 6, 14, 86; ethnic cycle of, 111–12; on race relations, 22–27, 86, 122

Parmenides, 60

Peace of Westphalia of 1648, 52

Pearson, Charles H., 40–41

Pedagogy of the Oppressed (Freire), 93–94

People v. George W. Hall, The (California), 149–50

performance of identity, 112–13, 156–57

Pietro Martir de Anghiera, 73

Pinochet, Augusto, 83

"The Pitfalls of National Consciousness" (Fanon), 179n59

Plato, 61

Plessy v. Ferguson decision, 100

positivism, 125

post-1968 ethnic studies, 1–3, 166, 173n1; Arizona's banning of, 2, 135; black-white binary in, 158–59, 185n7; on class divisions, 168; comparative approach to, 3–4; on consciousness, 93–94; critical approaches to, 14; identity politics and, 110–13; on land and labor, 12;

post-1968 ethnic studies (*continued*)
on postethnic hybridity, 168; racial
formation theory in, 10–11, 122–24;
Reagan-era attacks on, 104–5; at San
Francisco State College, 27–31, 159; segregated formations within, 2–3, 13–14,
158–59; self-determination movements
and, 2–3, 5, 8–10, 12, 31; Third World
studies and, 156–66; trivialization of
internationalism by, 19, 31; undefined
theory and methodology of, 2–4; at
University of California—Los Angeles,
4–5; at University of Chicago, 6, 10;
white ethnic revival movements and,
135–36, 167–68
postcolonialism, 81, 166, 168–70; focus on
diversity in, 169–70; Western culture as
basis of, 168–69
postethnicity, 168
poststructuralism, 10, 109–13, 125–26, 182n3
Power/Knowledge (Foucault), 108
Prashad, Vijay, 42
Pratt, Richard Henry, 9, 99
Prison Notebooks (Gramsci), 80–81
psychosocial development, 111–12
Puritan education, 95–97, 103, 105
Pythagoras, 58, 60

quadroon (blood quantum definition), 131
queer studies, 105, 110, 114; theory and
methodology of, 2; Third World studies
and, 156–66
Quit India Resolution, 44

race-neutral legal discourse, 126
race relations, 27, 36; Chicago sociology
and, 6, 10, 13–14, 17, 19, 22–25; civil
rights movement and, 12–13, 31, 36, 51,
126–27; as object of study, 21–22; Park's
study of, 24–27, 86, 122; whiteness as
protected category of, 10–11, 129
racial formation, 121–37; black-white
binary of, 3, 129, 158–59, 185n7; blood
quantum definitions in, 131; critical race
theory on, 124, 126–27, 129, 183n12;
legal production of, 127–29, 151–52,
162–63; mixing and miscegenation in,

122, 130–31; of nonpersons, 130; official
expulsions and exclusion in, 131–33, 147,
162–63; of problem races, 122, 162; reifi-
cation of racial identity and, 123; theory
of, 10–11, 122–24, 168; by US census
categories, 130–33, 147, 163, 183n15; of
whiteness, 11, 124, 129, 134–37
racial identity, 111–12, 123
racism, 10–11, 15–17, 25–26, 79–84; anticolonial movements and, 25, 41–48,
55–56; biological determinism and,
61–64; in citizenship laws, 124–28,
149–53, 155; critical race theory on,
126–27, 129, 193n11; geographical determinism and, 58–61, 63, 67; of the global
color line, 5–6, 19–21, 37–41, 57, 169,
174n18, 177n12; of Gobeineau's views on
pollution, 64–66; of Jim Crow segregation, 64–66, 89; of Ku Klux Klan terror,
33; mulatto marginality and, 111–12; as
natural survival mechanism, 24–25; of
Nazi policies, 25, 42, 102, 167, 177n23;
social formation of, 148–53, 148n24;
unassimilable problem races and, 111–12,
122, 162; in US education, 94–102,
105–6; wars of the twentieth century
and, 40–47, 167; white subjectivity and,
47. *See also* imperialism
rape, 84, 88
Reading Capital (Marx), 143
Reagan, Ronald, 102
Reel, Estelle, 99
relativism. *See* multiculturalism
reverse discrimination, 135
reverse racism, 135
Revolutionary Action Movement (RAM),
32–35, 37
Rich, Adrienne, 158
Robeson, Paul, 32
Rockefeller, John D., 100
Roling, B. V. A., 46
Roosevelt, Franklin D., 102
Russo-Japanese War, 20–21, 40, 46

Said, Edward, 185n22
San Francisco State College (SFS), 1–2;
Black Student Union of, 34–35, 51,

173n12; black studies at, 16, 27–31; ethnic studies at, 27–31, 159; student strikes of 1968 at, 27–28, 35–36, 175n59; Third World studies at, 36. *See also* Third World Liberation Front

Sartre, Jean-Paul, 25–26, 82, 170

Sastroamidjojo, Ali, 47

Saussure, Ferdinand de, 109

Sauvy, Albert, 38–39

Schleiermacher, Friedrich, 118

Scholar Denied, The (Morris), 174n35

Scott, Joan W., 114–15

Seale, Bobby, 34

Second Congress of Black Artists and Writers, 50–51

Second Sex (Beauvoir), 157

second-wave feminism, 157–58

Second World (as term), 39, 50

segregation, 25, 33, 64–66, 89. *See also* racism

self-determination, 167, 172; of American Indians, 52–55, 165–66; as basis for ethnic studies, 2–3, 5, 8, 12; in the black power movement, 32–37, 51; as goal of Third World studies, 2, 5–6, 9–13, 17–19, 31–36, 173n11; of indigenous peoples, 51–56; language and, 8, 12, 82–83, 181n18; nationalist discourses on, 6–7, 9, 12–14, 31, 37–56, 166; new humanism and, 5, 9–10, 13, 17–19, 94, 108–11; Wilson's Fourteen Points on, 37. *See also* anticolonial movements

self-hatred, 110

Seneca Falls Convention, 157

Senghor, Léopold, 50–51, 161

September 11, 2001, attacks, 147

settler colonies, 85–87, 124, 159–60

sexual violence, 84–85, 88, 181n24

Simmel, Georg, 32

slavery, 8, 25, 40; of American Indians, 88, 90, 181n24; Atlantic trade triangle and, 69, 72, 161; Chicago sociology on, 32; in colonial economies, 86–87; as inherited condition, 149; legal abolition of, 89–91, 160; in New Spain, 86; of Pacific Islanders, 90; prohibitions on literacy and learning in, 9; racial contract of, 10–11, 123–24; social formation of, 148–52, 185n24; in

US census counts, 130–31; in the Virginia Colony, 88–89, 148–50, 185n24

Smith, Andrea, 84–85, 181n24

Smith, Barbara, 140, 184n5

Smith, Beverly, 140

Smith, John, 88

Smith, Robert, 28–31

social formation, 15, 122–23, 139–53; on ability/disability, 172, 185n23; in ancient Greece, 148, 152; of binaries, 129, 158–59; colonial production of, 148–50, 148n24, 159; on convergent spheres of oppression, 145–47; on intersectionality, 11–12, 140–41, 146, 155–56; Marx's approach to, 141–43, 145; power as organizing principle of, 2, 15, 141, 143–47, 159, 184n21; production of citizens in, 149–53; property rights in, 150, 152–53; theory of, 11–12, 141–47, 155–56, 172; of third world women, 139–41, 153, 171

socialism, 11

socioeconomic class divisions, 168

sociology, 22, 174n35. *See also* Chicago sociology

"The Souls of White Folk" (Du Bois), 134–35

Soul Students Advisory Council, 34

Southern Christian Leadership Conference, 158

Southern Poverty Law Center, 136

sovereign nation-states, 36; citizenship as social contract of, 52, 53; colonial expansion of, 67–68; critical race theory on oppression in, 11; hegemonic production of subjectivities in, 81–83, 109; indigenous peoples' rights in, 51–56, 165–66; international institutions of, 7, 49–50, 54, 166; models of power of, 15; origin and development of, 48–50; patriarchal power structures of, 7–9; postcolonialist resistance to, 169; property rights in, 52–53; racial definitions of citizenry in, 124–28, 149–53; spatial and racial dimensions of, 6–7; subjects of, 10; world-system of, 7–9, 49, 55, 57–59, 74–75, 166–67. *See also* anticolonial movements; imperialism; nationalism

sovereignty (as concept), 52, 165–67, 179n62

space/time discourses, 12, 18, 58–67, 160–62; on ancient Egypt, 66–67; in borderlands theory, 164; challenges and refutations of, 65–67; on climate, 65, 180n26; in Enlightenment-era biological determinism, 61–64, 148; in Greek geographical determinism, 58–61, 63, 67; in nineteenth century views of blood and racial mixing, 64–66, 89; in performance of identity, 113; taxonomy and classification in, 7, 57, 108–9, 148

Spivak, Gayatri, 115–16, 118–19

Stanford, Max, 32–33, 37

Stanton, Elizabeth Cady, 157

Statue of Liberty, 163

Stoddard, Lothrop, 20, 41

structuralism, 10, 109, 122–23, 125–27

Student Nonviolent Coordinating Committee (SNCC), 139–40

subaltern (as term), 115

subjectification, 107–19; acts of recovery in, 110–11; definition of, 107; giving voice to difference in, 113–19, 182nn13–14; intentional work of, 107–8; language and translation in, 109–10, 118–19; new humanism of, 108–11; performance of identity and, 112–13, 156–57; poststructuralist identity in, 110–13, 119, 182n3; scholars' roles in, 115–16

subjectivity: of authors, 4–5; of black organic intellectuals, 32–36, 38; in feminist and queer theory, 12; hegemonic production of, 81–83, 107, 109; vs. identity, 110–13, 156–57; of oppressed people and communities, 15–17; positivist formations of, 9, 93; of students, 5; in Third World studies, 9–10, 12–13, 36; of traditional humanism, 10, 108–9, 113, 121; of whites, 12

subjects of Third World studies. See curriculum of Third World studies

Sukarno, Ahmed, 17–18, 36, 42, 47–48

Sumi, Pat, 16

Summerskill, John, 27–28

Sumner, William Graham, 122

Sun Yat-sen, 21

Survey Graphic (Locke), 139

Synthesis 1, 12, 156–66; on Asian-American migrant labor, 162–63; on binary social formations, 158–59, 185n7; on European conquest and imperialism, 159–60; on the Fourth World of Native Americans, 164–66; on gender and sexuality, 156–58; on Mexican American migrant labor, 163–64; on pan-Africanism, 160–62; on post-1968 ethnic studies, 158–66

Synthesis 2, 12–13, 166–70; on multiculturalism, 167–68; on postcolonialism, 168–70; on racial formation theory, 168

Systema naturae (Linnaeus), 62

Takao Ozawa v. United States decision, 128–29

Taney, Roger, 151–52, 177n12

Tape, Joseph and Mary McGladery, 100

Tape, Mamie, 100

Tape v. Hurley decision, 100

taxonomy and classification, 7, 57, 108–9, 148. See also space/time discourses

Taylor, Nathaniel G., 53

testimonios, 114, 117–18, 182nn13–14

Thind, Bhagat Singh, 128–29

Third Space of Sovereignty, The, 179n62

third-wave feminism, 171

Third World (as term), 17, 38–39, 50

Third World independence movements. See anticolonial movements

Third World Liberation Front (TWLF), 1–2, 15–17; culture wars sparked by, 8–9, 102–5; focus on imperialism and colonialism of, 7–9, 13; on miseducation and oppression, 26; on new humanism and self-determination, 9–10, 13, 17–19; strikes at San Francisco State College by, 35–36, 105; Third World curriculum demands of, 1, 5, 13–14, 18–19, 27–31, 36, 93, 102, 105–6, 155, 173n12

Third World studies, 1–4, 155–72; black organic intellectuals and, 32–36, 38, 57; Chicago ethnic studies and, 6, 10;